A Man That Looks on Glass

Derek Guiton

Published in 2015 by FeedARead Publishing

British Library C.I.P.

A CIP catalogue record for this title is available from the British Library.

Cover design by David Botwinik
Cover illustration: *The Message* by J. Walter West (1922), courtesy of Library of Society of Friends, London

A Man That Looks on Glass

Standing up for God in the Religious Society of Friends (Quakers)

Derek Guiton

A man that looks on glasse,
On it may stay his eye;
Or if he pleaseth, through it passe,
And then the heav'n espie.

George Herbert (1633)

Acknowledgements

Thanks are due to Gerard Guiton for his many insights and suggestions in the drafting of this book, his constant moral support and his ability to put me in touch with relevant academic sources. Grateful thanks also to Rachel and David Britton for their friendship, encouragement and stimulating conversation, and to Rachel particularly for allowing me to publish the full text of her talk to Colchester Friends, 'God as Energy or God as Person', as an Appendix. Thanks also to my readers, Margaret and David Heathfield, Edward Hoare, James Hogg, Roger Iredale and Noël Staples for their perceptive criticisms, textual corrections and points of information. And, of course, a special thank you to my wife, Brenda, for her patience, companionship and good spirits throughout. Needless to say, any errors are my responsibility alone.

Contents

Introduction

WHICHEVER WAY ONE looks at it, the Religious Society of Friends is in crisis. The main features of this crisis are growing secularisation, the emergence of incompatible belief systems and a readiness, in very many cases, to embrace ideology as a substitute for faith. Although all of these features have come up for discussion at various times in *The Friend* and other Quaker journals there has been no attempt since Alastair Heron's brave little book, *Our Quaker Identity* (1999), to address them as the single existential crisis that they represent. Quaker writing on this subject has tended towards a 'wise reticence'— doubtless from fear of provoking conflict. The effect has been to leave the field open to one side in this debate and allow the impression to develop that those who hold to the traditional Quaker faith have no answer to the arguments of secular rationalism.[1]

Consider, for example, the 2013 and 2014 Swarthmore Lectures. Both are excellent in their exposition of Quaker spiritual values. But in each case the authors discourage any engagement with current realities by appealing to Friends to abandon the 'empire of the mind' and plant a 'garden of the heart'. 'Heart-knowledge', it is suggested, encourages spiritual transformation, 'head-knowledge' leads to rational argument which will only worsen the crisis by driving us further towards the secular.

This book is written in the conviction that we need both kinds of knowledge. The Inward Light and the light of reason are complementary, not opposite. We have nothing to fear from

---

[1] Here I should like to stress that I am referring mainly to Britain Yearly Meeting which follows the unprogrammed (silent) tradition of Quaker worship. Other Yearly Meetings, particularly in the southern hemisphere, follow a tradition of programmed meetings with services organised by a pastor. Since these Yearly Meetings tend to be more committedly Christ-centred, problems around secularisation are not usually an issue.

theological and philosophical debate if we are firmly rooted in our own God-centred and deeply inspiring mystical tradition. But we have a lot to fear from refusing to engage with those for whom reason is the only guide. There is nothing to be gained and much to lose by burying our heads in the sand. As the great Anglican theologian Austin Farrer said, "what no-one defends is soon abandoned".

Leading Friends have warned against this gradual and now burgeoning crisis almost from its beginnings in the 1950s but their warnings for the most part have gone unheeded. It is probably this that led Alastair Heron to address the problem head-on and in a form "as free as possible from ambiguity and equivocation". What did he see as the problem? Essentially our inertia in the face of a threat that would put an end once and for all to something we hold to be the most significant and central focus of our lives, that precious experiment in practical mysticism that began in earnest on Firbank Fell in the summer of 1652. Heron's call to Friends was to overcome this inertia and put into action a programme of Society-wide spiritual renewal, and (crucially) not to let up until the drift from Religious Society to friendly society had been decisively reversed. For, as he pointed out, "if nothing effective is initiated soon, in thirty years' time the membership of the Society will need to be described by terms such as ethical, humanist, secular. By then only a minority will affirm personal experience of the living power of the Spirit of God in their daily lives".

We are now half-way through Heron's thirty-year term and it looks as if that disquieting prognosis is turning out to be grimly accurate. According to the *British Quaker Survey 2013*, the number of Friends and attenders professing belief in God has been decreasing (down from 74% in 1990 to 72% in 2003 and 57% in 2013 — considerably lower than in the population as a whole) while the number identifying as fully declared atheists has been increasing (up from 3.4% in 1990 to 7% in 2003 and 14.5% in

2013). There is also a large undecided contingent which has remained constant at around 25% over the same twenty-three year period. Overall, the trend appears to be moving towards a rejection of belief in God but not necessarily towards non-theism as a theologically fixed position since not all of those in the undecided group would accept the 'non-theist' label.[2] However, there is no doubt that Heron's fears have been amply vindicated. What we are looking at is a Religious Society in flux.

In his Swarthmore lecture, *Open for Transformation*, Ben Pink Dandelion draws attention to our anxiety about falling numbers.[3] That is a different concern and in his view perhaps a false one. "In dwelling on the end of Quakerism", he says, "where is our faith?" He urges us not to worry — fear and anxiety are themselves symptoms of the secular. Faced with falling numbers "we can adapt our structures as we need to, and as we have done in the past". All very true — but who are 'we'? The end of Quakerism may bc about more than falling numbers; it may also (despite appeals to an all-embracing but undefined 'Quakerness') be about our increasingly divergent and doubtfully compatible identities. How is it possible to adapt our structures to halt, and hopefully reverse, the decline in our numbers without further widening the theological basis for membership? And what is the advantage in *that* if the net result is yet further to dilute our core beliefs and Quaker identity and make it all the easier for others to step in with a wholly different set of beliefs and values?

I am not aware of any research into the reasons why people resign from the Society or the rate at which they are leaving; nor

---

2 According to the survey, the undecided contingent has remained constant at around 25% over the same 23 year period. This seems odd in view of the changes in the other figures but suggests other factors may be involved. *The British Quaker Survey 2013* is available online.

3 Membership of Britain Yearly meeting has been declining by an average of 167 people per annum over the past ten years. See Simon Best and Stuart Masters, *The Friends Quarterly* (August 2014), p.39.

of any comparison between the numbers and beliefs of those who have left and those newly admitted to membership. As numbers continue to fall, it seems we are losing more members and attenders than we are gaining. But again, what about the changing *composition* of the Society? It is possible that what we are seeing here is a process of positive feedback (what environmentalists call 'catastrophic bifurcation') where the more secular we become the more secular we become. As Friends and attenders of Christian and/or theist conviction die off or quietly withdraw from the Society, the proportion of those who do not share their convictions grows larger and this in turn attracts yet more people of similar outlook for whom our traditions can have no more than a passing historical interest.

What all this means is that for many Friends today George Fox's claim to have known God's presence 'experimentally' was a mistake and the Society was founded on nothing more than a delusion. This is a view which categorically denies any possibility of encounter with the Real Presence of God whether as individuals or corporately in our meetings for worship. Further, it undermines 'gospel order', the decision-making process without voting by which our business affairs are conducted, and makes it less likely that any future 'adaptations' will be considered and introduced under guidance. Some Friends continue to speak of the Society as 'the great survivor', but it is doubtful that any religious institution, however worthy, could survive such total abnegation of its basic and founding principles. If we go down this route we will most certainly, and probably very soon, be speaking about 'the end of Quakerism'.

Today one is likely to be accused of intolerance and dogmatism for insisting on any principles at all as being central to our faith. "Variety", we are assured, "is the spice of Quaker life." At the risk of appearing intolerant and dogmatic I would question this. Some variety is undoubtedly good for Quaker life, but variety is not a good in itself as anyone who has ever made a cake will know. Ingredients have to be chosen with care or the cake will have a very peculiar taste indeed. Only the right *blend* of ingredients will make a whole that is acceptable to the discerning cake lover. Or we may be advised to heed the words of Damaris Parker-Rhodes: "Truth is a path, not a possession". But note, she is talking about a *path*, not a trackless wilderness, and a path that has a Guide — the Light that is sought within and which is *more than* our finite selves. Not variety, but the search for God is the spice of Quaker life.

Alas, Alastair! He knew that his efforts to avoid ambiguity and equivocation would open him to accusations of dogmatism, for ambiguity, as he was well aware, is the *lingua franca* of modern Quakerism. It is the language of an over-stretched diversity. A diversity which was genuinely Spirit-led would (for that very reason) be a cause for celebration; but one that 'just happens' or results from accommodation to the pressures of secularity is simply a cop out. As I shall argue in Chapter 3 there are good reasons for thinking that the diversity we are being urged to celebrate today is mainly of this second type. It may have introduced a note of greater tolerance but also, by an interesting paradox, have opened us to a new dogmatism.

From our present standpoint, the encouragement of diversity could be seen as preparing the way for something harder-edged and more ideological — a particular expression of the secular. I am referring here to the so-called 'religious' humanism which is explicitly based on the post-structuralist philosophy of non-realism — or as it is sometimes called 'objective nihilism'. This teaches that since there is nothing beyond human language there is no objectively existing God and therefore the God we worship is no more than a human concept. However, the philosophical arguments which support this conclusion are themselves open to question.

There are probably many Friends who embrace diversity as an "expression of the searching and free-thinking spirit of modern Quakerism" who find in this theory of language a certain intellectual excitement without ever fully realising the implications for their religious faith and the future of the Society. Perhaps they feel it is just one among the many philosophical courses that are on offer in the Quaker prospectus and they are free to change from one course to another as the mood takes them. But this is not how non-realism is presented by the leading Quaker non-theist, David Boulton, nor by his acknowledged mentor, the Anglican theologian, Don Cupitt. In the works of both these writers it is presented as the only intellectually adequate, indeed the only *possible*, view of the nature of reality and of God; and whilst they extol non-realism as a courageous and liberating philosophy, they are not above putting emotional pressure on their adherents to draw them further into the closed system it actually is. It may come as a surprise to some of these Friends to learn that non-realism is not a popular perspective among academic philosophers, at least in Britain — nor for that matter among scientists. Perhaps we need to ask ourselves why this is.

It is one of the aims of this book to counter the extraordinary persuasive power that the Cupitt-Boulton version of non-realism has exerted in the Religious Society of Friends over the last thirty years by showing that there are other options which are just as adequate and for many of us far more attractive. I am not an academic theologian or philosopher, just one of that numerous class of people whom Virginia Woolf dubbed 'the common reader'. So rather than rely on my own capacity for philosophical argument I have marshalled the thoughts of others who can progress my case for me — people like Bryan Magee, Keith Ward, Rowan Williams, Janet Martin Soskice, Michael Polanyi, and even some of those admired by Cupitt himself — Ludwig Wittgenstein and Jacques Derrida. Magee alone provides sufficient evidence for most sensible people to reject non-realism — see Appendix A. Language just isn't *capable* of representing our direct experience in all its complexity and depth, and the whole argument that the humanist brand of non-theism relies on collapses as soon as the possibility of a reality which transcends language is admitted. From our point of view as Quakers, it follows that the way is then open to trusting our own *and others'* religious experience as evidence for a non-delusional belief in God.

I deal with the philosophical questions around non-realism in Chapter 8. Parts of this chapter may be difficult to follow for Friends who are unfamiliar or impatient with philosophical terms, but I would urge them passionately to make the effort. However, if abstract reasoning is not to their taste, I suggest they skip this chapter or just read its introductory section and its conclusion.

Another important aim is to explore the opposed concepts of theism and non-theism (Chapters 10, 11 and 12) which have given rise to so much controversy in the Society as we see from the many letters in *The Friend*. I discuss these in the light of a distinction to be found in Charles Taylor's ground-breaking study, *A Secular Age*, between what he calls the open and the closed reading of immanence. I argue that this corresponds to a distinction between *humanist* non-theism which would naturally favour the closed reading, and a more *mystical* non-theism which would presumably opt for the open reading, since it allows for the possibility that there may be something 'more than' the reality we think of as the world we live in. Whereas the first kind of non-theism is alien to our traditions, the second is more in keeping with our self-perception as 'seekers' and 'humble learners in the school of Christ'. In Chapter 10, I suggest that this may have implications for the way we revise our admission criteria in the future. It is as minimalist as it is possible to get without fundamentally changing the nature of the Society. It points not to a creed or an already established belief but to no more than an *attitude* of openness to no more than the *possibility* of transcendence as a minimum requirement for membership.

The principal advocate of *humanist* non-theism in the Religious Society of Friends is, of course, David Boulton. His views, persuasively written up in two books specifically addressed to Friends, *Real Like Daisies, or Real Like I Love You?* and *Godless for God's Sake*, have had a huge influence. A founder member of the Sea of Faith Network and its first general secretary, he has given talks up and down the country, as well as in the United States, held workshops, organised Conferences, developed an online network and created almost singlehandedly the Nontheist Friends Network (NFN), all with the objective of moving his 'religious humanism' from the margins of the Society to the centre ground. Since 'religious humanism' is "wholly secular in the root-meaning of the word" (*Real Like Daisies)* all this activity must be regarded as *anti-faith* and therefore directed against the very basis of our religious life.

In the tradition of Friends, therefore, this book is intended as a rejoinder to Boulton. Here, however, I am faced with a difficulty. Friends today are reluctant to challenge the views of other Friends in public. But how can one write about any of these matters insofar as they affect Friends without mentioning David Boulton? It would be like trying to write the history of ancient Egypt without reference to the pyramids or writing about quality tea without mention of Darjeeling. It would have been much easier if Boulton had confined himself to writing about his *ideas*, but as we have seen he is far more than a writer. The NFN is not primarily a 'special interest' or 'support' group; it is a campaigning organisation operating within Britain Yearly Meeting with clear (but significantly divided) objectives and a vigorously pursued counter-agenda. Those who write about non-theism, religious humanism, the philosophy of non-realism or the future of

Quakerism in Britain without reference to Boulton and the NFN are failing to identify, let alone address, the real nature of the challenge.

I have been asked on several occasions who is the book intended for? Who am I addressing? Part of the answer would be 'the same audience that David Boulton is addressing'. But that would be only part of the answer. Another or overlapping audience would be those Friends who yearn for or have experienced the direct Presence of God in their lives but are left with a dismaying sense that the arguments from the non-theist side are unanswerable. And lastly, it addresses the pool of highly trained Friends with professional expertise in theology, philosophy and other relevant disciplines who in their different ways are contributing to the debate around the forthcoming revision of the book of discipline.

Alastair Heron rightly emphasised that the way to avoid our disappearance into the secular and move the Society forward is through spiritual renewal which starts with ourselves and our personal and corporate openness to the Light, and it is very encouraging to see this already beginning to happen with (among other things) the publication of the Kindlers series of booklets on spiritual practice. But the Society is now poised at the very edge of the abyss. If we wish to stand up for God (the God of Quaker theistic mysticism) and rescue this once incomparably beautiful resource, we also need to remember Richenda Scott's words of prophecy in her 1964 Swarthmore Lecture: "we can be rescued only by a fresh and deeper experience, *and a clearer realization in thought* of what that experience means".[4]

[4] Scott, *Tradition and Experience* (London: Allen and Unwin, 1964), p. 56. My italics.

1

Believing nothing in particular

The doctrine of the inner light sometimes issues in an amiably hospitable frame of mind which presumes some measure of truth in any view sincerely held, and which is content to give an equal welcome to incompatible ideas.

— H. G. Wood

FOR SOME TIME now ecologists have been warning us that the Earth is at a tipping point, that the catastrophic changes brought about by global warming are in danger of becoming irreversible. It is not, I think, too fanciful to suggest that something similar is happening in the Religious Society of Friends. The trend towards non-theism[5] and atheism is growing stronger with each passing decade with the most worrying changes occurring in the decade 2003-2013.[6] If this trend continues, we can foresee a time when the wonderful spiritual tradition handed down to us by Fox and the early Quakers, the tradition that Evelyn Underhill once described as 'this unique experiment in corporate mysticism', will have disappeared forever — to be replaced by a far less interesting experiment in humanist ethics.

No-one will deny that change can bring enormous benefits, and the Society of Friends has shown that it is able to embrace change at key moments in its history. Perhaps the most far-reaching change the

---

[5] I use the term 'non-theism' to denote a weaker form of atheism which reduces God to an impersonal force or energy and is highly ambivalent towards or explicitly rejects any notion of the transcendent. For further discussion of non-theism, see Chapters 10 and 11.

[6] The *British Quaker Survey 2013*, available online. See also J. Hampton, 'British Quaker Survey', *Quaker Studies* 19, 1 (2014), *passim* and two articles by L. Murgatroyd, *The Friend* (20th/27th March, 2015), pp. 6-7/12-13 respectively.

Society has had to face was the shift from an evangelical to a liberal theology following the Manchester Conference of 1895. This in turn brought greater tolerance of differing theological viewpoints, openness to and willingness to learn from other faiths and changed attitudes to gender and sexuality. But along with these came other less promising developments which are now threatening the cohesion and (though few like to say it) the very existence of the Society — the emergence of special interest groups with their own insistent agendas, the erosion of any concept of a core Quaker theology based on Christianity, and the widespread individualisation of belief. The Society today is criss-crossed with divisions and it appears we now have no alternative but to 'celebrate' a diversity that, far from being the strength it is ritually affirmed to be, is in danger of destroying the unity which Friends have always felt to be there, regardless of the differences in their outward lives. Theists, non-theists, atheists, Christians, pagans, Universalists, humanists, Friends who welcome this diversity, Friends who regret it, we sit in the same room and share the silence. But they are different silences and our minds are in different places. As a religious society, we are like W.B. Yeats's long-legged fly that drifts in silence upon the water, the long legs holding together as much of the surface fabric as it can. The question is, what are we drifting *towards*?

The desire to treat everyone's beliefs as equally valuable, equally expressive of genuine Quakerism, has led to a situation where we have great difficulty knowing how to present ourselves to the world outside the Society. 'Simple. Radical. Contemporary' looks good on the poster but whilst we can all agree on the meaning of 'simplicity', it is clear we have very different understandings of words like 'radical' and 'contemporary'.

For some Friends these terms are no more than descriptions of our social and political witness. For others they speak of the distance we have travelled from our supposedly outmoded Christian roots. For still others, they signify a commitment to the values of postmodernism — the rejection of the 'grand narrative', the dismissal of any reliable ground for religious (and some would say even scientific) belief. For such Friends truth is relative, plural and subjective. Moreover, it seems that in recent years this kind of ambiguity has developed into a conscious style. Thus we have a poster proclaiming Quakerism as "belief in action", the double-entendre skilfully encapsulating the main theist/non-theist divide in the Society and leaving it open to the reader to choose his or her preferred interpretation. We may soon find the same ambiguity running through the whole of *Quaker Faith and Practice* as we 'move gently' towards a shared language that has no theologically agreed meaning.

Clearly this is a new situation, unlike anything Friends have encountered before. It is a situation that leaves many of us with the uncomfortable feeling that we may be inviting people to join us on the basis of a partially true, or even an untrue, picture of the Society.

This was brought home to me some years ago when I took part in a discussion around publicity for Quaker Quest, then a fairly new initiative to extend our outreach to the wider world. Most of the group wanted to avoid words like 'God' and 'worship' in the promotion material in case they "put people off" — this despite the fact that a majority of Friends still describe themselves as Christian and/or theist, and that *Quaker Faith and Practice* uses words like 'God' and 'worship' on almost every page. Even if it were not so obviously misleading, it is not at all clear that such a strategy actually works.

The enquirers I spoke to outside the formal sessions were looking for a more mystical expression of their faith, a further stage in their search for God. But what they were presented with was an invitation to join a diverse group all speaking from different scripts and with apparently very little idea of what united them. The main speakers were intended to illustrate this diversity rather than feed the spiritual needs of the listeners, and this they did most effectively. There was the apologetic Christian, the non-theist who "didn't do God", and the "disappointed seeker" who had given up on her seeking and was now a confirmed 'religious humanist'. There were Friends whose references to God were accompanied by embarrassed hand gestures and such phrases as 'whatever you want to call it', or 'if you believe in that kind of thing'. Others spoke movingly of their simple faith in God and Jesus, or conversely of their certainty that Christianity was an unpleasant anachronism which had had its day, and others again of their belief in 'something' they knew not what, a life force or energy. The prepared ministry took the form of a reading from *Quaker Faith and Practice* which noticeably stopped short at the mention of God. There was in all this no sense of a deep, shared experience, no real spiritual authority, and no sense of being led by a power greater than ourselves. I don't recall that we made a single recruit and we had to be content with the less than comforting thought that we had brought the Society and its work to the attention of a tiny fragment of the general public.

In my own small meeting over the past three years at least six Friends and Attenders, including one ex-clerk, have left for other churches or returned to the churches they came from. If this is the pattern across Britain Yearly Meeting, it is hardly surprising that recent surveys have shown a sizeable decrease in the percentage of Friends believing in God, until it is now below that for the population as a whole. So far as I am aware, there has been no in-depth research into the reasons why people leave the Society.

Some of the leavers have written to me, explaining the 'real' reasons for their leaving, often more pointed than those politely set out in their resignation letters. Emily, who with her husband, Peter, had been in membership for two or three years, writes: "I feel that Christians are being sidelined in the Religious Society of Friends at the moment and that actually in a strange sort of way, the Society is too equal. For me the lack of structure of Friends means that anyone can believe anything. For all its faults (and I acknowledge there are many) the Anglo-Catholic church that we attend now at least respects people with different opinions while there is a clear understanding of what the church believes. I felt that being a Christian within the Friends was becoming a source of ridicule and lack of respect. Thank you for your invitation for dual membership. I did consider it, as so did Peter, but we feel that either we are Quakers or we are not and sadly, and we ARE VERY SAD, we are not Quakers."

Madeleine, a new Attender who has been with us only a few weeks, already has her doubts: "if I had been told there were people in important positions in the Friends who did not believe in God, I think I would have fled. I wouldn't object to people who do not believe in God, but want to believe, sharing with us and expressing their beliefs or non-beliefs, but I would feel uneasy sharing with Friends only to find they had come to a decision not to believe in God. I would not know what to say. It is becoming difficult for me to grasp how the modern Friends operate. It seems comical now but I recall coming to the first meeting and taking off my necklace outside because I thought it might offend."[7] Madeleine's story clearly underlines the gap between what newcomers have learned about Quakerism based on past reputation, or in some cases their reading, and the reality actually encountered.

The problem is not so much the *diversity* of belief in the Society, but more the widening and unbridgeable gap between the different kinds of belief. Diversity, as the early Friend and mystic, Isaac Penington, pointed out, is the sign of a healthy church: it makes us seek for the true unity in the things that are eternal:

> For this is the true ground of love and unity, not that such a man walks and does just as I do, but because I feel the same Spirit and life in him, and that he walks in his rank, in his own order, in his proper way *and place of subjection to that*; and this is far more pleasing to me, than if he walked just in that track wherein I walk.[8]

This is a well known passage and one that is close to every Friend's heart; when used in ministry, as it often is, we listen with a sense of relief, for it breathes the spirit of tolerance, opening the prison gates of dogma and allowing in a variety of opinion and expression.

---

[7] All names have been changed.

[8] *Quaker Faith & Practice* (hereafter *QF&P*. London: Britain Yearly Meeting), §27.13. My emphasis.

But unfortunately it has also been misused, quoted out of context to justify a diversity that goes far beyond anything Penington could have conceived. It is a difficult text to transplant into our own era when we no longer share a common framework of belief and when the word 'Spirit' itself has such different and even contradictory meanings for different groups of Friends. Penington didn't have to deal with that kind of radical ambiguity which is fast becoming a new form of 'Quaker-speak' and which is justified by the claim that all we are doing is using different language to refer to the same thing, when it is obvious that we are using the same language to refer to different things.

For Penington, feeling "that same Spirit and life" in the other was a matter of seeing "the true image of God raised in persons, and they knowing and loving one another in that image, and bearing with one another through love". The true image of God was the spirit of Christ which he found in full measure in the man Jesus, and he warns us that "care must be had that nothing govern in the church of Christ, but the spirit of Christ." So this was a much more in-house and circumscribed diversity than that advocated today by those who would misappropriate his words in the cause of an *abstract* diversity — a diversity which should never be questioned as it is so obviously a good in its own right.

A closer reading of the text shows that Penington was much more concerned with unity than with diversity. Indeed, he believed that the patient acceptance of differences was only a stage on the way to an even deeper unity which would eventually include the 'outward'. He felt passionately that such a régime must not be imposed by human agency but come naturally and gradually through the silent working of the Spirit (meaning the Holy Spirit or 'the Christ'): "The intent and work of the ministry (with the several ministrations of it) is to bring into the unity, Ephes. 4:13, as persons are able to follow: and not to force all men into one practice or way . . . the unity being thus kept, all will come into one outwardly also at length, as the light grows in every one, and as every one grows into the light; but this must be patiently waited for from the hand of God . . . and not harshly . . . by the rough hand of man".[9]

Sadly, we can no longer assume that the fellowship and unity described in the beautiful and spiritual language of Penington will be available to us in Britain Yearly Meeting in the foreseeable future. On the contrary, we may be destroying whatever hope we have of recovering the sort of precious gifts Penington describes through our strident individualism, competing group identities, and our preference for a secular notion of equality over the real equality of all before God. The indiscriminate welcome we have given to a host of divergent and contradictory theologies has put us in the awkward position of having to extend this secular equality to everyone and everything, so that now we have to say as a Society that we hold them all to be equally true — and then, the logic of diversity being what it is, to justify this position by claiming "there is no Truth but only truths", our secular notion of equality being as much opposed to the 'hierarchy' of truth as to social or any other hierarchy.

So it goes on. We no longer speak Truth to power, we each speak 'our own truth' to power, a change which will ultimately prove disabling to our social and political witness. Nor can we say with confidence that we are seekers, each from our different standpoint converging on a deeper unifying Reality. Instead, we identify ourselves as members of special interest groups who occupy fixed positions, each with its own 'mission statement' and exclusive vision of '21st century Quakerism'. In these circumstances, it may indeed be safer and more honest to say that religious beliefs are 'relatively inconsequential'[10] and that all we hold in common are certain secular values, and that religious faith is relatively inconsequential too. What

---

[9] M. Keiser and R. Moore (eds.), *Knowing the Mystery of Life Within* (London: Quaker Books, 2005), p. 165. The passage from Ephesians reads: "So shall we all at last attain to the unity inherent in our faith and our knowledge of the Son of God — to mature manhood, measured by nothing less than the full stature of Christ".

[10] P. Dandelion and P. Collins (editors), *The Quaker Condition: the Sociology of a Liberal Religion* (Newcastle,: Camridge Scholars Publishing, 2008), pp. ix -x.

about *Quaker Faith and Practice*; isn't that an expression of our faith? Of course, but in these times a very changeable one. It is difficult to have faith in *Quaker Faith and Practice* when we know that it is soon to be revised to accommodate 'new insights' regardless of whether they are compatible with one another or with our tradition and that the pressure for change is all in one direction.

It is an inconvenient truth that where we see 'unity in diversity', the general public is likely to see confusion and self-contradiction. Here, for example, is one reader's reaction to David Boulton's 'Face to Faith' article in the *Guardian* (intended to promote the Society during our first 'Quaker Week' in 2007): "they are a 'religious group' apparently, but he's a humanist, and there are loads of 'non-theists'. Is it self-worship, mutual worship? Is it knickers in a complete twist to try to accommodate the views of every confused person in the world?"[11]

Catherine Deveney of the Melbourne newspaper, *The Age*, questions the honesty of our campaigning methods. "They're the Claytons religion. The religion you have when you don't have a religion. Because they're not a religion. They're a 'religious society of friends'. You don't even have to believe in God to be a Quaker. You don't even need to be a Quaker to be a Quaker . . . I keep thinking about the comedian Bill Hicks talking about the anti-marketing dollar being a good market."[12]

This may be dismissed as cheap journalism, but I suggest that it contains more than a grain of truth. I find it sad to think of the Society being lampooned in this way. It prompts the question, how are we living up to the reputation established for us by past generations of Friends? Can we still think of Quakerism, in the words of William

---

[11] See 'Face to Faith', *The Guardian* (22nd Sept., 2007). The quote is one of a long string of comments that follow the article. Many of these, of course, are positive.

[12] Deveney in *The Age* (Melbourne, 5th Aug., 2009). According to Wikepedia, 'Claytons' is the name of a non-alcoholic beverage coloured and packaged to resemble bottled whisky. It was the subject of a major marketing campaign in Australia in the 1980s when it was promoted as 'the drink you have when you're not having a drink'. The name has come to mean a 'poor substitute', 'an ineffective solution to a problem' or something that masquerades as something it is not.

James, as “a religion of veracity in a day of shams”?[13] Do we still deserve the accolade bestowed on us by the admirable Dean Inge: “The Quakers, who of all Christian bodies have remained nearest to the teaching and example of Christ”?[14]

Deveney clearly sees our avoidance of terms like ‘God’ and ‘worship’ as a mere ploy. Of course, what she doesn’t see is the modern Quaker desire to be inclusive, the other side of the coin of pluralism which I shall consider later in this book. We pride ourselves on excluding no-one on grounds of creed. But I think many Friends would agree that our current opposition to *all* credal boundaries emerged only when it seemed that we needed to widen our appeal and reverse the decline in our numbers. In other words, as a marketing strategy. “The anti-marketing dollar is a good market.”

But is it? In his Introduction to *The Trouble with God*, David Boulton points a mocking finger at our present day churches, synagogues and meeting houses which he describes as being in a state of “unstoppable slide”: “this one emptying because it believes in nothing in particular, that one keeping up numbers only by selling false certainties and comfortable lies”.[15] Clearly, as ‘modern creedless Quakers’, we fit neatly into Boulton’s first category. A recent study of ‘the Quaker condition’ makes much of the fact that “for Quakers, belief is relatively inconsequential”[16] and although our meeting houses are not exactly emptying, our meetings are noticeably in decline. If present trends continue, it has been calculated, British Quakerism has a projected endpoint somewhere around 2035.[17] Having nothing in particular to ‘sell’ except our ‘diversity’, it seems we are heading for eclipse in a market where specific selling features are everything.

---

[13] James, *The Varieties of Religious Experience* (Harmondsworth: Penguin, 1985), p. 7.

[14] W. Inge, *The Platonist Tradition in English Thought* (London: Longmans, Green and Co., 1926), p. 113.

[15] Boulton, *The Trouble with God*, (Winchester: O Books, 2005), p.xii.

[16] L. Woodhead in Dandelion and Collins, p. ix.

[17] Dandelion, *An Introduction to Quakerism* (Cambridge: CUP, 2007), p. 247.

What about Boulton's second category? It is not quite clear who he has in mind — 'lies' is a very strong word to use in this context. I will assume he means any church which is founded on the orthodox beliefs of Christianity. But some of these are doing more than keeping up numbers, they are growing exponentially, especially in the United States and the developing world. We may not agree with aspects of their theology or like their style, but they are clear proof that abandoning traditional beliefs for the sake of market advantage is not necessarily the best way forward.

Nor can they be casually dismissed as centres of neo-con fascism. The strength of the religious right in the United States is real and frightening, but improbable as it may seem to some, there are many so-called 'fundamentalist' churches in the US and across the world which happily combine theological conservatism and political liberalism. Jim Wallis, the evangelical Christian activist and editor of *Sojourners* magazine, heads a considerable movement in the United States and was an adviser to Barack Obama in the early, more optimistic, days of the latter's presidency. Wallis is an environmentalist, a supporter of gay marriage, and his wife was one of the first women to be ordained a priest in the Anglican Communion. Timothy Keller, who founded a new inner city mega-church for a largely non-churchgoing population in Manhattan, has grown his congregation from nothing to 5,000 in a few years. He wanted his church to have a strong focus on issues of social justice, but one "grounded in the nature of God" rather than secular political preferences.[18] The Evangelical Quaker, Richard Foster, whose book, 'Celebration of Discipline', has sold more than a million copies worldwide, describes the religious life as a call "to wage peace in a world obsessed with war, to plead for justice in a world plagued with inequity, to stand with the poor and the disinherited in a world that has forgotten its neighbour". We don't expect all of these trends and

---

[18] Keller, *The Reason for God: Belief in an Age of Scepticism*, (London: Hodder & Stoughton, 2008), p. xiii.

currents to agree on every issue but in general their understanding of the gospel story impels them more to the political centre-left.

Meanwhile, in the UK, the Pentecostal and evangelical churches have seen a proportionately similar growth in numbers. And one could add to this the rather quieter movement known as the 'emerging church' whose social composition, concern for social justice and environmental issues, and use of silence as well as prayer in worship, make it seem almost like an earlier version of ourselves — the main difference being that the emerging church is growing and prospering around a loosely Christian theology whilst we, '*believing in nothing in particular*', continue in a state of 'unstoppable slide'.[19]

The 'emerging church' is one expression of a wider trend within institutional Christianity which is gaining adherents from groups of unchurched younger people who want to explore their spirituality independently but who have seen the need for anchorage within an established framework which can offer spiritual direction and stability. What we are seeing is a fluid movement of the Spirit which is open and inclusive, free in its interpretation of Christian doctrine and yet theistic in *orientation*. Clearly the culture is changing in some indistinct way, and it is to be hoped that the emerging church and its counterparts will bring adjustment and change to the institutional structures that support them. None of these developments fits neatly into either of Boulton's categories, and the question we should be asking ourselves is why — despite all the effort we have put into Quaker Quest — these young people are not coming in greater numbers to us?

Indeed, there is some evidence of movement in the opposite direction, away from the Society of Friends to groups like the 'Centre for Action and Contemplation' founded by US Franciscan Richard

---

[19] The 'emerging church' is not to be confused with the 'emergent church' with which, however, it is closely linked. The first is the broader, informal, global, ecclesial (church-centred) focus of the movement, the second an official organisation in the U.S. and the U.K. The Quaker counterpart is the international group known as 'Convergent Friends', the term 'convergent' representing a happy combination of (theologically) 'conservative' and 'emergent'.

Rohr and the 'Julian' Meetings, named after the great English medieval mystic, Julian of Norwich. I know of a number of Friends, including one Swarthmore Lecturer, who regularly complement their attendance at Quaker Meeting by seeking fellowship with Christians in other settings who share the same mystical bent and in many cases the same form of worship. Friends who once remained in the Society because they had nowhere else to go, now have a choice of destinations. A brochure by the Julian Meetings entitled *Waiting on God in the Silence* describes contemplative prayer as "listening for God, opening ourselves to God, waiting silently upon God". It continues:

> If we feel we need to learn how to be still with God, we might start with some ways that other people have found helpful. Belonging to a group of people who meet regularly to pray in silent contemplation can be a great help and encouragement. We do not feel isolated. Prayerful silence is greatly helped when two or three are together, and this complements our daily personal prayer . . . A Julian Meeting provides these opportunities.

In the past we would have considered the kind of people who support these groups to be among our natural constituents, but not any longer. Now it is Quakers who are among *their* constituents. Friends can offer the ambience of a silent meeting room but all too often, only obfuscation and denial where the search for God is concerned.

I am not suggesting that Quakers return to being orthodox Christians — partly because uniformity of belief is neither desirable nor enforceable, but more important because Quakers were never that to begin with. Early Friends had some notably unorthodox ideas on the divinity and uniqueness of Jesus, most of them deemed heretical by their Protestant contemporaries.[20] For many, especially among the

---

[20] Research suggests there were "several (at least) Quaker 'Christologies' in the seventeenth century" and that it was only after the death of Fox that the more orthodox views of Penn and Barclay took root and became "the normative interpretation of Fox's inward Christ among a new generation of leadership".

leadership, Jesus was a man like any other but divine to the extent that he was filled with the Christ. This allowed them to take a Christian Universalist view of 'salvation', itself often defined in terms unacceptable to orthodoxy, and to see human life as perfectible here on earth. Just as they saw the Christ as both *within* and *beyond* the human person, so they saw the Kingdom (or, if you prefer, the 'Covenant') of God as a continuum stretching from our present earthly existence into the mystery of the Eternal. Jesus was like a prism through which the pure, absolute light of the One was broken into the colours which are the fruits of the Spirit.[21] It is consistent with this theology to see God as taking the initiative and consummating the incarnation in Jesus, not bodily but in the spiritual sense that Friends have known themselves in worship — a continuing incarnation, not exclusive to Jesus, as the gospel of John affirms[22], nor even requiring knowledge of Jesus, but available to all who follow in the path of faith, hope and love.

Although the early Friends teased out the implications of their theology to an extraordinary extent, they did so, naturally at that time, within the context of Christianity alone. It is open to modern Friends to extend this teaching to the holy men and women of other faiths and none. When one reads the life story of the Buddha, for example, there is a strong sense of something similar taking place; and the Vedic notion of the *atman* touches on the same conceptual ground. But only in Christianity do we get the sense of a fully human personality open to the spirit of God to such an extent that in Jesus we see God's true

---

See R. Bailey, "Was Seventeenth-century Quaker Christology Homogeneous?" in Dandelion (ed.), *The Creation of Quaker Theory: Insider Perspectives* (Aldershot: Ashgate, 2004), pp. 65, 77.

21 In the words of Anglican theologian/philosopher Keith Ward: "Jesus is a man who is filled with the Spirit and wholly obedient to the Father; whose humanity is transformed by inward power and open to the supreme perfection of the unconditioned source of all." See *Religion and Creation* (Oxford: Clarendon Press, 1996), p.54.

22 Jn. 1: 12-14: "But to all who did receive him. . . .he gave the right to become children of God, not born of any human stock, or by the fleshly desire of a human father, but the offspring of God himself".

nature revealed. Without this revelation, God remains for most of us an abstraction, and the gospel values of 'mercy, pity, peace and love' (as the poet Blake summarised them), as well as our own Quaker testimonies, are no more than relative truths, capable of being swept to one side when circumstances alter. On the other hand, we can say of *this* Jesus that through his life and death, Love is revealed as the one absolute Truth, subsuming all others, and that in him truly "heaven walks among us".

The idea of a 'spiritual incarnation' in which we can all participate, 'each in his or her measure', may be dismissed as a contradiction in terms, but if we think of it as the indwelling 'Christ Spirit' we are on more familiar Quaker territory. As Melvin Keiser explains in a note on Penington, "Christ, for Penington is God, 'the infinite eternal Being' which was most fully present in the man Jesus but '*cannot be confined to be nowhere else but there*'. Keiser continues:

> Penington's approach is experiential. He knows Christ is God and was fully manifest in Jesus because he knows in some measure that 'Being' in his being: God 'did all in him [Jesus], as it is a measure of the same life which doth all in us . . .' He rejects, therefore, the frequent accusation thrown at Quakers that they spoke of 'two Christs, one manifested without, and another revealed within', for the 'mystery of life, and hope of glory' was manifest in the earthly Jesus that is 'revealed and made known within unto us, by the same eternal spirit'.[23]

Considered from this point of view, the difference between Jesus and us is that in Jesus the presence (or gift) of the Christ was continuous, fully experienced and absolute in its demands. It evoked in him the response of complete surrender and obedience. In us, the same Spirit may be experienced in its fullness only momentarily but the same process is at work. When George Fox was accused of blasphemy

---

[23] Keiser in Keiser and Moore, p. 249.

in claiming he was equal with God, he replied: "he that hath the same Spirit that raised up Jesus Christ, is equal with God: and the Scripture saith, that God will dwell in man, and walk in man; as Jesus Christ, which is the mystery, hath passed before, so the same Spirit takes upon it the same seed, and is the same where it is manifest."[24] So Jesus is God in so far as he is filled with the Spirit of God, and we likewise in so far as we are united with (Fox uses the words "sanctified by") the same in-dwelling Spirit.

A theology of this kind is not what today we call 'fundamentalism'. It is theistic without necessarily being Trinitarian, and therefore has the potential to unite Friends in the essentials. It provides an area of *acceptable* belief, being neither Christian orthodoxy with its more problematic dogmas like the virgin birth, miracles and the physical resurrection, nor flatline atheistic humanism, but a coherent and open theology filling the broad space between these extremes and expressing the rich vein of mystical Christianity which lay at the heart of early Quakerism. Finally, and not least, a theology of this type, tested over more than 350 years in the crucible of corporate and personal *experience*, might enable us to benefit numerically as people search again for hope and meaning in a world dominated by greed, corruption, militarism and violence.

---

[24] Fox and Nayler *et al*, *Saul's Errand to Damascus* (London: Calvert, 1653), p. 8.

2
Prophecy and change

I will speak to this nation through men of strange tongues, and by the lips of foreigners; and even so they will not heed me, says the Lord.
— 1 Corinthians, 14: 21

All the great prophets . . . have appeared in the history of the world as so many stormy petrels, as warning voices, calling man back to God, the Eternal.

— Von Hugel

IN GREEK LEGEND, Cassandra was a gifted prophetess, condemned by Apollo always to be disbelieved. We don't have patron saints in the Religious Society of Friends, but Cassandra could well be adopted as the Quaker Muse, if not for Britain Yearly Meeting as a whole, then at least for one of its most outstanding institutions — the annual Swarthmore Lecture. Looking back over the last few decades, it seems that our Swarthmore lecturers have been fully aware of the dangers facing us from an over-extended diversity, but their carefully-chosen words of warning appear to have been only half listened to and then forgotten. Let us look at what some of them have said.

Thomas Green, 1952

Observes "a tendency in the thinking of many to replace religion by ethics".[25] We can become so immersed in our work for peace and social justice that we forget we are a religious Society devoted to the love and worship of God. While early Friends had to endure torture

[25] Green, *Preparation for Worship* (London: Quaker Home Service 1983 [1952]), p. 5.

and imprisonment , "the dangers which beset us are more subtle". Chief among these is our "vulnerability to the current intellectual fashions".[26]

Richenda Scott, 1964

Fears that "once again, as in the 19th century, we may find that we have lost any clear sense of direction [and] have no real grasp of what it is we have to offer as the constructive Quaker contribution".[27] Richenda Scott further warns that "if the two elements of the historical and mystical are not held closely together, the Society of Friends will always go astray". She insists that "both as Christians and as Quakers, we cannot sever ourselves from our historical roots".[28]

Kathleen Slack, 1967

Identifies the key question before the Society as "the extent to which it could offer membership to those of differing beliefs without so compromising itself that it should be unable to maintain its cohesion and unity". After presenting a careful and balanced review of the state of the Society, she concludes: "a religious society, as the Society of Friends is, cannot be an open society in the fullest sense of that term. That would involve a categorical impossibility for the very fact of membership of a religious body — any religious body — presupposes the acceptance, implicit or explicit, of some beliefs or convictions . . . If Friends were persuaded at any time that those convictions were ill-founded and untenable, then with their rejection would go the rejection of the Quaker faith itself".[29]

---

[26] *ibid*, pp. 4-5.

[27] R. Scott, *Tradition and Experience*, p. 56.

[28] *ibid.*, pp. 71-72.

[29] Slack, *Constancy and Change in the Society of Friends* (London: Friends Home Service Committee, 1967), pp. 53-4. Slack looks for a balance between an 'open' and a 'closed' Society, terms clearly derived from Karl Popper who was enjoying some popularity at this time.

Maurice Creasey, 1969

Draws our attention to Hugh Barbour's comment that "British Friends . . . face terrible problems of aimlessness". Creasey, like Barbour, is calling for a "corporate expression of a common vision", but has to recognise that as things stand this is unlikely to be forthcoming. Friends are in danger of "simultaneously pursuing mutually incompatible aims", treating them all with "the same impartial benignity".[30] (Today the incompatible aims are united in a new synthesis called 'diversity', embracing which not only makes it extremely difficult for the Society to maintain a living relationship with the past but to move forward into the future 'under guidance'.)

Janet Scott, 1980

During the seventies, the warning voices subside. Change however continues beneath the surface — a 'silent revolution' to use Dandelion's ironic phrase. Throughout this period the Society sees an increase in the numbers applying for membership who have only a passing interest in Christianity or quietly reject its 'privileged' position as the centrepiece around which other beliefs are expected to cohere. Finally, in 1980 Janet Scott delivers her Swarthmore Lecture, *What canst thou say?* This completely reverses the earlier trend and proves to be a major turning point for late twentieth century Quakerism, possibly as far reaching in its effects as the Manchester Conference had been for the earlier part of the century.

As Janet Scott's lecture is the exception to the more general trend, and the only one that appears to have been listened to and acted upon by Friends, it requires more extended discussion which I leave until later in the chapter.

[30] Creasy, *Bearings or Friends and the New Reformation* (London: Friends Home Service Committee, 1969), pp. 62-3.

John Punshon, 1990

Coinciding with the Thatcher era, the 1980s are marked by an emphasis on individual choice. 'What canst thou say?' is replaced by 'Thou shalt decide for thyself'. The 1990 Swarthmore Lecture highlights the new trend. John Punshon, directs our attention to what he describes as 'supermarket Quakerism'. We move around the "Friendly emporium" selecting whatever items coincide with our individual interest, one shopping list for the activist, another for the contemplative.[31] The result, he says, is that modern Quakerism is experienced as a personal needs-centred movement rather than one anchored in a well-tested mystical tradition which involves inward struggle and transformation. Separated from this tradition, our commitment is less enduring and our ideas of equality, peace and social justice are subject to the familiar distortions of secular ideology. Our testimonies can then claim no more authority than any other corporate mission statement or party manifesto:

> Newcomers need to understand that the testimonies are not pragmatic responses to the spirit of the age, being neither political principles nor programmes, but the outcome of the Quaker religious tradition, the greater whole against which they have to be evaluated and practised . . and that there is a basis for them which is not necessarily sympathetic to the presuppositions of rationalism and humanism.[32]

Margaret Heathfield, 1994

Like Kathleen Slack , Margaret Heathfield looks at the advantages and disadvantages of the 'closed' and 'open' phases in the history of the Society. She concludes that the pendulum now needs to swing a little more towards the 'closed' end of the spectrum. "How many variations can we hold together before we cease to feel any coherence ourselves, or before we begin to appear incoherent to others outside?" The

---

[31] Punshon, *Testimony and Tradition* (London: Quaker Home Service, 1990), p. 23.

[32] *ibid.*, p. 19.

Society is now at a crossroads. We can choose between being a People of God able to speak with a united voice or becoming an 'open spiritual movement', capable of absorbing a wide range of theological viewpoints without the need to test the individual's Light against that of the group:

> . . . we do not seem fully to understand that when we take actions such as opening our membership more widely, encouraging relatively inexperienced Friends to take responsibility in our life together, shortening periods of service, or encouraging special interest groups, we are implicitly choosing the route towards a religious movement, and making it more frustrating for ourselves when we try to speak with a united voice. Each step needs to be understood for what it means in terms of the implicit choice we are making; otherwise we will find that we have gone so far down one route that there is no easy way back.[33]

The real warning is contained in the words "each step needs to be understood for what it means in terms of the implicit choice we are making". They are very carefully chosen. Ignoring them, we choose to drift and the Society today is divided along yet another fault line.

Jonathan Dale, 1996

Asks if we have now gone too far along the liberal path, led not so much by the Spirit as by the 'spirit of the times'.

> We cannot be content with the individualistic and relativistic and fragmenting Quakerism of this time. It drifts on the times when the times are for resisting. It undermines our confidence in our coherence, often without good foundation. It weakens our corporate life. Unchecked it could destroy our understanding of faith in action. The spirit of 1895 has been betrayed.

---

33 Heathfield, *Being Together: Our Corporate Life in the Religious Society of Friends* (London: Quaker Home Serviice, 1994), pp. 51, 109.

One senses the desperation in his voice as he surveys the trends of the past forty or fifty years:

> Up to the 1950's there was . . . little reason to question the new Quaker liberal consensus. Even now the question for us is not whether the Enlightenment was or was not a good thing, nor whether the 1895 Conference was or was not a right turning point for the Society of Friends in Great Britain. Both these liberations were essential. The question is rather: have those trends now gone too far? Have we followed them under clear guidance as to their rightness or have we simply followed the times? In 1895 London Yearly meeting gave impetus to the new direction in which it was being led. It is time to pause and consider whether we have travelled too far along that path.[34]

His message might be summed up in G.K. Chesterton's famous quip, "those who marry the spirit of this age will find themselves widows in the next".

Christine Trevett, 1997

An expert on the divisions which racked the early Christian movement, Trevett warns that the future of the Society is hanging in the balance and will be forfeited "if we assume too readily that anything and everything can be embraced within its motherly arms without extending these too far for well-being". We need to act now if we are to avoid a total collapse into anarchy and sectarianism:

> Above all, as the end of the millennium approaches we must not allow to become reality the (doomsday?) scenario which Ben Pink Dandelion presented . . . It is one I would also characterise as a special danger deriving from niche marketing — advertising our wares as of special interest for Universalists or crypto-Buddhists, unitarian Christians or whatever, without due holistic care for the what and why of Quakerism. What Dandelion pointed to was the Religious Society of

---

[34] Dale, *Beyond the Spirit of the Age* (London: Quaker Home Service, 1996), pp. 121, 46.

Friends becoming a collection of method-oriented groups in schism: individualism pushed beyond denominational bounds into the 'anarchist extreme' of sectarianism.[35]

The Janet Scott Lecture — 'What canst thou say?'

I now return to Janet Scott's Lecture which was notable for the conspicuousness with which it stood out against the fears and predictions of previous lecturers — and, as we have seen, some of those who came after her. Although in her personal life she has remained a Christian and a theist, her Lecture was a decisive factor in turning the Society towards the stance which Ben Pink Dandelion later characterised as 'liberal-Liberalism'. Described by Martin Davie as no more than the "logical outworking" of trends that already existed, her approach was essentially one of accommodation to the changing face of the Society which was itself a reflection of the spirit of the age. Perhaps for that very reason it struck a chord within Britain Yearly Meeting, making it the first theological production by a member of the Society in recent times to be widely read with interest and enthusiasm.

It is likely that Janet Scott conceived her lecture as a much needed healing ministry, since by 1980 the struggle between 'Christocentric' and Universalist Friends was intensifying and out in the open. Her response was to welcome the new pluralism, making room for Quaker Universalism in particular by rejecting the uniqueness of Jesus and his role as Saviour. This, of course, was to reject Christian *orthodoxy* only; there was no attempt to appraise the various Christologies that were circulating in the early period of Quakerism. Yet she proceeded as if it were to reject Christianity as a whole. Her answer to the question, 'Are Quakers Christian?', was that it didn't matter: "What matters for Quakers is not the label by which we are called or call ourselves, but the life":

[35] Trevett, *Previous Convictions* (London: Quaker Home Service, 1997), pp. 93-4.

> The abandonment of self to God means also the abandonment of labels, of doctrines, of cherished ways of expressing the truth. It means the willingness to follow the spirit wherever it leads, and there is no guarantee that this is to Christianity or to any 'happy ending' except the love, peace and unity of God.[36]

These words contain both a challenge and an assurance, and our first instinct may be to give them our unqualified approval. When we come to look more closely, however, we find that they cannot be taken entirely at face value. They seem to be suggesting that we abandon any sense of self-identity that owes anything to tradition and start again from scratch, trusting only in God — ignoring the possibility that God too might be considered by some as part of the tradition needing to be abandoned.

'Labels' do matter, not ultimately, of course, but most definitely in theological enquiry, in matters of church government, in dialogue with other churches, and in ordinary discourse. And Friends continue to regard them as important. Witness, for instance, the periodic surveys (a telling innovation) to discover how our members and attenders continue to define themselves. Janet Scott refers to herself as a theist. Of course, some labels are disparaging of others and should never be used — 'Christocentric', for example, which draws on the social guilt associated with terms such as 'ethnocentric'. But if we discard all such distinguishing labels, how can we think and communicate?

At every stage in her Lecture, Scott reveals herself as a passionate theist. Her statements about God are expressed in the most sensitive and inspiring language. When she calls on us to be ready to abandon "labels, doctrines and cherished ways of expressing the truth", she is referring not to belief in God, but to Christianity itself, which, although a professing Christian, she sees as an obstacle to unity

---

[36] J. Scott, *What Canst Thou Say?: Towards a Quaker Theology* (London: Quaker Books, 1980), p. 70.

at a deeper level. She wants us *as Christians* to make the ultimate sacrifice: selflessly to abandon our Christian identity, our beliefs and the language in which we express them. And if I am not mistaken there is a suggestion that we become more authentically Christian by that very act of self-denial. She sees in our willingness to "follow the spirit wherever it leads" a supreme act of trust in which we place that which we value most highly into the hands of God "to make or break, to crown or destroy". But what if the spirit leads us to the denial of the Spirit, to humanism, and ultimately to nihilism? Does our act of trust still make sense? Has God then broken trust with us? When Janet Scott was writing, such questions might have seemed absurd; not so a decade later.

As she builds the case for accommodating to Quaker Universalism, Janet Scott appears to rule out any major concessions to atheism. For example, one of the arguments she employs involves the belief that there are many different models of the Truth. How do we choose between them — "have we any ways of showing that some models are better, or more true, than others?" One way, she suggests, is to ask: "What are its effects on the believer? Does it encourage maturity, does it strengthen, does it lead to freedom to hear and follow the leadings of God (under whatever name)?"[37] This allows no space at all for the atheistic model which by implication is defined as 'less true' than others.

An even more radical exclusion follows from her theory of 'simultaneous' and 'mutually destructive' models. Simultaneous models can co-exist, one alongside the other; 'mutually destructive' models, as the name implies, cancel one another out. Since theism directly contradicts atheism, it must be assumed that the theistic and atheistic models belong in the mutually destructive category.[38] But,

---

[37] *ibid.*, p. 20.

[38] *ibid.*, pp. 22-3. J. Scott also says that models may contradict each other and yet be individually valid. However, she is referring here to models within the compass of religious faith. To include theism and atheism among these would make a nonsense of the 'mutually destructive' category.

surprisingly, in her single extended reference to atheism, she arrives at exactly the opposite conclusion. She writes:

> Our theology must be inclusive towards other faiths and towards atheism. That is that it must take them seriously, respect their principles and concerns, and seek to find them a place which justifies and does not condemn them. Thus, although it is impossible for me to speak in other than theist terms and this contradicts atheism, I must not thereby maintain that people are wrong to be atheists.[39]

Perhaps the key word here is 'towards'. It assumes a position of leadership for what (despite her previous abandonment of "cherished ways of expressing the truth") remains a Christian based theology which can afford to be generous "*towards* other faiths and *towards* atheism". What it doesn't do is look ahead to a time when the minority (or minorities) might wish to challenge this leadership position, and the effects that such a development would have on the Society. From this point of view, the truly prophetic voice was that of Richenda Scott. But perhaps even she could not have imagined the disintegration and chaos that lay ahead.

In fairness to Janet Scott, it needs to be said that she was writing in the days before the 'new atheists' were swinging into action with their violently worded condemnations of all religious belief, the days before the 'Sea of Faith' atheists and the militant philosophy of 'religious' humanism. The atheists she had in mind, therefore, were likely to be individuals who could not (at this point in their spiritual lives) say that they believed or trusted in God but who still saw themselves as seekers in the Quaker tradition. Whatever the case, the damage had been done, and atheism in the Religious Society of Friends had gained a significant foothold.

It is important to emphasise that atheism is not in itself the problem. As a philosophy or belief system it is fully deserving of our

---

[39] *ibid.*, pp. 13-14.

respect. How could it be otherwise when so many great names in philosophy and literature are associated with atheism — Nietzsche, Heidegger, Sartre, Iris Murdoch, William Empson. It only becomes a problem for a religious group such as ours when it takes the form of a militant *anti-theism* and when its influence becomes so widespread that it affects the quality and depth of our worship. It could have been different. We could have been inclusive and welcoming towards atheists in a way that fulfilled all of Janet Scott's requirements by inviting them to worship with us as attenders, whilst restricting membership to those who felt able to embrace the faith and practice outlined in our book of discipline. Now it is the increasingly assertive and organised non-theist and humanist *members* who are applying pressure to relax our admission criteria and change the content and language of *Quaker Faith and Practice.*

The 1980 Swarthmore Lecture is one of the few *theological* treatises to gain a wide readership among Friends. It deserves recognition as the first serious attempt to develop criteria which could be used in judging applications for membership and which implicitly recognises the need for boundaries, while at the same time aiming for the greatest possible inclusivity. For this we should be grateful even if the author then ignored her own analysis and the criteria she had so thoughtfully developed. On the negative side, her lecture had the effect of moving us further from our roots in Quaker Christianity and reducing the tradition inherited from early Friends to one 'model' among many. That, surely, was to squander a great gift. Of all Christian theologies, the early-Quaker model is the one most suited to meeting the challenges of the present age, the one least in need of adaptation, and the one which holds out the promise of genuine solutions to the difficult questions around postmodernism which our own theologians seem to lack the will or capacity to take on. If we really mean to make our mark in the wider theological debate, drawing on the audacity and brilliance of that early Quaker blend of intellect and experience, we will need more than a sharp pair of scissors in our theological armoury.

Janet Scott not only gave theological shape to the changes that were overtaking the Society but provided it with what appeared to be a way out of its dilemma. From being an organisation which was struggling to manage and absorb diversity it became, almost overnight, one which positively welcomed and celebrated it as a new dispensation. One can almost hear the sigh of relief around the room as she utters the words "it does not matter". And yet it is probable that once the brakes were off, the ensuing free-for-all went far beyond anything she would have expected or wished to have seen. The next ten years saw a rapid proliferation of special interest groups and the stratification of the Society into what the sociologist Gay Pilgrim has described as 'exclusivists', 'inclusivists and 'syncretists'.[40] It was against this background, as we have seen, that the post-Scott Swarthmore lecturers raised their own voices in warning. However, like Cassandra they lived to see what they most cherished being progressively destroyed.

Christine Trevett's 1997 lecture marked the end of Swarthmore prophesying on this subject. For some years after this the lectures were more concerned with individual 'findings' and social and ethical issues of the kind Friends have always been deeply involved in. The torch now passed to others, but with as little practical effect as before. When Alastair Heron came to write *Our Quaker Identity* in 1999, he gave as his reason "to enlist the interest and support of my fellow-Quakers and active Attenders in stemming a slow thirty-year drift towards a humanist or secular Quaker identity, from a religious society to a friendly society".[41] Re-reading this short but perceptive little book recently, I was struck by something in its tone which told me he knew there were few attentive listeners.

Already by this time Ben Pink Dandelion had published his comprehensive analysis of the state of the Society, referring, as we

---

[40] Pilgrim, "Taming Anarchy: Quaker Alternate Ordering and 'Otherness'", in Dandelion (2004), pp. 219-21.

[41] Heron, *Our Quaker Identity: Religious Society or Friendly Society?* (Kelso: Curlew Productions, 1999), p.47.

have seen, to a 'silent revolution'. He maintained "a shift to diversity" had taken place almost unobserved as Friends refrained from ministry which might be open to specific theological interpretation from fear of being isolated or criticised or of hurting others.[42] This was followed by several other important sociological studies. However, these last cannot be regarded as 'prophetic' in the sense that our Swarthmore lectures are and have been. They start from a description and acceptance of the status quo and look for aspects of current Quaker life around which the Society might be able to unite in forging a new and *theologically neutral* identity.[43]

And that is more or less where things stand today. Except that, with the founding of the Non-theist Friends Network (NFN), an organisation within an organisation with its own mission statement and campaigning agenda, and the implicit threat of a humanist take-over, there have been some signs of unease and even revival in leading Quaker circles. Again it is the Swarthmore Lecture that provides a reference point and a sense of the direction in which change might now, at last, be moving.

Peter Eccles, Gerald Hewitson and Ben Dandelion, 2009-14

In 2009, Peter Eccles gave the Swarthmore Lecture on 'The Presence in the Midst'. Despite its title, the lecture takes the existing pattern of belief and unbelief in the Society as a given and in so doing legitimises the claims of the humanist and non-theist groupings who are now clamouring for full recognition. Surprisingly, it then gives way to an emphasis on traditional Quaker practice and the importance of spiritual discernment. Indeed, my reading of the lecture is that it is essentially an attempt to head off the growing influence of the non-theist groups with the author admitting his own preference for materialist explanations of the world whilst at the same time expressing his

[42] Dandelion, *A Sociological Analysis of the Theology of the Quakers* (Lampeter: Edwin Mellen Press, 1996). See also *The Creation of Quaker Theory,* pp. 229-30.
[43] I am thinking here of Dandelion and Collins.

continued faith in a God who is "both within and beyond us". He is saying in effect, 'Just because you're a scientific or philosophical materialist doesn't mean you have to embrace non-theism or atheism. I'm both, and as you can see, I believe in God'. In line with this approach, outright atheists like Daniel Dennett, John Searle, and Richard Dawkins are all given the stamp of approval. But how are these usually opposed positions reconcilable? While Eccles deserves credit for drawing attention to the really difficult *philosophical* questions, it cannot be said that he resolves them in any satisfactory way. Materialism and mysticism are not usually thought to be comfortable bed fellows and the lecture exhibits the kind of split thinking that has become characteristic of the Society as a whole.

Much has been written in recent years about 'the complementarity of apparently opposed truths', but for some minds the contradictions inherent in Eccles' position are a step too far. Ben Pink Dandelion tackles the problem head on when he writes in his 2014 Swarthmore Lecture: "As a group we need to be honest with ourselves. For example we cannot say we seek to encounter the Divine in our meetings for worship and also say categorically that there is nothing beyond the material world. We cannot honestly claim to discern Divine guidance as part of our understanding of corporate Quaker life and at the same time say that there is no such guidance to discern. We cannot both nurture our meetings for worship as a cohesive community experience and say to everyone, regardless of their understanding, behaviours and preferences, that anyone can be a Quaker". He concludes, "we have lost the heart of our faith, and have diluted basic and central Quaker understandings within a desire to appease all the varieties of doctrinal slants we now encompass".[44]

Dandelion's Swarthmore Lecture marks a new turn for the Society, a turn perhaps best described as a recovery of confidence. It is a process which began with the previous year's lecture by Gerald Hewitson. Both Dandelion and Hewitson emphasise the importance of

[44] Dandelion, *Open for Transformation* (London: Quaker Books, 2014), p. 4.

'heart-knowledge' over 'head-knowledge', Hewitson looking back to the early Quakers for inspiration, and in particular to Isaac Penington:

> How may the principle of truth be discerned? Answer: By its piercing, quickening nature . . . for it appears and works, not like man's reason or like motions of his mind which he takes into the understanding part; but it appears and works livingly, powerfully and effectually in the heart. [45]

The emphasis on the heart, on mystical experience, is essential to Quakerism and essential to any revival of the Quaker spirit. But it is an *emphasis*, not a prohibition on thinking, and it is unfortunate that in both authors it should be accompanied by what appears to be an outright dismissal of the claims of reason. "Arguing about beliefs", says Dandelion, " . . . is a red herring — a secular distraction". Hewitson speaks of 'dismantling the empire of my mind' and 'planting a garden of the heart' — an appropriate response when it comes to the experience of prayer and worship, but surely not quite appropriate when we are called to *reflect* on what that experience means? Why cannot we have both: a garden of the heart *and* mind?

One cannot help wondering if there is an element of fear in this — fear of the arguments being hammered home by the self-assured advocates of a secular spirituality, not one of whom receives a mention by either lecturer. But this, surely, is to ignore the elephant in the room? Friends who take refuge in the notion that the experience they point to is safely 'beyond words', beyond the reach of the rational mind, are making themselves vulnerable to a form of philosophical questioning which recognises no reality beyond language and therefore no inviolate 'experience'. It is important for Friends to resist this line of attack which I believe can only be achieved by drawing on the resources of mind as well as heart.

None of this detracts from the positive attempt on the part of all three lecturers to re-focus on the essential aspiration of Quakerism, the

---

[45] Hewitson, *Journey into Life* (London: Quaker Books, 2013), p. 10.

aspiration to a life lived in the atmosphere of God. Eccles' lecture is the most *informative* when it comes to the scientific and philosophical issues which confront today's 'thinking Friend' and in my view performs a very useful function in bringing 'head' and 'heart' together, even if the resulting synthesis is less than perfect. Hewitson's lecture is the most *spiritual*. The subtitle is 'Inheriting the story of early Friends'. Hewitson writes of those early times: "Many people saw the world as it is, and could see no further; Quakers saw the world as God wishes it to be — not a world based on might and strength, but on a long-suffering loving-kindness, imitating the cosmic patience which unceasingly offers its love to the world, wishes us no harm, is solicitous of our welfare, and wants nothing but infinite good". For me, that says it all. When I read it, I am reminded not only of the graceful language of James Nayler's dying testimony, which it echoes, but of George Herbert's beautifully turned poem, *The Elixer,* a verse of which provided the title for this book:

A man that looks on glasse
On it it may stay his eye;
Or if he pleaseth, through it passe,
And then the heav'n espie.[46]

"The absence of any sense of the mystical", I imagine the poet saying, "is a blind spot that the materialist is almost completely unaware of; all he sees is the surface of the glass itself, insisting that this is all there *is* to see. Yet it could all be so different. It is only a matter of faithfully nurturing 'the Light we have' and we can pass through the glass into the divine 'garden of the heart', the Kingdom of God".

Finally, Dandelion's lecture. This is the most *challenging* of the three. Dandelion invites us to re-engage with the central tenets of

[46] C. Patrides (ed.), *The English Poems of George Herbert,* (London: Dent, 1974), p. 188.

Quakerism, so that, growing together in community, we can become vehicles of the healing power of God's love in a destructive and cruel age. His lecture is, among other things, a manifesto for spiritual renewal and lists all the positive attributes and strengths that are present but dormant in our Religious Society, awaiting only the touch of faith to be re-kindled.

Taken together these three forward looking lectures comprise a powerful message of hope, but is it the image of the risen Christ or the ghost of Cassandra that hovers over the speakers? Are they to suffer the fate of previous Swarthmore Lecturers — to be listened to with rapt attention in the Yearly Meeting Conference Hall, only to be ignored and forgotten as soon as the room empties? Or will their words burn with the true Pentecostal fire in the hearts *and* minds of Friends, firing a vision of what Quakerism could be and what it could offer once it had overcome the individualism and secular drift which have led to the current situation?

3

Accommodation and discernment

Why has the heart so gone out of the Christian apologists that apparently they do not see that the maintenance, the justification, of their function is that they do not allow themselves to be swept off course by the fickle waves of fashion?

— Lorna Marsden

Do not be conformed to this world, but be transformed by the renewing of your minds .

— Romans 12: 2

BRITAIN YEARLY MEETING has changed and it is dawning on all of us that the changes now go very deep. It must be admitted that as things stand at present any movement in the direction of a Quaker Christianity, however loosely defined, seems unlikely.[47] Indeed, the direction of change is increasingly pointing the other way, that is, towards the secularisation that Charles Taylor defines as a "self-sufficing humanism" which acknowledges "no final goals beyond human flourishing, nor any allegiance to anything else beyond this flourishing".[48] So faithfully have we followed the intellectual fashions,

[47] A personal friend commented on reading this: "My limited experience of reading Quaker writers and life as an attender have taken me in the opposite direction. These have necessitated a re-exploration of Christianity. I've found it hard to be engaged without at least informing myself about Christianity historically and theologically. Where and how re-engagement is possible I don't yet know — only that for me this seems a requirement of continuing involvement with the *Religious* Society".

[48] Taylor, *A Secular Age* (Cambridge, MA.: Harvard University Press, 2007), p. 18.

that the division to be found in the wider culture between scepticism and religious faith has become part of the make-up of Britain Yearly Meeting itself.

In line with these changes, a new and stronger emphasis has been placed on the notion that we are "creedless", and the understanding of what it means to be creedless considerably extended. Acceptance of diversity is presented as an undisputed good. Instead of being seen as the backbone of the Society, true Christian discipleship is treated as a minority interest along with many others — and by some Friends it is even regarded as a sign of intellectual backwardness.[49] Social activism is valued as a Promethean undertaking unrelated to any sense of dependence on the Divine. And as Jonathan Dale observed, our sense of the sacramental is likewise diminished as the word 'sacrament' itself is dropped from our shared vocabulary.

Things have now gone so far that the question will arise in the minds of some Friends, why have a Religious Society of Friends at all? If celebrating our diversity and taking part in social action are all that provide us with a common purpose, why not wind up our affairs and donate the proceeds to efficiently run charitable organisations like Oxfam and Amnesty which are unambiguously secular? The thought is not new. The US sociologist, Peter Berger, makes the point that the major problem facing an ultra-liberal or secularised Christianity is how "to demonstrate that the religious label, as modified in conformity with the spirit of the age, has anything special to offer". Falling back on the market analogy, he asks: "Why should one buy psychotherapy or racial liberalism in a 'Christian' package, when the same commodities

---

[49] The philosopher, Roger Scruton, makes the same point. He says of Lord Gifford: "I doubt that he anticipated the culture that prevails today, in which belief in God is widely rejected as a sign of emotional and intellectual immaturity. But I think he would have endorsed the attempt to explore what we lose, when we lose that belief." See Scruton, *The Face of God* (The Gifford Lectures. London: Bloomsbury, 2010), p. I.

are available under purely secular and for that very reason even more modernistic labels".[50]

Of course I am not seriously suggesting that we should dissolve ourselves in the more extended and richer diversity of the world at large, since I don't believe the Society of Friends is about diversity, or for that matter, social action. Our social action is the *consequence* of our faith, not its source, although I agree with Jonathan Dale that "when we say that God is love, the integrity of our claim is known by the degree to which it is fulfilled in our lives", although again that fulfilment may be expressed in areas other than direct social and political activity (for example, in the creative arts). But to those who proclaim that "variety is the spice of Quaker life" and yearn for a more secular Society of Friends "based on science and reason" I do ask the question, 'What is so special about the Society of Friends that it should attract those who are already benefiting from the much greater diversity of secular ideas to be found in the world at large?' Or to put it another way, why should people who aspire to a more secular life based on science and reason *want* to be members of a religious society — rather than, say, a local astronomical or debating society? A religious society by definition is *not* secular, and one would have thought the last place to look for a more secular life based on anything at all. Yet the very fact that such attitudes are not only accepted but 'celebrated' in our modern Society of Friends speaks volumes about the way we have allowed ourselves to be invaded and taken over by what Lorna Marsden called the 'fickle waves of fashion'.

The process by which this tends to happen is known as 'accommodation'. As each step is taken in a liberal direction, the way is prepared for the next step. It is a process which has been going on for more than half a century, and one of the first to comment on it was again Peter Berger. In his book, *A Rumour of Angels*, which appeared in 1969, Berger accurately describes trends in US society which have emerged and consolidated within Britain Yearly Meeting since that

[50] Berger, p. 35.

time: evidence, if any were needed, of our susceptibility to 'notions' not of our own making. Referring to the Protestant denominations which he criticised for not resisting but accommodating to secularist influences, Berger remarked, "while this curious vulnerability (not to say lack of character) can probably be explained sociologically, what is interesting here is the over-all result — a profound erosion of the traditional religious contents, in extreme cases to the point where nothing is left but hollow rhetoric". He identifies pluralism as "the twin phenomenon to secularisation", an observation that helps to explain why the call to *celebrate* diversity comes loudest from those who want to move the Society in a secular direction.

Accommodation to secularist ideas has been criticised as self-defeating by other eminent figures in the sociology of religion. The distinguished theologian and cultural historian, Miroslav Volf, warns us that Christian communities who adopt this strategy are accommodating to what they have not shaped: "Reconstructions of the Christian faith guided by the strategy of accommodation carry in themselves the seeds of possible Christian self-destruction . . . The voice of the Christian communities has become a mere echo of a voice that is not their own". He continues, quoting two of the United States' most eminent theologians and thinkers, who are on record as opposing both Christian fundamentalism *and* liberal Christianity. Stanley Hauerwas and William Willimon, he says, "put the consequence of the accommodation strategy this way: 'Alas, in leaning over to speak to the modern world, we had fallen in. We had lost the theological resources to resist, lost the resources even to see that there was something worth resisting'".[51]

According to Volf the way to resist the forces of secularism is not to de-emphasise our differences from the wider community but actually to highlight them:

> Christian communities will be able to survive and thrive in contemporary societies only if they attend to their "difference" from

[51] Volf, *A Public Faith* (Grand Rapids, MI.: Brazos Press, 2011), pp. 84-5.

> surrounding cultures and subcultures. The following principle stands: whoever wants the Christian communities to exist must want their difference from the surrounding culture, not their blending into it. As a consequence, Christian communities must "manage" their identity by actively engaging in "boundary maintenance". Without boundaries, communities dissolve. The question is not whether there should be boundaries; it is rather what their nature should be (i.e. how permeable should they be) and how they should be maintained (i.e. by shoring up that which is specific to Christian communities or by strengthening that which is central).[52]

As I write, Britain Yearly Meeting is entering a period of reflection and preparation for the next revision of *Quaker Faith and Practice.* In the August 2014 issue of The *Friends Quarterly*, the current Recording Clerk, Paul Parker, maps out the vision which he believes should guide those entrusted with this important task. On the question of boundary maintenance, he tells us "we have to resist the temptation to draw fat black lines around what it means to be a Quaker, but that does not mean that you have no lines at all. I think there is a dotted line around what it means to be a Quaker, and we have to negotiate and be very sensitive about that."[53] I am not sure that 'negotiation' is the right word to use in connection with spiritual discernment, but I am *quite* sure there is something between a fat black line and a highly porous dotted line. For example, we might think of a continuous thin grey line as one requiring a criterion of openness to the *possibility* of the transcendent, an idea which I discuss further in Chapters 10 and 11.

'Boundary maintenance' is what Janet Scott began and then retreated from. But so thoroughly has Britain Yearly Meeting been 'penetrated' (the word is Gay Pilgrim's) by ideas and movements which run directly counter to its basic beliefs, it is doubtful that even this option is open to us any longer. What was a question of choice when Janet Scott told us we "must be inclusive towards other faiths

---

52 *ibid.*, p. 80.

53 Parker, *The Friends Quarterly* (August 2014), p. 6.

and towards atheism" has become an imperative that is now inclusive of even the most explicit anti-theism, and it should come as no surprise that in order to make room for these ideas we are besieged with calls to remove the last remaining boundary line, that between member and attender. However, if this is what we decide to do, we should proceed with our eyes fully open. As Patricia Loring has said "the consequence of having no standard [for membership] is that the Meeting conforms to the vision of those it has admitted".[54]

Accommodation is a gradual process and in a Society which welcomes new light *from whatever source*, there is always the danger that cherished concepts like 'discernment' and 'continuing revelation' will be used to justify and win support for changes that will lead us further towards the secular. Indeed the word 'discern' is itself undergoing a change in meaning and is likely to be used, even by those undertaking the revision, in both a religious *and* a secular sense, without any clear distinction as to which meaning is intended.

'Discernment' traditionally means 'seeking the will of God', but in the 2013 British Quaker Survey we are given a quite shocking statistic. It appears that "only 20 per cent of adult Quakers now say that they are seeking the will of God in Meeting for Worship, and clerks do not generally see their role as helping the Meeting to discern the will of God".[55] While this figure does not equate to the number of Friends who profess to *believe* in God (72% in 2003 down to 57% in 2013 — still a majority but a lower figure than for the population as a whole),[56] it does appear that a large section of the Society has decided that discernment in the traditional sense doesn't work. And how can

---

[54] Loring, quoted in S. Best and S. Masters, "What Can We Say Today?: Questions for the Revision of the Book of Discipline", *The Friends Quarterly* (August 2014), p. 39.

[55] Dandelion, 'The British Quaker Survey of 2013" in S. Best and S. Masters, *ibid.*, pp. 37-38. The same survey found that "41% of us see Quaker business method as seeking the will of God. Whilst 79% felt 'the sense of the Meeting' to be an appropriate description" (see also Dandelion, *Open for Transformation*, p. 46). The figures are not necessarily contradictory since seeing what the Quaker business method is about is not the same as believing in it oneself.

[56] Dandelion, *The British Quaker Survey 2013.*

important, and for many Friends deeply distressing, changes to our belief system and corporate procedures be justified by an appeal to the Quaker doctrine of 'continuing revelation' when the source of that revelation is conceived as having neither will nor purpose, nor in some cases any transcendent reality at all? Are we not accommodating here to a wholly subjective and wholly secular understanding of the 'Inner Light'?

Following on from his comments on boundary lines, Parker gives us little ground for hope that the trends of the last thirty years are going to be reversed to any great extent. On the contrary, our survival as a religious society is attributed, at least in part, to our willingness and continuing capacity to absorb such trends, including the now wide and deepening theological differences:

> The Book of Discipline needs to reflect the diversity among us, as well as the unity — both of which are positive qualities — and it needs to reflect the fact that Quakerism can accommodate such diversity. Since the time of the Manchester Conference our Liberal Quakerism has experienced demographic, theological and societal change, but remains the great survivor. Part of that is our ability to accommodate such diversity under a single umbrella.[57]

The word 'accommodate' in this context may mean nothing more than 'making room for'. But this in itself is not so far removed from Peter Berger's use of the term, meaning 'accommodate to' — for 'accommodating to' is surely what one is doing in order to 'make room'? What then of 'discernment', a process which one would expect to have little in common with the process of accommodation? Parker continues:

> Although we would not be seeking to reach a point where we all unite necessarily behind exactly the same things, I expect that the Yearly Meeting would want to seek out through discernment what texts

---

[57] Parker, *ibid.*, p. 6.

resonate sufficiently to be counted as central to current Quaker perceptions, and which are interesting but relatively peripheral. The eventual anthology would need to say "this is the closest we can get to being able to capture our historical and contemporary experience".[58]

It is interesting to find the words 'accommodate' and 'discernment' in such close conjunction. The idea being advanced here appears to be that of accommodating (and therefore accommodating to) as wide a theological diversity as possible within an undefined, elusive and paradoxically disunited 'unity' ("a single umbrella" but not one that unites us "behind exactly [or even approximately?] the same things").

Accommodation to diversity thus taken for granted, discernment, under whatever form, will be confined to selecting the texts that correspond to this diversity — more a literary exercise, one may feel, than a spiritual one. In fairness, there was probably no other diplomatically acceptable way the Recording Clerk could have put it; but I hope and pray that I am wrong, and that the process of discernment will be carried out more in line with our historical than our contemporary experience.

There are some grounds for optimism. In the same issue of *The Friends Quarterly*, Simon Best and Stuart Masters with admirable foresight set out all the really important questions, refusing to shirk even the most uncomfortable.[59] How we answer those questions will make or break Britain Yearly Meeting. Turning back is never going to be easy, even when we are so patently standing on the brink. But recognising honestly where we are 'accommodating to' and where we are being truly led by the Spirit is certain to be a good start. To attain this clarity of insight we will need not only the confidence born of trust. We will need, as Hauerwas and Willimon insisted, "the theological resources to resist".

---

[58] *ibid.* p. 9.

[59] Best and Masters, *ibid.*

4
The Quaker need of theology

The weaknesses of Quakerism lay, and to some extent still lie, in the tendency to distrust the intellect, to suspect the outward, and to neglect the historical.

— H.G. Wood

Not to philosophise is still to philosophise.

— attributed to Aristotle

WHAT IS THEOLOGY? For many Friends it is an abstract, sterile and unreal form of book knowledge which has little or no relation to the only authority they recognise as valid — direct personal experience. For these Friends, Fox's famous declaration, "This I know experimentally", has come to mean "I have no time for God-talk or any kind of systematic thinking about religion." Yet these same Friends are often among the most avid readers of whatever happens to be the popular theology of the day, which means their thinking is influenced and shaped by external theologies which are seldom countered or modified by anything coming from the Society itself, nothing that really addresses fundamental issues in a way that defines the Quaker perspective.

Theology of some kind is unavoidable in today's world. The most committed anti-theists, whether inside the Christian community, like Don Cupitt and Richard Holloway, or outside it, like Richard Dawkins and Christopher Hitchens, are theologising whether they acknowledge it or not. Friends are no exception. What Aristotle is reputed to have said about philosophising is equally true of theology — 'not to theologise is still to theologise'. As soon as we start *thinking* about our religious experience and the beliefs that arise from it we are entering the realm of theology. If we are in a state of crisis about our faith, unable to decide whether we are Christian-oriented or Universalist or humanist, we find ourselves grappling with the big questions, the theological questions, even as we express our hostility to all forms of God-talk.

The term 'God-talk' in Quaker circles as elsewhere is used to express impatience or contempt for what at its most sophisticated is a deeply reflective discourse about the nature of God and religious faith; a form of discourse that is not (at least primarily) concerned with proof but, as John Macquarrie says, with establishing the internal consistency of the faith position and "a coherence, so far as this is required, with all the other intellectual enterprises of the human mind."[60]

At this point I can picture the reader's eyes beginning to glaze over, but the unavoidable truth is that there is no future for a religion which stands in direct contradiction to the findings of science and the light of reason. Far from dismissing the arguments of rationalists and humanists as having no bearing on our spiritual lives we need to have the confidence, based on our experience of the real presence of God, to tackle them head-on. Inconsistency and incoherence will be cleverly exploited by those who feel the need to undermine the faith positions of mainstream Quakerism. Indeed, it would be difficult to exaggerate the importance of the task that Macquarrie so clearly sets before us. Take, for example, Peter Eccles' 2009 Swarthmore Lecture, one of the few that openly acknowledges the force of the rationalist position. Eccles tells us that he rejects dualism, being convinced by the materialist views of people like Daniel Dennet, John Searle and Richard Dawkins that "consciousness is an ordinary biological phenomenon comparable with growth, digestion, or the secretion of bile" but that nevertheless there is "a Spirit within us *and beyond us*" to which we can turn for leadings and guidance. Without conceding anything to dualism, these appear — at least on the surface — to be

---

[60] Macquarrie, *Principles of Christian Theology* (London: SCM Press, 1966; rev. edn. 1977), p. 3.

quite contradictory ideas, but if they are not, then a consistent and coherent explanation as to why they are not is needed if we are to take his claims for the reality of the Spirit seriously — and that is a theological task.

The assumed division between reason and spiritual experience is at the root of much Quaker thinking around theology. I believe this is a weakness rather than a strength, and for this reason I find I am not fully in agreement with Ben Pink Dandelion's position in his otherwise excellent 2014 Swarthmore Lecture. It is surprising to me that one of our leading intellectuals should share in the distrust, amounting almost to phobia, that many Friends feel with regard to the intellect. In his lecture Dandelion appears to equate the rational mind with a full-blown secularism. "Arguing about beliefs", he maintains, ". . . is a secular distraction", and we are reminded that Friends are "not like-minded, but like-hearted". Similarly, spirituality is "not about head belief but heart experience". Fears about the future of Quakerism are seen as "a symptom of the head alone taking over from the heart, of logic supplanting faith", and although there is here a gently applied pressure on the word 'alone', the overall effect is to reinforce longstanding anti-intellectual attitudes and leave the fundamentals of our faith undefended.[61] While it is undoubtedly right to highlight the centrality of spiritual *experience,* the danger with this approach is that some of our members and attenders may be left with the uneasy feeling that Quakers are afraid to engage with the *rational* arguments because they believe them to be rationally unassailable. That is to leave the field open to the non-realist, language-based, thinking which would question even the experience itself.

For those who engage in it, theology is felt to be an urgent and necessary form of service which we ignore at our peril. Even Christian social action, Macquarrie points out, "will become aimless and

---

[61] Dandelion, *Open for Transformation,* pp. 37, 22, 14, and 5 respectively. Dandelion does say (p.74), "My desire to live out of a heart place rather than a head one does not take away the place of enquiry and thought, it simply means not starting and ending there", but he gives no hint as to what the role of enquiry and thought in relation to the religious life should be.

sporadic unless it is illuminated by clear theological understanding". The effect on church membership of ignoring theology may be equally serious. The great Anglican theologian, Austin Farrer, maintained that failure to defend the reasonableness of faith would leave it exposed to the pressures of the surrounding culture with inevitable consequences:

> Though argument does not create conviction, the lack of it destroys belief. What seems to be proved may not be embraced; but what no one shows the ability to defend is quickly abandoned. Rational argument does not create belief; but it maintains a climate in which belief may flourish.[62]

Many Friends nowadays take the view that 'belief is relatively inconsequential'. It is hard to say whether that is a cause or effect of the rapid decline in our numbers in recent years, but whatever the case there can be little doubt that the low status of theology in the Society of Friends has been a contributing factor in its decline since the early eighteenth century. Edward Grubb, one of the architects of the Manchester Conference, believed that the absence of a Quaker theology to defend Quaker belief had made the Society weak and ineffectual. It was a view shared by H. G. Wood and the Anglican champion of Quakerism, F. D. Maurice. Grubb complained that so much emphasis had been placed on the Inward Light "that every exercise of reason or judgement seemed an obstacle that must at all costs be cleared out of the way":

> Hence arose a fear of the use of reason in relation to 'Divine things' which is a chief secret of the mental poverty that soon overtook the Society of Friends. Since Barclay, it has produced not one profound thinker. The idea became prevalent that all that was needed, in the way of religious teaching, would be supernaturally provided; and the third and fourth generations of Friends were left, to a very large extent, to grow up in ignorance.[63]

---

[62] Quoted in A. McGrath, *Mere Theology* (London: SPCK, 2010) p. 71.
[63] Grubb, *Authority and the Light Within* (London: James Clarke, 1909), p. 85.

Grubb believed that this also helped to explain why, after the first phase, the Quakers made so little impact on the religious life of the nation. "The early Quakers failed, then, to see through some of the fallacies that were universal in the religious thought of their day, and hence were unable to find a true way of expressing the new truth they had discovered. It is probable that this is one great cause of their failure, after the first generation had passed away, to move the religious world. While it is true that many of their thoughts are now held by spiritually-minded people in all the Churches, this can hardly be put to their credit, as though it were mainly due to missionary toil of theirs. The Friends had been known as quietists and philanthropists, but to the vast majority of people their spiritual ideals and experiences have been almost completely unknown."[64]

Later writers took up the theme, but with the focus more firmly on warnings about society's impact on us than on whatever impact we might have on the religious thinking of the age. As we saw in Chapter 2, Thomas Green as early as 1956 commented that a religious society which devalues theology is likely to have weak defences and be vulnerable to the current intellectual fashions.[65] Little more than a decade later Richenda Scott observed:

> The danger for the Quaker at this time is that his experience may be so slight, his thought so vague and confused, that he will merely batten on the fresh ideas burgeoning around him, absorbing them piece-meal without discrimination, and thereby producing in himself further mental indigestion and conflict. So, once again, as in the 19th century, we may find that we have lost any clear sense of direction, have no real grasp of what it is we have to offer as the constructive Quaker contribution . . . Once more we may discover that we have been swept into a backwater, from which we can be rescued only by a fresh and deeper experience, *and a clearer realization in thought of what that experience means*.[66]

---

[64] *ibid.*, p. 86.
[65] Green, *Preparation for Worship*, pp. 4-5.
[66] R. Scott, *Tradition and Experience*, p. 56. My emphasis.

So it is a paradox that having no tradition of doing theology ourselves, and rejecting 'notions', we are all the more susceptible to theologies and notions we have had no hand in shaping. The leading example of this in our own time is the 'modernising theology' of Don Cupitt whose ideas began to influence Friends in the mid-eighties through the 'Sea of Faith' movement and continue to have an influence today through the writings and activities of the Quaker humanist, David Boulton, and the Non-theist Friends Network (NFN), the special interest group he was largely instrumental in setting up.

Cupitt is a 'liberal postmodernist' and 'non-realist' who argues, as a point of irrefutable logic, that the only reality available to us is that which we ourselves construct through the medium of language. It follows from this by no means universally accepted reasoning that God is no more than a 'human construct'.[67] Initially, Cupitt proposed the idea of a God beyond being, "a something prior to being that may be called a background of radical otherness and difference". In this he was much influenced by the continental philosophers up to and including Derrida. Not all of these have been atheists. Derrida himself was deliberately ambiguous about his attitude to theism. The Christian existentialists, Karl Jaspers and Gabriel Marcel, and the eminent Catholic philosopher and theologian, Jean-Luc Marion, have all resisted the atheist attack with particular emphasis on two key theological concepts, transcendence and revelation. These are concepts which lie at the very heart of the Quaker experience but are anathema to humanists. But while most Friends of the Sea of Faith school will have read much that Boulton and Cupitt have written, how many will have taken the trouble to read the works of any of these writers? Marion's most famous book, *God Without Being*, takes us directly into the territory defined by the early Cupitt, but without the ambivalence that a reader may have expected from the title.[68] Marion, in other

---

[67] The idea is not new but proceeds from the work of two related schools of linguistic philosophers, the structuralists and post-structuralists — more of them later!

[68] Marion, *God Without Being* (tr. T. Carlson. Chicago, IL.: University of Chicago Press, 1991). In his Preface to the English edition, Marion acknowledges that the

words, comes down firmly on the side of God. Cupitt was to lead his followers in a wholly different direction.

It's quite possible that Cupitt's own philosophical development was too far in advance of many of his followers. Some appear to have held their ground, accepting his depersonalization of God but holding on to the element of transcendence. Others went further, affirming the kind of 'immanence without transcendence' that merges God with the natural universe — making God a sort of cosmic force for good (though without distinguishing whether this was a natural force like, say, dark matter or a supernatural force). Probably both these sub-groups would accept the term 'non-theist' as an accurate description of their position. Cupitt himself, however, was unable to hold on to anything so provisional. Such half-formed ideas, he knew, were open to philosophical and even commonsense objections. So he continued his journey, his liberal postmodernist theology taking him step by step to an unqualified atheism and ultimately to nihilism.

Rowan Williams says that Cupitt "gives his readers very little sense of the range of intellectual options involved in this debate".[69] By this he means that Cupitt's less aware readers might feel trapped within the well fortified system, amounting to an ideology, that he has constructed on a particular view of language. Cupitt does in fact discuss and set out other philosophical viewpoints but almost always within a historical framework which makes it appear as if they are all leading inexorably towards his particular brand of anti-realism, and for the most part he refrains from taking on his more formidable *contemporary* critics, such as Rowan Williams himself. Boulton, in contrast, has no time at all for other points of view. His books,

---

title is open to misunderstanding: "was it insinuating that the God 'without being' is not, or does not exist? Let me repeat now the answer I gave then: no, definitely not. God is, exists, and that is the least of things. At issue here is not the possibility of God's attaining to Being. But, quite the opposite, the possibility of Being's attaining to God."

[69] Williams, "'Religious Realism': on not quite agreeing with Don Cupitt" (1984) in M. Higton (ed.), *Wrestling with Angels: Conversations in Modern Theology* (London: SCM Press, 2007), p. 247.

although lively and popular, are seamless examples of tunnel vision. But in either case the 'ordinary' reader is denied choice; she or he is inducted into the author's extreme subjectivism and anti-realism without any fair and proper discussion of alternative perspectives which may be every bit as credible and as 'theologically and philosophically adequate' (to use a favourite Cupitt expression) as their own. Two such examples are 'critical realism' and the 'personalist', extra-subjectivist philosophy of Michael Polanyi — more of them later.

Perhaps all of these divergent views are openly and fairly discussed within the Sea of Faith Movement, but I imagine there are also powerful inhibiting factors at play. The ordinary thinking 'Sea-of-Faither' may feel too cowed to question such strongly worded sentiments as "today all the traditional supernaturalist ideas about the religious life are dead, and must be got rid of. Above all, we should be tireless in hunting down and driving out all forms of the repulsive distinction between 'material' and 'spiritual' things and concerns".[70] This, incidentally, illustrates how far Cupitt has travelled since the days when he could say with equal conviction that theism and non-theism are "both so stupendously grand that we would not even wish either of them to be wiped off the map. We actually prefer pluralism".[71]

Cupitt's literary output since the early 1970s has been prodigious and it is obviously impossible to summarize or do justice to his views in a few paragraphs. One could say, like the Anglican theologian, Keith Ward, that "he has done theology a service in voicing the inner doubts and hesitations of many churchgoers, forcing them to greater honesty and clarity and exposing the main problems that have to be faced". But Ward, a member of the Council of the Royal Institute of

---

[70] Cupitt, *The Old Creed and the New* (London: SCM Press, 2006), p. 51. It may be objected that what is being 'hunted down' is merely an abstract theological or philosophical concept, not a person. Nevertheless, the violence of Cupitt's language seems excessive when one considers that included among those who hold to this 'repulsive' distinction are his own colleagues, academic and clerical.
[71] Cupitt, *Creation out of Nothing* (London: SCM Press, 1990), p. 114.

Philosophy, disagrees that the 'modern mind' is compelled to accept the uncompromising solution Cupitt offers. There are other options open to the religious seeker.[72] My point is that these other options are seldom brought before Friends in ways that might help them to relativise Cupitt's arguments, and that this is due in part to our tradition of marginalising theology. Paradoxically, by insisting on this stance, we have allowed ourselves to be the passive instruments of a theology that strikes at the very heart of our Quaker faith.

This may go some way to explain, what has always been a puzzle to me, why Friends' mistrust of 'notions' does not extend to secular theologians of the 'death of God' school who produce abstract systems by the spadeful, but are welcomed with enthusiasm as deliverers from an allegedly infantile, theistic belief system. Indeed, the assertion that God is a *human construct* (a 'notion' if ever there was one) is now far more likely to be received sympathetically in Quaker circles than the assertion that God exists, even though the first cannot be validated 'experientially', and therefore *remains* at the level of a 'notion', while the second has been grounded in our corporate experience and history for more than three hundred and fifty years.

Friends like to see themselves as trail-blazers and they often are; but in the field of theology they are more likely to be trailing behind, and trailing dismally. The mindset of the free-thinking, independent Quaker, as described in the paragraph above, is nothing new. Peter Berger, as far back as 1969, points out how "Protestant theologians [in the United States] have been increasingly engaged in playing a game whose rules have been dictated by their cognitive antagonists":

> The self-liquidation of the theological enterprise is undertaken with an enthusiasm that verges on the bizarre, culminating in the reduction to absurdity of the 'God-is-dead theology' and 'Christian atheism'. It is no wonder that even those clergy, younger theologians, and, with particular poignancy, theological students who are not simply eager to be 'with it' in terms of the latest ideological fashions are afflicted with

[72] Ward, *Holding Fast to God* (London: SPCK, 1982), p. x.

> profound malaise in this situation. The question 'What next?' may sometimes be the expression of an intellectual attitude geared to fads and publicity; but it may also be a genuine cry *de profundis*.[73]

And he shows how ambiguity and denial as well as this genuine *cri de coeur* can be covered over and concealed by an over-determined emphasis on social and political action:

> In the [US] situation the option of political activity, made morally reasonable by the unspeakable mess of our domestic and international affairs, can serve as a welcome relief, a liberating 'leap' from ambiguity to commitment. I do not for one moment wish to disparage this option, but it should be clear from even moderate reflection that the fundamental cognitive problem will not be solved in this manner.[74]

What does this say about the modern Quaker emphasis on social action as the ground of our lost unity? Does it reveal us as a Spirit-led community or as merely reflecting developments taking place elsewhere, a decade or two behind those in the United States?

If we Quakers could overcome our distrust of the intellect, as Edward Grubb and H.G. Wood advised, and apply ourselves seriously to the study of philosophy and theology, we might be better equipped to evaluate the ideologies that threaten our very existence. We have nothing to fear from taking such a stance and everything to gain. If we have experienced God in our lives or in the gathered Meeting for Worship we can afford to explore ideas freely at the intellectual level without in any way shaking our convictions at the spiritual level. Thus strengthened, we might again find ourselves in a position to offer guidance and leadership, showing that there are rationally coherent alternatives to humanism which are not reductionist and which keep open the possibility of transcendence.

Moreover, far from 'intellectualising' our spiritual lives in ways that would desensitise us to the love and presence of God, such

---

[73] Berger, *ibid.*, pp. 23, 25.

[74] *ibid.*

explorations are likely to lead to discoveries that will enrich and strengthen our lives. Melvin Keiser, reflecting on the theology of Isaac Penington and early Friends, tells us "there is a power, I have found, in the life as it is contained in theological language that can nourish our spiritual growth — if we will confront, rather than avoid, this strangeness, and find a way through its forms into its life. Not simply discerning the life there but thinking about its relevance to the life in our lives can enhance the quality of our spiritual existence. We need such religious thinking not only to clarify for ourselves who we are, but to nurture the next generation and to share with others our deepest life-orientation"[75]

It will be clear from what I have said so far, that I believe the term 'notion' to be a stumbling-block preventing the Society from engaging effectively in the theological controversies of the day and reducing it to the role of passive observer and ultimately consumer. If we go back to the time of Fox, we discover that the term 'notion' was applied only to those ideas which were not 'in the Life'. By this, Fox meant chiefly the ideas of his opponents, the Calvinists and other Protestants, who believed in such life-denying doctrines as predestination and justification by faith alone — notions indeed — which guaranteed salvation to the few and consigned the rest to the fires of hell. The Quaker faith, by contrast, was based on personal experience of the Christ within, which was available to all without distinction, revealing to them the imperfections of their own nature, and through this opening them to the transforming power of love.

So when Fox challenged us by asking 'What canst *thou* say?' he wanted us to consider whether it came 'inwardly from God' or was received second hand from 'the hireling-shepherd's tent'? He certainly didn't mean to imply that it was a virtue to have no conceptual understanding of what that inward experience meant. It needs to be remembered, too, that the question was addressed to those (including Margaret Fell) who had not yet been 'convinced'. The theologising of convinced Friends, like Edward Burrough and Francis Howgill, was

[75] Keiser in Keiser and Moore, p. 244.

never in doubt as it was founded on their personal and collective experience of the Light, that is, the Spirit of Christ in their hearts and consciences, through which they had entered into a new covenant with God.

In *Quaker Faith and Practice* (19.08), there is a wonderful passage from Howgill describing the effect on his listeners, including Howgill himself, of Fox's great sermon to the Westmorland Separatists on Firbank Fell. The passage includes the words, "We met together in the unity of the Spirit, and of the bond of peace, treading down under our feet all reasoning about religion". Readers might be forgiven for interpreting this as yet further evidence of early Friends rejecting any kind of systematic thinking about their faith. But when we turn to the original text, we find that the sentence doesn't stop at 'religion' but continues with the words '*as to any external thing*'. What Howgill is repudiating is not reasoning as such but "debating and contending" among themselves about "external forms", that is to say, practices and institutions which were mere human creations, or doctrines and scriptural texts that were valid but used without spiritual understanding, and therefore not 'in the Life'.[76] Among themselves, as they waited in "pure silence", all disputation over these matters miraculously ceased. But towards the outside world, they showed a different face — reasoning, questioning, debating and contending for all they were worth, seizing every opportunity they could to spread their liberating gospel, "*by Doctrine, by Practice, by holy conversation.*"[77] Howgill says of his friend, Edward Burrough, described as a 'Son of Thunder': "God filled his mouth with

[76] The full passage reads: "And from that Day forward our Hearts were knit unto the Lord, and unto one another, in true and fervent Love; not by any External Covenant, or External Form; but we entered into the Covenant with God, and that was as a strong Obligation or Bond upon all our spirits, which united us one unto another; and we met together in the Unity of the Spirit, and of the Bond of Peace; treading down under our Feet all reasoning, questioning, debating and contending about Religion, or any part or parts, or practice or practices thereof, as to any external thing." See Howgill's 'Testimony Concerning . . . Edward Burroughs' in G. Whitehead (ed.), *The Memorable Works of . . . Edward Burrough* (N.p.: n.p., 1672), Sig. C[4-5] .

[77] *ibid.*, Sig. E[4]. 'Conversation' in those days also meant 'behaviour'.

Arguments . . . his Tongue was as the hand of a ready Scribe, and yet he had the Tongue of the Learned."[78] No fear of the intellect there!

In the ten years between 1652 and 1662, the early Quakers produced approximately one thousand publications, some of which were large volumes like Fox's *The Great Mystery* and Fisher's *Rusticus ad Academicos*, others mere tracts like Burrough's *A Declaration to all the World of our Faith*, writings which were free of 'notions' (the dead forms embraced by their adversaries) but crammed with contentious ideas of their own. The works of these early Friends raised issues around Christology, ecclesiology, theodicy, eschatology, pneumatology and biblical exegesis, often in vigorous debate with the great Puritan theologians of their day. Their mode of writing, as was the custom in the seventeenth century, was polemical, page after page ferociously attacking the 'notions' (and often the characters) of their opponents with 'the weapons of Truth'.

An exception to this characteristic literary style is the early 'second phase' Friend, Robert Barclay, whose *Apology for the True Christian Divinity* was described by Sir Leslie Stephen as "in many respects one of the most impressive theological writings of the [seventeenth] century". The novelist, George Eliot, considered it "among the richest gems of our language".[79] Barclay is the only theologian of truly *European* stature that the Society has produced, and it says much for his reputation and the discoveries of early Friends that it is only now that the rest of the world is catching up.[80] New Testament scholars like Gerd Thiessen and Marcus Borg, along with Hans Kung and many others, are recovering an early Christianity which in many respects is identical to that presented in *The Apology* and fully justifies the early Friends' description of their beliefs as 'primitive Christianity revived'. It is ironic, tragic even, that this is

---

[78] *ibid.*, Sig. E6.

[79] Dean Freiday (ed.), *Barclay's Apology in Modern English* (Newberg, OR: Barclay Press, 1991), p. xxxii.

[80] This was first pointed out to me in conversation with David Britton.

happening when many in the Society in Britain are shrugging off the inspiration of the past.

Barclay has been, and remains, one of the most neglected figures in our Society's history. In the eighteenth century, instead of building upon the contribution of Barclay, with the Society of Friends leading the way as might have been expected, we entered on a long period of theological quietism which continues to this day, squandering the wonderful head start he gave us with his *Apology*. Today, we lack a sound theological base and we could do worse than turn to Barclay for new compass readings as we consider the Society's precarious future.[81]

In defending Quakerism against the movement's detractors, at a time of great persecution, Barclay attempted to make his theology acceptable to orthodoxy on one sensitive point: the nature of Jesus and his relation to the Christ. He describes Jesus as the Son, "with God through all eternity, being himself God, and also in time partaking of the nature of man".[82] However, later in the *Apology,* he criticises both Protestants and Catholics for the 'error' of relating the Eucharist, or participation in the body and blood of *Christ*, to the "outer body" of him "that walked and suffered in Judea".[83] This replicates 1650s Quaker teaching, for it is apparent that Fox and the early Friends did not believe that Jesus was literally God. They looked upon him as the 'garment' of the Christ, a man like all men who had within him the Spirit in 'full measure'. As Melvin Keiser says of Isaac Penington: "Christ, for Penington, is God, 'the infinite eternal Being', which was most fully present in the man Jesus but '*cannot be confined to be*

---

[81] A commendable start in delineating a Quaker theology has been made by Patricia Williams in her *Quakerism: A Theology for Our Time* (York: The Ebor Press, 2007).

[82] Freiday, p. 24. Barclay's views on this subject are complex and perhaps ambiguous. He says of Jesus: "He is the head and we are the members. He is the vine and we are branches. Just as the soul is more immediately present in the heart and the mind than it is in the hands or the legs, as the sap and life of the vine is present *in greater quantity* [emphasis added] in the stock and root than in the branches, so God dwells differently in Jesus than in us (Freiday, p. 86).

[83] *ibid*, p. 337.

nowhere else but there'".[84] They went further, quoting among other texts, John 17.22 ("The glory which thou gavest me I have given to them, that they may be one, as we are one") to show that through the Christ we all have the potential to be the Sons and Daughters of God.[85] For the early Friends, Jesus' claim that "no-one comes to the Father except through me" was a life-affirming reference to the Spirit of God within him, not a self-aggrandising claim to uniquely divine status.

Early Friends tended to spiritualise the events of the gospel story. For example, they were inclined to speak of the resurrection, transfiguration and ascension of Jesus not so much as historical facts but as spiritual realities unfolding in the individual soul. So advanced were their ideas, that it could be said they anticipated the 'Honest to God' debate of the 1960s by some three hundred years. Thus they mocked the Puritans for telling the people "that God, and the Kingdom of God is without them, or in a place in heaven a great many miles above their heads, making the ignorant people think that God is as some great man sitting in a throne in the natural heavens".[86] In contrast to this, Barclay explains that "the proper nature and essence of God" is "pure and uncomplicated being, devoid of all composition and division . . . a spiritual, celestial, and invisible principle".[87] A measure of this divine principle, he says, "exists as a seed in all men which by its nature draws, invites, and inclines the individual towards God". But the claim that God is sought *within* the person does not mean that the divine principle does not also transcend the individual (or group): "Because we have earnestly desired people to sense the presence of God in and near themselves, they have maliciously inferred that we

---

[84] Keiser in Keiser and Moore, p. 249.

[85] See, for example, James Nayler, *Love to the Lost* (London: Calvert, 1656), p. 21; also George Fox, Epistle 35 (1653) in *A Collection of . . . Epistles* (London: Sowle, 1698), p. 31.

[86] B. Nicholson, *A Blast from the Lord*, p. 5 quoted in G. Guiton, *The Early Quakers and the 'Kingdom of God'* (San Francisco, CA.: Inner Light Books, 2012), p. 34. These aspects of early Quaker theology are explored in detail in Chapter 8 of Guiton's book.

[87] Freiday, p. 85.

deny God, except that of him that is within us. But what we have really being trying to tell them is that their notion of God as being beyond the clouds will be of little use to them if they cannot also find him near them".[88]

Equally attractive to our modern way of thinking are early Friends' views on universal redemption. Quoting John 1: 9, "The true light that enlightens every man was coming into the world", Barclay says, "This passage so clearly favours our assertions that some have called it the Quaker text". He has much to say on this subject, the chapter dealing with it being the longest in the book, but I will confine myself here to one rather endearing argument which demonstrates the spirit of his writing. He asks, "If it is absolutely necessary to know the name of Jesus in order to be saved, why do those who maintain this make an exception in the case of deaf-mutes and children . . . why isn't this excuse also valid for the man in China or India who has never heard of Jesus by an accident of geography rather than because of physical infirmity?"[89] A good if lighthearted example of logic *confirming* faith.

Finally, consider their views on the role of women in the church. Barclay devotes a separate chapter to this question, explaining that "since male and female are one in Christ Jesus, and he gives his Spirit no less to one than to the other, we do not consider it in any way unlawful for a woman to preach in the assemblies of God's people when God so moves her by his Spirit".[90] He dismisses "Paul's reproof of the inconsiderate and talkative women who caused trouble in the church at Corinth", pointing out that in the same text Paul lays down rules on how women should conduct themselves when preaching and praying in public and refers as a matter of course to a woman who laboured alongside him in the ministry. Other women mentioned in the New Testament, Barclay says, are described as having a gift of prophecy; and he concludes by referring to the many souls converted

---

[88] *ibid.*,p. 438.

[89] *ibid.*, p. 114.

[90] *ibid.*, p. 218.

in his own day, presumably to the Quaker cause, through the ministry of women. "Certainly this demonstration of actual practice should place the question beyond controversy".

With a tradition like this to draw on, which denies (or at least qualifies) the divinity of the man Jesus, while upholding his status as "the garment" of the Christ, the uncreated, eternal Word which shines in everyone regardless of race, gender, or creed, we have the beginnings of a theology which has the potential to unite most of us today, and one that could be intellectually acceptable to Universalists and feminists who are not simply anti-Christian. In its tendency to internalise the miraculous and interpret historical events figuratively, and in its intuitive understanding of God as Divine Essence, it is a tradition which places us well within the frame of contemporary theological discourse. Moreover, we have here the foundation for a theology that would enable us to respect and value our Christian roots, and their continued capacity to grow, flourish and bear fruit, without locking us into the kind of irresolvable problems that are currently plaguing the mainstream churches. It would open us again to the inspiring visions of the past, and perhaps most appealing of all, in these days of uncertain identity, provide us with a context and a home into which we could invite others without feeling the need to give up important aspects of our faith, as if they constituted a barrier rather than a channel of peace and love. This is the true universality, the true inclusivity, which, as Rabindranath Tagore said, consists not in "breaking down the walls of one's house, but the offering of hospitality to one's guests and neighbours".

If Richenda Scott is right and we have indeed been swept into a backwater "from which we can be rescued only by a fresh and deeper experience, and a clearer realization *in thought* of what that experience means" (my emphasis), we are in dire need of help from the handful of Quaker theologians and historians we have got. It applies as much to our Society as to any other denomination that "what no-one shows the ability to defend is quickly abandoned". This means confronting rather than evading the difficult philosophical questions which early Friends didn't have to face — whether there is any sense in which we can speak of ultimate Truth; and whether it is ever possible to experience or even point to a Reality which is not a construct of our own language-ruled imaginations. And second, since most of this work has already been done with admirable clarity by theologians belonging to other denominations, we will need our own theologians to contextualise the case for God within a Quaker framework that is unashamedly appreciative of our traditions and experience. I believe that the aim should be to develop a theology which is firmly based on our historical faith and practice and, while it may overlap with non-theism at the more moderate end of the spectrum, is broadly theistic in scope. I am convinced that only when this is truly underway can we hope for the re-kindling of the Spirit that will sweep us out of the backwater, rebuild our numbers, and give us the unity and strength to go out and remake the world in healing partnership with God.

5

The behavioural creed

Turning and turning in the widening gyre
The falcon cannot hear the falconer;
Things fall apart, the centre cannot hold . . .

— William Butler Yeats

JONATHAN DALE POINTED us to the fact that we had gone a stage beyond liberalism, a stage which Ben Pink Dandelion has called 'liberal-Liberalism' which recognises no authority or any boundaries to belief except those imposed by the 'behavioural creed' — that is, the way we worship and conduct our business and the rules, structures and arrangements by which the Society continues to be governed.

It is the 'behavioural creed', popularly known as the 'Quaker way', which, according to Dandelion, now holds the Society together and prevents it from disintegrating as diversification gathers pace. However, Gay Pilgrim, a Quaker sociologist whose specialism is religious identity, points out that a new intake of members, who regard traditional Quaker methods as anachronistic, is putting even this constraint under pressure, opening up the possibility of "serious splits": "Liberal Quakerism has set its boundaries through the correct observance of the ways in which the group 'does' religion, rather than by a shared liminal rite of passage. The behavioural creed has allowed Friends to be very permissive about belief, but, as diversity of belief proliferates, acceptance of the behavioural creed with its distinctive Quaker forms is being eroded, both in the regular Sunday Meetings for Worship and in the Meetings for Worship for Church Affairs . . . as the Society of Friends is steadily penetrated by those seeking a place to express their personal spirituality rather than follow a religion, sustaining unity and a shared identity is becoming increasingly problematic."[91]

Today, the attack on 'the behavioural creed' revolves around the notion of discernment and the real presence of the Spirit as the Inward Guide which will lead us into Truth. With a growing number of Friends who regard the real presence of the Spirit as delusional now occupying important positions within the Society, how much longer can this last remaining bond hold before the centrepiece drops out of Quakerism?

Historically, Friends have described the 'traditional Quaker methods' and 'distinctive forms' in terms which to newcomers may seem somewhat negative — more about what we are not than what we are, and what we deny than what we affirm. As John Wilhelm Rowntree said at the beginning of the last century this has led to a supposition that Quakerism is a system of negations: "We do *not* baptise, we do *not* take the Supper, we do *not* have a separated ministry, we do *not* consecrate our Meeting-houses, we do *not* take oaths, we do *not* fight; what have we here, says the outsider, but a bundle of negations? And too often Friends have lent colour to this view. They have laid stress upon the things they do *not* believe or do *not* do, and have failed to lay bare the positive basis of the faith which is thus expressed. The supposition is, of course, mistaken. The Quaker faith, rightly understood, so far from being negative, is the profoundest affirmation."

A faith which *appears* to be based on negations is vulnerable to a whole series of *ad hoc* changes if what underlies the appearance, what Rowntree here calls "the profoundest affirmation", is forgotten by a later generation. Rowntree's list is by no means exhaustive. We could add, for example, that we have no liturgy or symbolic acts of worship, we do not adorn our meeting houses with pictures or statues, we have no sacraments, and not least we have no voting. So what *is* the 'profoundest affirmation' that redeems and explains this lengthy

[91] Pilgrim, *ibid.*, p. 218.

'bundle of negations'? For Rowntree it is the need to preserve and enhance our focus and sense of dependence on the Inward Light. "Symbolism in worship having shown a universal tendency to obscure the truth it once revealed, [the Quakers] disregarded all forms, fearful lest the spirituality and inwardness of their worship might suffer. They built their meeting houses in simple fashion, that no sensuous aesthetic delight in outward beauty might displace the dependence on the inward light in the temple not made with hands. The underlying principle of their worship was the responsibility and the priesthood of each worshipper, and his immediate dependence upon the Spirit of God."[92]

It is the contemporary loss of belief in this underlying principle that is today undermining the behavioural creed. For what possible justification could there be for keeping these negations without the kind of spiritual grounding that Rowntree draws to our attention? If we take as an example the simple interior of the meeting house, why insist on this if there is no sense of the presence of God to be 'displaced' by objects which give us 'sensuous aesthetic delight'? Why not fill our meeting houses with sculptures and paintings that express and celebrate the diverse spiritualities which congregate in the modern Quaker meeting? I am sure we have enough artists in the Society to fill them ten times over. And if a good number of those participating in our local and area business meetings no longer believe in divine guidance, but only in their *own* guidance, however 'connected' or reflective, how can we justify not voting? Why continue with a clerk whose personal sense of the meeting relies entirely on her own judgement — or worse still, her own 'highest ideals' which may be different from yours or mine? Would it not be better to install a 'chair' whose powers were well defined and acceptable to all? Finally, if the priesthood of all believers has become no more than a shibboleth without that sense of dependence on the Inward Light that for

92 Rowntree in Joshua Rowntree (ed.)., *Essays and Addresses* (Ashford: Headley Brothers, 1905), p. 98.

Rowntree was the justification for *not* having a "separated ministry", why not resolve the problem of sharing the workload in meetings by appointing a full-time administrator? Isn't that the logic of diversity — and aren't we already halfway there? In setting up Boards of Trustees to take over the administrative functions formerly carried out by Area Meetings are we not already on the way to making Area Meetings themselves obsolete? As it is likely to be the more high-powered Friends with professional expertise who sit on these Boards, how long will it be before the Area Meeting becomes little more than a rubber stamp? How long before it loses its *raison d'être* altogether and falls into disuse as fewer Friends bother to attend? And where will this leave the Local Meeting? No longer 'preparative' in its relation to Area Meeting, its only course is to interface with the Board of Trustees which will have the same function as any other board of management in a medium sized charity.

In all probability this will mean exposing the Society to all the dangers associated with modern management methods in the corporate sector. 'Management' can be a form of manipulation. People who manage others frequently have to be economical with the truth; or they may find themselves having to say what they know to be untrue or true in a very qualified sense. For example, it is not uncommon for managers to offer words of encouragement and support when really all they seek is to edge the person in their way to the margins of whatever operation they are managing; and when the moment of opportunity comes, they can show themselves to be ruthless. What we have done through Recast (the body charged with restructuring our systems for church government) is exchange a system which allows maximum participation, and where business is conducted throughout in a spirit of worship and absolute trust, for a system which relies on the more conventional methods of the Board Room, albeit with a brief moment of silence 'to settle the mind' before proceedings begin. The inevitable result will be to change the nature of relationships between people in the Society, paradoxically (since the aim is equality) making them subtly more hierarchical.

It could be argued that this major change was forced on the Society by the Charity Commission, but the fact is we chose not to fight it. There were, of course, good reasons for not doing so, and some would say even for welcoming it — the recognition that we were not as efficient as we should be, the demands of new government legislation, the depletion of our skills pool. But there was one very persuasive argument which was sometimes used, and which amply confirms Gay Pilgrim's analysis. It is the argument that in relieving the burden on Area Meetings they and local meetings would be freed up to concentrate on more spiritual matters.

An important strength of the Society in the past, and an essential element in the behavioural creed, was that it made no distinction between the spiritual and the administrative in that sense. That is why we still stand when we *minister* in our meetings for church affairs. The dangers should be obvious, and again it is Rowntree who points them out, this time with reference to the history of the early church. The most notable feature of the early Christian meetings, he tells us, was "the immediate activity and controlling influence of the Holy Spirit . . . Every Christian had the right to take part, and the woman's right was equal to the man's."[93] But already by the end of the first century, officials were appointed, "and the movement which was ultimately to establish a hierarchy had begun." Things never happen twice in quite the same way, but with each loosening of the knot which binds the spiritual and the temporal, the behavioural creed is weakened, and the Society is more vulnerable to the combined pressures of individualism and secularism.

Clearly, there has been no shortage of well-informed, far-sighted Friends to alert us to 'the widening gyre' of diversity, but as we have seen, their voices have been largely ignored by a religious society which has grown careless of its own identity and even sees concern about such matters as evidence of psychological insecurity.[94] In a

---

[93] Rowntree, pp. 95-6.

[94] See D. Boulton and J. Lampen, "Gently Move", *The Friend* (16th January, 2009), pp. 14-15.

sense the whole debate from the 1950s onward has been about boundaries of belief, a difficult one for Friends who pride themselves on having no credal test of membership. When we are prevailed on to "celebrate our diversity" we are being asked to express our actual *joy* in having no beliefs or boundaries, for this is what welcoming an ever-widening diversity means. Yet without boundaries or beliefs it becomes increasingly difficult to discern who *we* are and at the same time to see the *other*.

Indeed, there is no escaping the importance of the issue. It affects the Society at every level from Yearly Meeting, with its increasingly evasive Yearly Meeting epistles which of course have to please everyone *equally*, down to the Local Meeting where attenders are gently pressured to apply for membership but no-one is quite sure what they are being asked to join. When we start looking for our unity not in "Christian love" but in 'external forms' which are emptied of theological content what is there to attract the person who is seeking a deeper experience?

But perhaps the greatest impact is on the individual member who is struggling with the contradictions and dissatisfactions of belonging to a religious group which has lost its bearings and yet has retained enough of its former appeal to make leaving it an agonisingly difficult decision. Gay Pilgrim's experience as she struggled with her research into pluralism and Quaker identity is, I am sure, typical of many. She found doing the research painful both from an academic and a personal point of view:

> It was personally painful because I was forced to reflect on whether I wished to be part of a religious group that had so slight an acquaintance with its own distinctive theology, or indeed *any* coherent theology. Could I even continue to see the group as religious in any way that had meaning for me at all? As I struggled to achieve the necessary distance from my identity as a Quaker so as to undertake a good academic sociological study, I was simultaneously struggling with what that Quaker identity meant to me, and what my life would feel like, be like, without it . . .

> My ambivalence about Quakerism also led me to feel uncomfortable about the roles I inhabited in my Quaker life. Some of these were central to the organisation: an organisation I was not sure I felt I belonged to, or even wanted to belong to. Furthermore, Quaker business is conducted as a worship event, yet I was now questioning what that 'worship' really represented. In fact, I found myself in a curiously paradoxical situation. My head observed with some wryness my participation, but my heart entered fully into the event with all its erstwhile passion and conviction. This was a context in which it was not necessary for me to keep my state of mind hidden, and I had some useful discussions which decided me to continue in the roles I had been appointed to, at least until I could come to some firmer conclusions.
>
> Which brings me to where I am now. I still find a lack at the heart of present-day Quakerism in terms of a spiritual rigour and discipline. My research has brought me to recognise my personal requirement in this respect. My difficulty lies in the fact that, like most Quakers, I find the notion of an external human authority unacceptable, which leaves me with very few, if any, alternatives. So despite the lack of a shared religious enterprise and the nebulousness of present-day Quakerism which I find profoundly unsatisfactory, I continue to identify myself as a Friend.[95]

It is tragic that any individual Friend should find herself in the conflicted state of mind expressed here with such vulnerability and openness, but even sadder to think that the Society today is full of people who are in exactly Gay Pilgrim's position. Those who are Christians may eventually leave the Society, and their places will be taken by others with little knowledge of its traditions and no interest in the religious beliefs of its founders which are confused with the orthodox Christianity which many of them have left behind. The result is that the balance of Christians and theists to others who define themselves in non-theist or humanist terms is slowly tilting in favour

[95] Dandelion (Ed.), *The Creation of Quaker Theory*, p.224.

of the latter, helped along by the fact that the older generation of Friends who are more rooted in Christianity are gradually dying off.

If Dandelion and Pilgrim are right and the Quaker Way is now all that holds the Society together, it is clear that the Quaker Way is unsustainable without the Quaker theology; and if it is objected that Quakers don't have a theology, then (1) that is clearly untrue — we have simply moved away from it; and (2) I am here speaking about the theology that *underpins* the Quaker Way — faith in the Inward Light, and trust, as *Quaker Faith and Practice* urges, that "we have a common purpose in seeking God's will through waiting and listening, believing that every activity of life should be subject to divine guidance".

6

Belief and Quaker non-credalism

For Quakers, belief is relatively inconsequential. Different Quakers believe a whole host of very different things before breakfast, and the attempt to find some essence of Quakerism in a set of shared beliefs is doomed from the start.

— Linda Woodhead

In 1895 London Yearly Meeting gave impetus to the new direction in which it was being led. It is time to pause and consider whether we have travelled too far along that path.

— Jonathan Dale

HAVING OPENED OUR membership to people of very different, indeed contrary beliefs, it becomes distasteful to bar anyone from membership, even those whose stated aim is to replace what they have found with a wholly different belief system of their own. But while it is right we should 'welcome the stranger' — excluding no-one who wants to worship with us — it is wilful blindness not to recognise that in taking this approach we are opening the door to a multitude of other problems. Our testimony to equality, in the secular sense which it bears today, requires that beliefs, once they are widely represented amongst the membership, are given equal status; no one belief can be regarded as more fundamental or more valid than another. The logic of diversity then requires that we treat beliefs as 'relatively inconsequential'; what counts, what unifies, is our action in the world. In this chapter, I shall be taking the opposite view, arguing that beliefs are very important to all of us, individually and as a religious society.

The only way we can counter the secularising tendencies within the society and maintain its faithfulness to God, as revealed in the personality and example of Jesus, is to stand up for those beliefs as part of a progressive movement of spiritual renewal.

What do we mean by a 'belief'? Friends tend to use the word in three quite different senses. The first sense is that I *know* something to be true on the basis of my own and others' *experience*; the second, that I have *faith* in a particular conceptual understanding of that experience; and the third refers to formulated statements of belief — what Friends often refer to as 'credal statements'. Most of the time we move between these different usages without giving much thought to their individual meaning; at other times, when greater clarity is called for, we try to separate them out.

Belief and experience

Many Friends would say that the first kind of belief is not a belief at all. Belief implies adherence to a concept, while here we are talking about religious *experience* — direct, unmediated *knowing.* William James, in his book *The Will to Believe*, called this 'knowledge of acquaintance' to distinguish it from 'knowledge about'. Admittedly, 'knowledge of acquaintance' is an unusual, rather dated, term to apply to religious experience, but all James is really saying is that those who have left accounts of their experience know what they're talking *about* because they have experienced it directly. Another who has written about this is Don Cupitt (and here, for once, I agree with him). He says, "when you have really worked through it, when your belief has become deep enough — then you no longer believe! Faith has given way to sight, and mediation to immediacy. Thus church Christianity actually works by progressively conducting us beyond itself, to a greater light on the far side of it".[96]

---

[96] Cupitt, *Reforming Christianity* (Santa Rosa, CA.: Polebridge Press, 2001), p. 59. Unfortunately, the 'greater light' here is no more than the light of secular society

Despite this one often hears it said, particularly in non-theist circles, that God is a human concept. This implies that the only knowledge of God that we can have is a conceptual knowledge: knowledge about. But the traditional Quaker view is that God is not a human concept but a Presence — a Presence that can be known directly through contemplation, the practice of silence. This is James' 'knowledge of acquaintance'. A good example of contemplation in the Quaker tradition can be found at the start of Janet Scott's Swarthmore Lecture:

> In the silence, waiting, Quakers know God. We feel the presence, sometimes as a gentle comforter, sometimes a firm assurance, sometimes a light that illuminates our thoughts and gives us new words, sometimes a fearful reality whose loving, tender, awful power enters our pounding hearts and trembling bodies . . . This is the essential truth of Quakerism, held not as a belief but as experience. However, our experience is wider than this and carries with it other discoveries which we must express in words but which we know first as living truth.

Held not as a belief but as experience. The experience can be personal or communal, and if communal, as in worship or corporate discernment, it will be both. However, it is very difficult, and perhaps pointless, to try to detach the experience from the belief. I remember as a child trying to detach the word 'kettle' from the object 'kettle' and failing completely, although I knew intuitively that the object existed apart from the word that was merely a signifier. But perhaps what Scott means is that belief is a kind of secondary or conceptual knowledge, like James' 'knowledge about'. She is not intending to dispense with belief altogether — the experience "carries with it other discoveries which we must express in words" — but wants to stress the priority of the direct personal and communal encounter with God. The words may change and therefore, to some extent, so may the way

---

which has fully absorbed Christian values and therefore no longer needs the church to preserve them.

in which the belief is held, but that doesn't mean the belief can be altered or discarded just to suit our personal or corporate whim. In this sense the relation between the words and the experience is analogous to that between the scientist's hypothesis and the reality being investigated. The hypothesis may change or need to be adjusted but that doesn't just happen arbitrarily. As we shall see in Chapter 8, where we discuss this relation in more depth, it happens in response to some hidden aspect of the unknown in nature. In other words, it is accountable to a reality that may always remain at least partially beyond the scientist's grasp.

Janet Scott presents the experience of the Divine Presence as "the essential truth of Quakerism". If that is true, and it certainly appears to have been true until very recent times, should at least an *openness* to the *possibility* of that truth be an essential criterion for membership? One might agree and yet dispute that what we are talking about here is a belief. Scott herself says, 'held *not* as a belief' — although I have interpreted this as an emphasis rather than an absolutist position. For surely it *is* a belief that the experience is available to us, *inter alia*, in the silence of worship? And it is an attitude of openness to the belief, and not to any claim to have experienced the Divine Presence itself, that I am suggesting might be considered as a requirement for membership.

Is it possible to have a beliefless experience? Scott is a little unclear on this point. She gets round the question by saying that "*our experience* is wider than this and *carries with it* other discoveries that we must express in words". 'Our experience' is now a catch-all term and not clearly distinguished from the mystical experience itself. Moreover, 'carries with it' says nothing about the actual *relation* between (presumably) the mystical experience and the words. But Scott would have found powerful support in William James even if he saw things in slightly more sequential terms. For James, 'knowledge about' arises from and affirms 'knowledge of acquaintance'. He says that while "religious experience is immediate and primordial, it is ultimately productive of beliefs". Belief — conceptual belief — is still important.

Indeed, there is some doubt that the 'sense of presence' that Scott describes as 'God', and sometimes as a 'fearful reality', can he 'held' for very long at all. I think that those like William James and Alister Hardy who have researched it would say that the mystical state can only be 'held' for a relatively short time. As soon as we begin to reflect on the experience, it leaves us. So 'knowledge about' immediately succeeds 'knowledge of acquaintance', thereby affirming it in conceptual terms. And if belief in and a sense of being guided or prompted by God *arises* from such an experience — a transformative experience *of God* — then it cannot be said not to matter. On the contrary, it is of the highest importance, not only in itself, but in its consequences, and cannot be placed on the same footing as a merely *conceptual* belief in the *non*-existence of God — a 'notion' if ever there was one.

Belief and faith

This takes us to the second use of 'belief', which identifies it with 'faith'. It is not always clear what Friends mean when they use the word 'faith' even though it is there on the title page of our book of discipline. The usual meaning is 'a set of beliefs and practices', but faith can also refer to trust or loyalty. Since it involves a *conceptual* understanding, an understanding of that which is known 'experientially', it tends to be avoided in modern Quaker writing, rather like the word 'belief' itself with which it is virtually synonymous. Modern Friends tend to stress the 'ineffability' of religious or mystical experience which places it beyond words or conceptualisation and therefore (they hope) out of the reach of rational argument. While this may help to avoid division, it opens the way to a host of other problems which are even more divisive.

The typical Quaker view today is forcefully illustrated by Linda Woodhead's remark, "Different Quakers believe a whole host of very different things before breakfast, and the attempt to find some essence of Quakerism in a set of shared beliefs is doomed from the start". She is referring not to an *agreed* set of beliefs (a creed) but to any set of *de facto* beliefs which claims to represent the essentials of Quakerism. But without any shared beliefs whatsoever, can we still speak of a Quaker faith?

My own understanding of faith is that it is best understood as response, the response of the individual believer or community of believers to God's self-revelation, and this, I suggest, requires a shared belief of some kind — even, perhaps, a set of shared beliefs. For example, in the case of Scott's "essential truth of Quakerism" faith would involve the willingness to place one's trust in that truth, both as an individual and as a community, and allowing it to guide us. This would imply some shared understanding of what the act of trust signified and the nature of the relationship it presupposes, and this could only be represented in conceptual terms. So faith, I believe, is indispensable to the religious view of life and to any *religious* society which still regards itself as such.

Faith is also associated with hope and so the definition of faith could stretch to an attitude of openness to the *possibility* of experiencing "the essential truth of Quakerism" (as already suggested, a possible criterion for membership). In this sense, faith is less of a certainty than belief. When the apostle Paul says, "Faith gives substance to our hopes, and makes us certain of realities we do not see" (Hebrews 11.1), he meant by 'certainty' a gradually growing conviction, not certainty in the positivistic (proof laden) sense in which we deploy the term today. Faith is not about certainty in that sense at all. Indeed, it would be truer to say that faith and certainty in that sense are opposites. It is in *rejecting* faith that we choose certainty over uncertainty or a gradually growing conviction. The great Anglican divine, William Temple, said that he valued faith because it made religion 'interesting', that is, an adventure, and because he believed it drew out the best in us. "As soon as the reality of God was an intellectual certainty, there would no longer be any spiritual merit in faith. From the point of view of religion, not only of the Christian religion, faith is something nobler in its own kind than certainty. For us finite beings in this world that which most of all calls forth our noblest capacities into action is always a hazard of some kind, never a certainty. It is when we are ready to stake our lives on something being so, or to make something so that is not so, that nobility begins to appear in human nature."[97]

There are those among my family and friends who are adamant atheists, and naturally I have the greatest respect for their views — as, I hope, they do for mine. But I have come to the conclusion that many atheists prefer the certainty of 'there is no God' to the faith which involves trusting oneself to the uncertain and demanding task of spiritual struggle. There is a strand in the psychology of atheism that is afraid to hope, afraid to take risks, afraid to plumb the depths because of the swirl of uncertainties it might stir up. The more courageous and mature approach, despite the uncertainty involved, is surely to commit oneself to 'going forward in faith'? However, commitment of this kind is difficult for Friends today. We have opted instead for a different kind of uncertainty, the uncertainty not of faith but of a deeply disabling loss of confidence. We know we cannot live up to the accolades showered on us in the past, of being a religion of spiritual inwardness nourished by the truths of Christianity.[98] Today we are constantly 'challenging' ourselves with questions like 'who are we?', 'where are we going?', 'what can we say?', and are unable to arrive at any shared understanding of what a religion of spiritual inwardness would look like.

It is often implied that the person of faith is someone who has made an act of will or taken an arbitrary decision to think what s/he knows is unlikely to be true. The technical term for this is 'fideism' — the idea that religious belief is based on faith alone. I think most of us would find this intellectually and even morally unsatisfying. Nietzsche said of a friend who was advocating 'faith' as the solution to all his

---

[97] Temple, *Christian Faith and Life* (London: SCM Press, 1931), p. 10.
[98] James, *The Varieties of Religious Experience*, p. 7.

problems: "Faith in what, I ask . . . But perhaps he means *faith* in *faith* — I would prefer a slice of bread and butter to anything so vague." Nietzsche, of course, was a philosopher, and as the theologian, John Milbank, observed, "much modern philosophy is built on what appears to be a very unsophisticated and unmystical account of God."[99] For the mystic or religious seeker, faith begins not primarily with an act of will but with an absence, a longing and desire deep within our human nature. Only later, sometimes by means of a spiritual discipline, sometimes directly by revelation and divine 'grace', will s/he find grounds that give it support. It is not the fideism derided by Nietzsche but perhaps a weaker kind of fideism where a willingness to believe or an act of faith is not a leap in the dark but a kind of intuitive probing beyond the mundane reality.

There has been a tendency in Quaker writing in recent years to avoid the word 'belief' at almost any cost, as if it carried with it some awful bacterial infection. Instead of 'basic or core beliefs', we find terms like 'basic tenets' or 'core insights' being used, not as occasional variants but as regular substitutes, even though they mean virtually the same thing. But if beliefs are 'relatively inconsequential' for Quakers, why should tenets and 'core insights' be less so? It may be thought that the term 'basic beliefs' has credal overtones, but hasn't also the term 'basic tenets'? In some cases the word 'understanding' is used, although again it is not altogether clear what the difference might be between saying, for example, it is my *belief* that Dawkins is of sound mind and it is my *understanding* that he is so. In his 2014 Swarthmore Lecture, Dandelion uses the term 'heart-understanding', but again I think one would be hard put to explain the difference between that and a 'belief', since beliefs, although conceptual, also have an *emotional* component. The only real difference that comes to mind is that 'belief' may suggest a corporately held *faith*, whereas 'understanding' is, or may seem to be, more personal and to subjectivise faith. An unacknowledged consequence of opting for the latter term, however,

---

99 R. Shortt, *God's Advocates: Christian Thinkers in Conversation*, (London: Darton, Longman & Todd, 2005), p. 110.

may be to reinforce the strident individualism that is now one of the main threats to the unity and cohesion of the Society.

All this simply underlines the fact that belief in religion is unavoidable; it cannot be said not to matter. Some Friends will use the word 'trust' rather than 'believe' — I trust in an experience, I believe in a concept. But trust in the religious sense implies *receptiveness* to experience and an expectation that the experience will have a quality that is usually described as transcendent. It is difficult to imagine trust of this kind not being bound up in some way with prior belief — with some kind of conceptual starting point — however inadequate it may be to the actual experience; and as I have argued above, it would be very difficult, having once had a profound religious experience, not to hold some belief about it. 'Trust' in the sense in which Friends tend to use it would belong to the weaker form of fideism in which some element of belief is necessarily present but is supported by other factors, including (crucially for Friends) religious or spiritual experience.

The classical Quaker view of the relation between faith and experience has been set out for us by Isaac Penington. One of the most profoundly spiritual of early Friends, Penington takes his place in a long line of Christian mystics in thinking of God as beyond language and beyond thought. The mainstream Christian of his day, he said, "reproacheth and blasphemeth the incomprehensible Wisdom, in its incomprehensible ways, and would restrain life to what they apprehend, or can comprehend by the Letter concerning it." There is but one way to the knowledge of God, he maintained, and that is through experience. Spiritual things cannot be known but "in union with them [and] in the receiving of them".[100] And for Penington and the early Quakers, this meant union with and surrender to the Christ, without whose personal saving touch God remains remote and unknowable. For them the Christ is the only mediator, the living Word "which was before the world was", before the historical Jesus was. It is

---

[100] Penington, *A Question to the Professors of Christianity* (London: n.p., 1667), p. 6.

from this 'principle' that we receive our capacity for spiritual discernment, and by modelling our lives on him who had the Christ in full measure, by trying to live as much like Jesus as possible, we come to the greater understanding of that which sent him: "Our knowledge is in a Principle [the Christ], wherein we receive our capacity of knowing, and wherein the Father (from whom the Principle came) teacheth us. And this is his way of teaching us, to wit, by making us one with the thing he teacheth. Thus we learn Christ, by being born of him, by putting him on. Thus we know his Righteousness, his Life, his Wisdom, his Power, by receiving a proportion of them, which giveth an ability to discern and acknowledge the fullness".[101]

Penington's views on the incarnation and the nature of Jesus were unorthodox and, in places, confused and self-contradictory, but he clearly believed that *in some way* God had 'sent' Jesus to teach and guide us and that this teaching was something we were meant to receive not only from scripture but from the Spirit and the self-sacrificing action that flowed from it. Scripture was the 'outward' teacher; the Christ, as expressed in the life of Jesus, the 'inward teacher'; and we could only truly possess the former by means of the latter. Faith and religious experience, therefore, were *both* necessary. Spiritual experience could not be cut off from belief, nor should belief be cut off from 'the substance'. "Now we believe", says Penington, "because we have seen and received the thing which the Scriptures speak of."

It is generally acknowledged that the early Quakers were far ahead of their time, but during the long years of theological quietism the rest of the world has been catching up, and as we slowly drift into apostasy the lead is now being taken by others. Here, for example, is Laurence Freeman, a Benedictine monk and Director of the World Community of Christian Meditation. It is worth noting that the book from which this extract is taken bears the title, *Jesus: the Teacher Within*.

---

[101] *ibid.*

> Faith or Experience? For many today the tension between the two has led to an unhappy polarisation of their spiritual journey. There is a great interest in spirituality but also great confusion about what it means. Polls show that increasingly we prefer to call ourselves spiritual rather than religious. Is this because spiritual means experience and religious means faith? And so we feel that as experience has the higher claim to be authentic, it is better to be spiritual than religious . . . The problem is that faith and experience cannot be polarised so easily. Faith means more than belief in the dogma or tenets of religious systems. Experience means more than the good or bad vibes I get when I do this or that: it means the lifelong journey of becoming fully who we *can* be, who we *really* are. And religion is not so easily dispensed with either. We cannot be truly spiritual without encountering others on the same path and relating, with them, to those who went before us. Tradition is also a form both of faith and experience.[102]

Far from experience and faith being separate, therefore, so that the one is said to matter but the other not, they are interdependent. For Friends faith and belief both arise from, are built upon, experience, and this is because, as the Scottish philosopher, John Macmurray (a Quaker in later life), put it, "faith refers to an inner experience, a living apprehension which carries with it an immediate conviction of its own validity."[103]

Faith of this kind is based on the direct apprehension of the real presence of God in our lives; being based on actual experience it is unassailable in the face of argument, a kind of certainty which is different from that demanded by the critics of faith. When the Quaker poet, John Greenleaf Whittier, in his beautiful hymn, 'Dear Lord and Father of Mankind', pictured the peaceful hills above Galilee

---

[102] Freeman, *Jesus: The Teacher Within*, (NY and London: Continuum, 2005), p. 15.

[103] Macmurray, *The Self as Agent* (London: Faber and Faber, 1957), p. 41.

Where Jesus knelt to share with thee
The silence of eternity
Interpreted by love

he was not referring to self-evident truths (which do not require faith) but to mysteries beyond the reach of scientific, historical or philosophical proof. Certainty in the sense in which the critics use the term usually demands external evidence. Such a presumption would seem wholly inappropriate in relation to the figure of Jesus who is not concerned to justify his inner state with an appeal to reason. What is being described is a way of being, a state of relationship with that which is experienced as real and transcendent. It requires no evidence; we recognise it immediately and know it to be true.

It was faith in the reality and meaning of the 'Teacher within' that separated the first Quakers not only from the Calvinists and other 'professors' of Christianity, but from the Ranters who held pantheistic beliefs that in the last analysis were indistinguishable from materialism. It is my personal view that if Friends are to survive as a religious society, and avoid descending into a modern form of Ranterism, we will need to re-discover ourselves as a community of faith as well as of experience. That faith can be broad in scope, but at the very least it must contain some element of the transcendent, by which I mean an acknowledgment that the experience of which we speak is of something both deep within and at the same time beyond our finite human nature. Atheistic humanism denies this and by definition cannot share in such a faith.

While religious experiences which involve no conceptual starting point are possible (William James provides us with many striking examples), they are relatively rare. This is why in the preceding pages I have argued that we also need faith, not the faith that requires us to believe "twelve impossible things before breakfast", but the faith that I have described as the weaker form of fideism. In contemplation, according to the author of *The Cloud of Unknowing*, "the mind is a mirror; void of images and thoughts but filled with faith, it is in darkness; and in the darkness we meet God." I think it will be agreed that this is a fairly good description of what Quakers mean by 'centring down'. Instead of 'faith' we might say 'expectant waiting', but it amounts to the same thing. Whether we want to use the term 'faith' or not (and it is there in the title of our book of discipline), we are essentially a faith community. We are 'expectant' because we believe, and we believe because, as Penington said, we have seen and received the thing which scripture, that is, revelation, speaks of. For this, if for no other reason, it cannot be true to say that for Friends belief is unimportant. We only *say* that it is because the logic of diversity requires it.

Belief and credal statements

This being so, it is hardly surprising that we find in much Quaker literature of the present day an over-determined emphasis on the Society's traditional opposition to *credal statements*, the third use of the term 'belief' which I now want to consider. A typical example is the following, from an Area Meeting Newsletter:

> The Spirit is leading us in some very exciting ways, but do I sometimes try to put the brakes on and even go into reverse? Do I always try to go behind the words and seek where they are coming from? The same experience can be expressed in many different ways using very different language. We are not a credal church, on paper or in spirit.

The writer is clearly unimpressed by Jonathan Dale's words of caution: "In 1895 London Yearly meeting gave impetus to the new direction in which it was being led. It is time to pause and consider whether we have travelled too far along that path" (see below, pp. 23-24). I shall be looking at the question of language in my next chapter. For the moment I will confine my comments to the claim that "we are not a credal church".

It is true that Friends have always been reluctant to place their faith in particular formulations of Christian or indeed any other belief. Our spiritual literature abounds in protestations to this effect which are the other side of our belief in the primacy of religious experience. How often do we hear in ministry words like those of Thomas Story in 1737: "The unity of Christians never did nor ever will or can stand in uniformity of thought and opinion, but in Christian love only"? And the similar words of Isaac Penington: "For this is the true ground of love and unity, not that such a man walks and does just as I do, but because I feel the same spirit and life in him"? We warm to these words not just because they lift the dead weight of dogma from our shoulders, but because we feel that they open us to the direct influence or 'teaching' of the Spirit — and perhaps nowadays because they appear to speak the language of inclusiveness and tolerance. All this is very much part of our tradition and to be cherished. But doesn't it distort the meaning of these texts to use them as justification for a diversity that extends far beyond the boundaries of a Quaker Christianity, the conceptual framework in which they were articulated and which they were intended to illumine?

One of the more authoritative statements of the Quaker position on creeds is *The True Basis of Christian Unity*, a paper addressed to the World Conference on Faith and Order and presented to Yearly Meeting in 1917. Here we are told that Quakers "conceive of Christianity not as a collection of 'notions' or doctrines . . . but as essentially an experience, and a way of life based on that experience"; but the paper then goes on to say: "To us [the unity of Christians] consists in the one Divine life that is reproducing in them the character of the historic Person, Jesus Christ; which, while it is something far deeper than any definition of His Person, is for Christians the final manifestation of the character of God Himself".

So for Friends in 1917 this way of apprehending 'the character of God' is not an idea, a notion, a doctrine or a creed, but a truth derived from their common Quaker-Christian *experience*. A notion or doctrine might have been some particular theological proposition, for example, a corporate statement on the Trinity or the meaning of the crucifixion. Here, however, the writers seem to be saying, "We are touched by the Spirit of God who reproduces in us the likeness of Jesus, as the most perfect expression in human form of the divine nature. So much we can know experientially, and beyond this we are not prepared to go". It was in this highly contextualised sense that they understood themselves to be non-credal.

This places those Friends who constantly invoke "our traditional opposition to creeds" in something of a dilemma. How could they possibly claim that this thoroughly Christian self-understanding is non-credal?

It could be objected that the claim to be non-credal is not meant to be applied retrospectively, but in that case it loses almost all its force. Or again, that the claim is intended to be made only in a very qualified sense, but then, when the issue is diversity, it never *is* presented in a qualified sense! In fact, just the opposite. It tends to be explicit and categorical: "We have no creed. We never have, never do and never will insist that those who join us believe this or that — or if we do we betray our own tradition."[104] "Modern creedless Quakerism" is presented as the apotheosis of our "traditional opposition to creeds."

When the 1917 document set out the Quaker position on credal statements, it wisely conceded the role of the intellect in "formulating the ideas implicit in religious experience" and then emphasised that all such formulations are provisional, "and can never be assumed to possess the finality of ultimate truth."

> There must always be room for development and progress, and Christian *thought* and *inquiry* [my emphases] should never be fettered by theory . . . Among the dangers of formulated statements of belief are these:
>
> a. they tend to crystallise thought on matters that will always be beyond any final embodiment in human language;

---

[104]Boulton (ed.), *Godless for God's Sake* (Dent: Dale Historical Monographs), p.15.

b. they fetter the search for truth and for its more adequate expression; and
c. they set up a fence which tends to keep out of the Christian fold many sincere and seeking souls who would gladly enter it.

Sentiments such as these have formed the basis of the liberal consensus since the Manchester Conference and few Friends would disagree with them today. But note that the writers are not saying we should refrain from formulating statements of belief altogether, only that they should not be written in stone so as to obstruct 'Truth', that is, the word of God, and its *more adequate expression.* It is the *expression* that changes, not that which is ultimately beyond words. When the language we use becomes worn out and jaded, we can again use our intellect to re-formulate our understanding of God's word, but in a way that is sensitive and strives to be faithful to God's continuing purpose, that gives more space to the Light, and at the same time recognises that these new formulations or statements may themselves be provisional. What we should not do as a religious society is deny that there is a God whose Truth is always available to us.[105]

The True Basis for Christian Unity was written when the liberal reaction to evangelical, bible-based Christianity was in full swing. It has to be understood in the context of that reaction and should not itself be given the stamp of permanency. It was seen as opening the gate to Christian believers who had difficulty with orthodox Christian teaching on matters such as the atonement and the physical resurrection. It was *not* seen as the thin end of a wedge leading the Society into error. Nor does its significance stretch backwards in time: early Friends were strong on statements of belief; their contempt for 'notions' was intended to distinguish their own statements which were 'in the life' (and therefore not 'notions') from those of their Calvinist opponents which they condemned as dead forms.

For all these reasons, it is an over-simplification to say that Quakerism is and always has been non-credal. Consider the statement

---

[105] On the question of Truth, see above, pp. 158-78.

'there is that of God in everyone'. There is no rational proof of this; it is an article of Quaker faith and is the usual response to the question 'what do Quakers believe?' It is therefore unmistakably a credal statement. The writings of early Friends like Edward Burroughs and Francis Howgill are full of credal statements. Barclay's *Apology* is one long credal statement. Even where there has been a conscientious attempt to eliminate them as in the periodically revised *Quaker Faith and Practice*, they keep cropping up. "Worship is the response of the human spirit to the presence of the divine and eternal, to the God who first seeks us". This says (i) that there *is* a God, a divine and eternal presence, separate and distinct from the human spirit, and (ii) that worship is our response to an initiative which is not of our own making. What is this but a theological proposition and a statement of belief? To take another example, this time from what used to be accepted Quaker opinion, that what distinguishes us from other Christian denominations is the claim that every individual can have a direct, unmediated experience of God. Isn't this too a credal statement, along with the related proposition of a 'priesthood of all believers'? We have only to imagine a Quakerism without any credal statements of this kind to realise the extent to which we *rely* on them for our very identity.

The cry of the Manchester Conference was 'back to Barclay'. How could this be if we are not, and never have been, a credal church, "on paper or in spirit?" In part, it is explained by Barclay's stress on the Light as the Inward Teacher; partly again by the fact that Friends at that time understood a 'creed' to be a string of theological propositions, such as the Nicene Creed, which claims to define Christian teaching for all time. In accepting Barclay, they were accepting a form of theology which, although systematically worked out, still left room for the Light; and certainly the idea that a simple profession of faith in God or Christ could be dismissed as 'credal' would have been a cause of serious alarm.

The reality is that a Quaker belief system has always existed; it was first articulated by early Friends and subsequently taken for granted. Dandelion points us to the obvious fact that "until recent times, the non-credal belief system was informed by, and contained within, a Quaker-Christianity". He cites Edward Grubb, one of the key figures in the turn to Liberalism, who thought it safe to define Quakerism as non-credal where the emphasis was on loyalty to Christ. Where this emphasis existed, "correctness of belief would largely take care of itself". There is a clear difference between 'non-credal' in this sense, which is more an *attitude* or *orientation* than an absolute prohibition, and being 'creedless', that is, having no beliefs at all. Dandelion drives the point home further when he says: "The concept of non-credal has been *reinterpreted* [my emphasis] to accommodate an increased diversity of belief". In other words, the argument that we should accept diversity because we are not a credal church is itself the product of the diversity it is defending and promoting — it is not a legitimate argument.

The idea that credal statements "fetter the search for truth and its more adequate expression" is linked to the Quaker doctrine (or creed, if you like) of 'continuing revelation'. It is assumed by many Friends and Attenders today that continuing revelation gives us unfettered freedom to think what we like, even to the extent of replacing one set of core beliefs with another as society and cultural conditions change. But this has never been the Quaker position. Gospel order, that is, the system of church government without voting which is at the centre of our faith, requires us to wait upon God, suppressing our own egos and elevating God's will and desire for us in order to discern the way forward. It is reflective of the 'Jesus way', the path into unity and wholeness, and presupposes our yielding to 'love as the first motion'. Continuing revelation — the revealing of God's word — is not, therefore, a kind of permission to go our own way, and credal statements are only wrong in so far as they frustrate this process, leading us away from God's truth and back into our own.[106]

[106] In the same way, Fox's question, "What canst thou say?" cannot — or should not — be used to justify the notion that 'anything goes' or 'we all have our own truth', *vide* the new Quaker poster brought out for National Quaker Week —

Belief and social action

David Boulton has said that he wants a religious society which "sits lightly to theological difference" and finds its unity in a common commitment to social and political action.[107] That should not surprise us as the ultimate beneficiary of such a lighthearted attitude to theological difference will undoubtedly be humanism. 'Sitting lightly' can mean a number of things: openness, tolerance, or not taking any ideas about what we stand for in a theological sense seriously at all. The question arising from Boulton's perspective on the Society, a perspective which is itself unavoidably 'theological', is whether social and political action is now the only thing that really matters and is a sufficient substitute for the undefined 'essentials' on which we have traditionally based our faith. If a common commitment to social and political action is to be the acknowledged source of our *unity* then shouldn't we in all honesty present ourselves to the world as a social and political organization?

Before dismissing this as quaint or melodramatic, consider the following exchange between a friend of mine, a fairly new attender, and 'old Bill', a longstanding member who introduced himself as "a Quaker and a secular rationalist". I am not in any danger of identifying the Friend concerned since there are numerous 'old Bills' around the place although not many who would describe themselves in such punctilious terms. My friend was understandably puzzled. "In that case — I'm just curious — what made you want to become a member of the *Religious* Society of Friends?" The answer came back, "Because it's better than the Labour Party". In the same way, I am sure many

"Thou shalt decide for thyself". When Fox challenged us with this searching question he wanted us to consider whether it came "inwardly from God". What he meant of course was that scripture had to be read and understood in the spirit and life which originally inspired it; otherwise it was a dead form and likely to give rise to error.

[107] See his 'Endpiece' in *The Friends Quarterly*, 3 (2012).

will agree, there are issues of *The Friend* that could serve with only minor edits as a supplement to the *Guardian* newspaper.

The story provides a good illustration of what is likely to happen when secular loyalties take the place of religious texts, like the Sermon on the Mount, as the source of our commitment. Old Bill, steeped in his secular rationalism, evidently saw the Religious Society of Friends as a kind of spiritually enhanced version of the *Labour Party*. There we already have the beginnings of disunity, for others will have different loyalties. Why should a secularised Society of Friends which is no longer centred in its *religious* tradition be any more immune to political disagreements that any other secular organisation? When have political and social activities *ever* been a sound basis for unity?[108]

There is, however, a more important consideration. What this perspective fails to take into account is the extent to which Quaker social and political action is the product of what we call 'fellowship', a Christian concept which is essentially theistic and dependent on a shared, if not systematically worked out, cluster of beliefs. One essential component of this 'cluster' is the idea that Friends do not take on challenges "in their own strength". Instead, they seek inspiration, strength and guidance in the transforming power of the Spirit, an exercise and discipline for which they need the fellowship of like-minded (and, as Dandelion would say, 'like-hearted') others.

Without God we can have friendship, but not true fellowship. As Richenda Scott puts it: "Real fellowship is possible only through the relation of each individual to God and so through God to his fellows, who are rooted and grounded in the same eternal life and love"; and Janet Scott: "We have found that this power, this light, turns us from evil to good and brings us into unity with God *and thence with our*

---

[108] It may be objected that Friends would never base their social and political action on party considerations, so disunity in that sense is unlikely, but one has only to think of an organisation like the Campaign against the Arms Trade (CAAT), which most Friends would support. where one faction wants to express their solidarity with the Palestinian armed resistance while another is opposed to the use of arms on any innocent civilians, including Israelis, to realise how quickly differences can develop within a purely political and secular framework.

fellows, into that 'spirit which takes away the occasion of all wars'" (italics added).

For a truly inspiring example of the way in which fellowship spills over into social and political action we need look no further than the 1922 edition of *Christian Life, Faith and Thought*. There, under the heading, "Seeing God in the Face of Jesus Christ", we find the following beautiful passage, full of enthusiasm, joy and dedication:

> In our hearts we must know this life of unity with God and our fellows, and we must then, from our hearts, live it out in God's way of life for the world. It will open our eyes to the oppression caused by many of the economic and other privileges which we have often taken for granted, and in opening our eyes will abase our hearts. It will send us forth to break down the social and educational barriers and to abolish the servitudes, which mar the fellowship of the human family. It will take us with Jesus not only into lowly service but also into clear-sighted truth. We shall find our lives brought alongside the lives of others in practical fellowship. We may have to give up what the world counts most dear, but we shall be lifted into the joy of love. Our feet will be beautiful with reconciliation as we go in and out among men with the gospel of peace.[109]

As in the Quaker tradition generally, the encounter with God is primary and leads to action in caring for others and the world. For Quakers, this balance expresses the right relationship between religious faith, personal conduct and social witness, between 'belief' and action. It is for this reason that Rufus Jones described the Society of Friends as "a religious body which has made a serious attempt to unite inward, mystical religion with active, social endeavours."[110] However, in recent Quaker writing, and in line with the tendency (perhaps now a necessity) to treat religious belief as 'relatively

---

109 *Christian Life, Faith and Thought in the Society of Friends* (hereafter *CFT*. London: The Friends Bookshop, 1923 [1922], p. 88.

110 Blamires, "Eckhart, Rufus Jones and the Quaker Tradition", *The Friends Quarterly* (July, 2006), p. 103.

inconsequential', there has been a move to tip this 'balance' decisively in favour of social action. While this is clearly evident in Quaker sociological writing, we may find that in a weaker form it has also been creeping into the more theological subject areas. Benjamin Wood, for example, in a thoughtful article which reaches out to non-theist Friends in a spirit of Christian reconciliation, emphasises the practical aspects of Jesus' ministry over and against his teachings. But is it conviction or a desire to placate that leads him to say: "this pragmatic emphasis on 'what we do' and not 'what we think' should structure our response to questions of God"; for when Jesus said "Come, follow me", he was not (I am convinced) inviting his disciples to follow his example only by performing good works. He had some very important things to say about the nature of God and the Kingdom. And although he emphasised that faith without charity is worthless, there is nothing in the Christian Testament to suggest that he regarded his own teachings as secondary.

Another example is provided by David Blamires, a prominent Quaker and well known Eckhart scholar, who tells us that for Eckhart, "the evangelical acts of mercy take precedence over the enjoyment of mystical experiences". He bases this conclusion on Eckhart's saying, "Even if one were in a rapture, like Paul's, and there was a sick man who needed help, I think it would be far better to come out of the rapture and show love by serving the needy one."[111] But this is not the only way of interpreting Eckhart's words since for Eckhart the love which leads to 'the evangelical acts of mercy' is precisely the self-giving love that *is* God, a love which cannot be denied, especially when one is wholly absorbed in God (enraptured) as Eckhart frequently was. The experience of God therefore *compels* the contemplative to acts of mercy and in this sense may be thought of as primary.

Later in his article, Blamires turns to Lorna Marsden for support, recalling a talk she had given to the Quaker Universalist Group in April 1990 on 'the inward journey and outward activity' in which she

---

[111] *ibid.,* p. 104

quoted Eckhart “to good effect”. He felt that the talk supported his view that in Eckhart the contemplative and the active life went hand in hand (a slight shift here), but that the spiritual disciplines, which included silent waiting upon God, could not be regarded as in any sense primary. The Eckhart passages quoted by Marsden, however, seem to be saying just the opposite — that the active life flows from the contemplative:

> We ought not to think of building holiness upon action; we ought to build it upon a way of being, for it is not what we do that makes us holy, but we ought to make holy what we do.[112]

The second of the two Eckhart passages is given here not in the abbreviated form in which it appears in Blamires’ article but in the more extended version to be found in Marsden’s *The Prepared Heart*:

> The interior work contains in itself all time, all vastness, all breadth and all length. The interior work receives and creates its whole being out of nowhere else than from and in the heart of God . . . It is not so with the external work, for it has its divine goodness brought and poured into it by means of the interior, as the divine nature stoops and clothes itself in distinction, quantity, in division.[113]

In both cases, the impulse to perform acts of charity is rooted in the relationship with God as the origin and source of love, a relationship which is described as ‘a way of being’; and it is in this sense also, the sense in which Jesus gently corrected Martha (Luke 10, 38-42), that Quaker social action has traditionally been understood.

This is not to say that non-theist Friends are less likely to be involved in social and political activity than their theist counterparts. From a Quaker-Christian standpoint the grace that leads into costly self-sacrifice is offered to all regardless of their beliefs, a position which follows from the Quaker doctrine of universal salvation. But

---

[112] *ibid*,. p. 107.
[113] Marsden, *The Prepared Heart* (London: Quaker Home Service, 1988), p. 81.

whether intended or not, the effect of arguing for a kind of equivalence between the contemplative and the active is to lessen the sense of our dependence on God. It is then all the easier to see in one side of the equation all that is necessary for our future fellowship and unity. Corporate social action which has no horizon beyond human flourishing becomes the sole content. We see the change in our Yearly Meeting Epistles where God is relegated to a footnote and the tone and emphasis is ideological rather than spiritual. No longer feeling any strong sense of the Divine will or of acting to fulfil God's purpose, we are focused on our own purposes, content to go forward in our own strength.

If we apply this emphasis retrospectively, then new Light can deconstruct the old. As Sue Glover Frykman points out in *The Friends Quarterly*, the Quaker Testimonies of peace, equality, simplicity, integrity and stewardship would then no longer be seen as "the outward expression of the inner experience of divine leading" but at best an expression of group sentiment in a particular cultural milieu: "I have experienced a subtle change in tone among Quakers, where the swing seems to be away from a collective experience and witness of the divine towards one of individual notions and expression . . . At first I simply accepted this as the fittings and furnishings of the Quaker home being freshened up to match and meet the needs of our times . . . But by emphasising individual notions to the detriment of a collective waiting in the divine Light and a collective witness to 'power' . . . are we not eroding the very foundations of that home?"

And she adds, rather sorrowfully, "To me, flinging individual notions into the nooks and crannies of the corridors of power is a waste of energy. We might just as well throw feathers. There is simply no weight behind them". [114]

---

[114] Glover Fykman, "United We Stand, Divided We Fall: Speaking Truth to Power", *The Friends Quarterly* 3, (2008), pp. 17-18.

Conclusion

The notion that belief is 'relatively inconsequential', and for the most part can be dispensed with, is a fairly recent extension of the notion that we are non-credal, and seems to have been arrived at without much thought as to what a belief is and its relation to experience. Moreover, the notion that we are non-credal is itself mistaken or at best misunderstood. How can it be true to say that because we have traditionally been wary of subscribing to formulated statements of belief we should have no corporate beliefs at all? How can this be in a Religious Society which has for more than three hundred years defined itself as Christian?

The consequences of 'non-credal' (interpreted in the Boulton sense of 'creedless') are the same as the consequences of an open-to-all diversity. No longer having a shared belief in God or in any transcendent reality beyond the human, and treating our core beliefs as outmoded constructs without relevance for our future, we are left pondering the question, 'Wherein lies our unity?' Social activism emerges as the most popular choice but with a nagging sense of 'something missing'. Paradoxically, what makes us different and still respected is the heroic past we are rejecting rather than anything we can put our finger on in the present. Sometimes we take comfort in the view that whatever our differences we are all agreed on the 'essentials' — now whittled down to two: the importance of Meeting for Worship and the value of silence. Never mind that your understanding of worship and mine may be poles apart and even (to use Janet Scott's term) 'mutually destructive', the *practice* is the same. Our loyalty, then, is to the external form, the very thing that Howgill and the Westmoreland Seekers trampled underfoot in that marvellous dawn which launched the Quaker movement. It seems that as long as we can preserve the ritual of a collective silence we can convince ourselves that nothing has fundamentally changed.

7

Gently move — the search for a common language

The eternal Word, which was in the beginning before all languages were, breaks in pieces all languages and . . . brings all into one language, for that which keeps in many languages keeps in confusion.
— James Nayler, 1653

A word must **mean** *the thing it stands for, not only in the logical sense of accurately corresponding to the intention of the writer but also in the visual sense of conjuring up a reflection of the thing in its completest reality.*
— Herbert Read

IN THE PREVIOUS chapter I argued that an over-determined emphasis on the 'non-credal' and the commitment to social action as the primary source of our unity were not the outcome of considered debate, still less of spiritual discernment, but a logical necessity to which we were driven by our decision to admit into membership people who do not share our basic and long-held Quaker beliefs. In this chapter I want to focus on a number of other important questions that have emerged as a result of the same pressures and are connected with religious language.

In January 2009, *The Friend* published an article by John Lampen and David Boulton which was notable for bringing together a declared Christian and a declared atheist in uneasy alliance. The uneasiness was evident in the elaborate way the article was constructed to avoid any apparent clash of ideas. Its title was 'Gently move', words taken from Herbert's great poem, 'The Church Porch', where the ambiguity of 'move' is skilfully exploited by the poet to advance the two themes of healing and restraint. As the poet and critic, William Empson, has famously demonstrated, there are at least seven types of literary ambiguity. Herbert's use of 'move' is an example of Empson's second type where "two or more meanings all add to the single meaning of the author". The kind of ambiguity being proposed in the article corresponds to Empson's seventh type: "the most ambiguous that can be conceived . . . when two meanings of the word . . . show a fundamental division in the writer's mind." [115] This of course was to be expected since the aim of the article was to search for an inclusive religious language that would be equally expressive of both positions and yet give an impression of unity to the general public when explaining what we stand for as Quakers.

The article began with a quote from a previous issue of *The Friend* which warned us against "an intolerance and over-zealousness regarding words and definitions that perhaps is not consonant with our ancient tradition of holding and living by a faith that is non-credal." With these words we were given advance warning that the views about to be expressed would be based on the same false premise (the assumption that 'non-credal' means 'creedless') as we have seen in other contexts.[116]

Who are these troublesome Friends who are 'over-zealous' in their use of definitions? The nearest we get to an explanation is that they may be people who in their early lives had "been bullied, intellectually or emotionally, in the name of some belief". Moreover, the authors write, "those who become distressed when their deepest beliefs are challenged may be feeling some threat to their own sense of identity, because of the way our convictions are linked to our sense of who we are." Friends who care about words and definitions are thus

---

[115] Empson, *Seven Types of Ambiguity* (London: Chatto and Windus, 1930), pp. 62, 244.

[116] As before, I understand 'non-credal' to refer to an attitude and 'creedless' to a fact.

pathologised in a way which makes it difficult for them to respond 'intellectually or emotionally' without incurring further labeling on the same lines. Although no doubt kindly meant, this type of characterisation also works rhetorically as a signal to the reader that it's not cool to be thought of as a Friend who worries about such matters.

But then, where does this leave someone like Alistair Heron who wrote a whole book on the subject of Quaker identity and another defining the word 'concern'? There is nothing in his autobiography to suggest that he was bullied emotionally or intellectually for his beliefs. And what does it say about our Swarthmore lecturers who have voiced similar anxieties and have shown themselves to be extremely conscientious in defining their terms? David Boulton himself has spent many hours defining terms like 'theism' and 'non-theism' without anyone suggesting that this resulted from the constant emotional bullying which, he tells us, he experienced as a child at the hands of the Plymouth Brethren.[117]

The opposite tendency to over-zealousness in the use of words and definitions is the desire to blur distinctions. However praiseworthy the reasons behind this, the result is likely to be the further degradation of our religious language. When language is misused, as T.S. Eliot has pointed out, words "slip, slide, perish/ Decay with imprecision".[118] This has the effect not only of making communication more difficult but of allowing further change to take place unnoticed — the 'silent revolution' becomes 'permanent revolution'. Moreover, to suggest that a concern with words and definitions violates our 'ancient tradition' of non-credal is to re-interpret that tradition in a way which, as we have seen, quite seriously misrepresents it. Indeed, the use of 'non-credal'

---

[117] Chapter 1 of *The Trouble with God.*

[118] Eliot, *The Four Quartets* (London: Faber and Faber, 1944), p. 12. The South American poet and critic, Octavio Paz, winner of the Nobel Prize for Literature, saw this as evidence of a decaying social order. "When a society becomes corrupt", he wrote, "what first grows gangrenous is language. Social criticism, therefore, begins with grammar and the reestablishment of meanings". See Paz, *On Poets and Others* (tr. M. Schmidt. London: Paladin, 1992 [1987]), p. xiii.

in this context, which is itself both a word and a definition, points up the need for *greater* clarity regarding words and definitions rather than less.

It is hardly surprising that the article should target verbal accuracy and precision when the question at issue is how to stretch our religious language to cover the increasing diversity of our member-intake. It seems that creedlessness, far from making the job easier, as one might expect, has made it virtually impossible:

> For most of its history, members of our Society shared a common (Christian) language in which to speak of these things [morality, religious experiences, fellowship, biblical narratives], even when they disagreed about them. Now that we no longer have a generally accepted language, it is easy to feel unheard or misunderstood. How can we get past this difficulty in a Society whose religious consciousness embraces non-theists as well as theists, post-Christians as well as Christians?

We are back with the intractable problems posed by the concept of 'equality in diversity'; having decided to demote our core beliefs to parity with minority beliefs, and in the process denied the importance of any beliefs at all, we are now faced with the problem of the language in which those beliefs are expressed. Those who feel that the beautiful language of *Advices and Queries* is more than adequate to the task must prepare themselves for a shock. Clearly the authors' intention is to pave the way for the next revision of *Quaker Faith and Practice*, and from this point of view 'Gently move' is an inspired choice of title.

The authors make a careful distinction between public and personal language. So far as our public language is concerned "we need to take scrupulous care to seek forms of words that are as inclusive as we can make them". For 'inclusive' read 'ambiguous' — for how else can words be inclusive of quite different and even opposite meanings? The development of this vocabulary is described by the authors as a "work in progress", which suggests a wider and more 'official' collaboration somewhere off stage, although exactly where is unclear. To the reader with a progressive mindset it may seem that we have here an interesting long-term project, but we need to be aware — and wary — of what we are consenting to. We are being asked not only to be inclusive (which we undoubtedly are) but to change the very language we use to include people and the very thing we are including them in. As Rachel Britton argues in an article in *The Friend* on the limitations of membership, it's rather as if a group of cricketers applied for membership of a football club and not only wanted to use the facilities of the football club to promote cricket but expected the football club members to adopt a form of language and a style of play which would encompass both sports on equal terms. The analogy is drawn from her own experience of the consultation on the revision of what was then *Christian Faith and Practice*:

> Sheffield Meeting divided itself into house-groups to send suggestions to, and read drafts provided by, the Revision Committee. The house-group I was in contained two attenders, who thought the revised document should leave out all reference to God, so as to make itself more comfortable for them, as they were atheists. The rest of the group took the view that if they wanted to play cricket, they shouldn't join a football club. 'We like the clubhouse and the grounds,' they could have said. 'Why shouldn't we play our game in the same field and with the same facilities? We could play in different corners or at different times — or, more radically, we could rewrite the rules of 'football' so that they could include people playing 'cricket'. 'Footballers' could interpret the rules one way, and 'cricketers' another. Or, why have rules at all? Let's all just play in whatever way expresses ourselves best.'
>
> An extravagant metaphor? Perhaps. But it illustrates the need for boundaries if any human activity is to flourish. Of course, people who don't know the basis, and want to try out the activity, can come in and try it. We would not exclude anyone from Meeting for Worship who

> could tolerate silence and was not a risk to others. But allowing *anyone* to have a say in what Quakerism is, would be ridiculous.[119]

What is clear is that if we accept the authors' proposal, we can no longer present ourselves to the world as essentially Christian or even theist — or indeed anything of a genuinely religious nature at all. In our public pronouncements, we must be "clear and open about our diversity, affirming it as our strength, not our weakness", and even "where traditional religious language is appropriate" (and where, in this scheme of things, is that even possible?) "we should seek ways of making it clear that we embrace our religious heritage and find ourselves enriched by different understandings and interpretations of it." But what if we *cannot* say that diversity is our strength and what if we are *unable* to feel enriched by a particular understanding and interpretation of our religious heritage? For example, how enriched would the majority of Friends feel by an atheistic understanding of the 'gathered meeting' or the 'Real Presence' — as enriched, let us say, as they would by reading Thomas Kelly on the same subject? Surely not more than they would expect a committed atheist to be enriched by a theist understanding of these same terms?

The rather touching belief that all that separates us is language is closely linked to the notion of 'non-credal'. Get rid of all the definitions and labels and beneath the variety of expression, if only we are sensitive enough, we will find that we are one in spirit, sharing a common focus and tapping into the same deep sources of inspiration. An example of this kind of thinking is provided by the extract from the Area Meeting newsletter quoted earlier: "Do I always try to go behind the words and seek where they are coming from? The same experience can be expressed in many different ways using very different language". A similar thought is expressed in an article by Michael Wright reporting on the conference held at Friends House in January 2014 on the subject 'Faith — What's God got to do with it?' "What emerged, for me, was that not only the speakers, but also the

[119] R. Britton, "Limits to Membership?", *The Friend* (18th April, 2014), p. 6.

participants I encountered during the day, share similar experiences — but they account for them in rather different language. It is words that cause us problems, rather than the experiences." But as Donna Morgan pointed out in a follow-up letter (28th March) there was one dissenting voice. "Halfway into the Q&A session, David Boulton said, 'naming our differences is hugely important . . . be straightforward and plain about what it is you are dialoguing about and name it . . . no we are not all saying the same thing'."

Leaving aside the fact that for Boulton there is *nothing* behind the words because "language goes all the way down",[120] the much greater danger is that we could end up using the same language to express very different experiences. Just to take the word 'Spirit' — the most likely candidate to replace the word 'God'. As Mehrdad Fatehi has pointed out, in Judaism generally, and in St Paul, 'Spirit' was "never conceived of or experienced as an entity distinct or somehow separable from God. The Jewish experience of the Spirit is always and essentially an experience *of* God . . . In fact, the Spirit-language is used precisely when God's own personal presence and activity, in distinction . . . from other agents, is in view".[121] And this was also, until fairly recently, the Quaker experience. However, if ambiguity is the new inclusive language, how can we be sure that it is the Spirit of God that is intended? For non-theist Friends, 'the Spirit is leading us' could mean that we are open to new light from whatever happens to be the current intellectual fashion. The 'spirit' referred to could also mean the "wholly human spirit" — not that of God in us, but that of us in us. The word 'Light' would be subjected to a similar multi-layered interpretation, and most certainly the word 'God'. Even now it is used 'inclusively' to cover the not-God of humanism and the immanent and

[120] See below, p. 112.

[121] M. Fatehi, "The Spirit's Relation to the Risen Lord in Paul: An Examination of its Christological Implications", *Wissenschaftliche Untersuchungen zum Neuen Testament* 2/128 (2000), p. 163. My emphasis.

transcendent God of Christian theism. To maintain consistency the recommended strategy should be to stay with the *surface* meaning of the words and *not* to go behind them. Going behind the words to seek where they come from is a worthwhile response where there is a large measure of unity in the group; it becomes problematic when 'the places they come from' are as diverse and as contradictory as these.

Returning to the "work in progress", the article says nothing about how it is to be achieved. How are we to gauge its feasibility? How to measure its success? When we've finally got rid of Christian language because it excludes the Universalists, theistic language because it excludes the non-theists, and some forms of non-theist language because they exclude the humanists, what will be left? Perhaps some kind of lowest common denominator, a non-language eviscerated of all the accumulated associations of the past, a PC language stripped to its barest essentials — in short, a 'religious' language that is fully acceptable only to 'religious humanists'. And if this is thought to be stretching matters too far, I am told that in a subsequent correspondence between the two authors, John Lampen's positing of the phrase 'something more'as a minimalist definition of the Mystery which some call 'God', was rejected by his co-author as too 'credal'. The work in progress clearly has a long way to go, and one cannot help wondering how many of the beautiful passages from Nayler, Howgill, Barclay and others will be left in a 2050 version of *Quaker Ethics and Social Reform.*

Finally, can the authors of this article really affirm, beyond any shadow of doubt, that diversity is indeed our *strength* — a diversity that embraces contrary and incompatible beliefs — rather than merely a present reality which we are all being asked to make the best of? And should this really be binding on all of us (the moral imperative 'should' is used throughout)? But then, if so, where do they stand who believe the opposite — that our present diversity has become so extended that it is now a weakness, one which could ultimately change the Society into something that would be unrecognisable to its founders? Too often the claim that "diversity is our strength and not our weakness" takes the form of an abstract principle without any thought being given to the real-life diversities that make up the whole and how they blend together.

The debate so far has been about public language. However, the article also looks at personal language, and here the authors take a very different approach. "Differences in personal language, especially when used in ministry", they maintain, "should not merely be accepted by Friends but cherished as a mark of the searching and free-thinking spirit of modern Quakerism". One's immediate reaction is to cheer, for who would not wish to be thought of as a 'searching and free-thinking spirit'? And who would dare dispute the statement "that when Friends speak personally from their own experience they must be free to express themselves in language appropriate to their own conviction"? As the article goes on to say, we all "have a responsibility to speak our truth with integrity". Yet attitudes like these are not as innocent as they first appear and could be just as damaging as the most ambiguous public pronouncements to the spiritual well-being of the Society. However suited to life in a secular democracy, they are not the sentiments one would expect of the 'humble learner in the school of Christ'; there is a note of self-projection in this way of speaking that seems curiously at odds with a professed religion of the Spirit. How would it have sounded, for instance, in the ears of those who compiled the 1922 book of discipline?

> Inward guidance does not mean unchecked individualism, for the follower of the light will be continually correcting his first perception of it by a fuller experience, and by that of others who have followed it more faithfully. Unity in diversity is thus achieved, because the light that guides the sincere and humble seeker is the light of God who is love. This is the path towards peace with all men, for there is no discord in the will of God. In His light we discover that He is at work in all others, and find unity with them in His love.[122]

---

[122] *CFT,* p. 84

Or if we are speaking of the language used in vocal ministry, consider this passage from Barclay's *Apology*. It appears in the section on Worship under the heading, 'It is a time for waiting upon God':

> When assembled, it should be the common task of one and all to wait upon God. It should be a time for turning away from one's own thoughts and for suspending the imagination .... No one limits the Spirit of God in such worship or brings forth his own laboriously assembled ideas. But everyone will state whatever the Lord has placed in his heart. And it will not be uttered from man's own will or wisdom, but in the evidence and demonstration of the Spirit and of power.[123]

Our hesitancy, then, is around phrases such as 'free-thinking', 'their own conviction', 'speaking *our* truth'. Friends giving ministry are accustomed to asking themselves, 'Does it come inwardly from God?' Even where the word 'God' is not used, they are asked to *pray* that their ministry may arise from *deep experience*, and to *trust* that words will be *given* (*Advices and Queries*, 13). It is not their own truth they are seeking but the Highest Truth. Without this assurance, Barclay warns us, they should remain silent.

When one thinks about it, it's a strange thought that one should go to Meeting to accept or cherish the *free-thinking* capacity of anyone. But this is clearly another, and logical, consequence of a heavily secularised notion of diversity. Later in the article, we are reminded that "none of us has a monopoly on truth". That, at least, is indisputable — if we mean by 'truth' the shapeless multiplicity of viewpoints "uttered from man's own will or wisdom"; but Barclay, with unmistakable authority and speaking for all Friends everywhere, reminds us that the One Truth, the word of God, is "over all".

---

[123] Freiday, p. 248.

8

Non-realism or Real Presence?

What is the ground and foundation of the gathered meeting? In the last analysis, it is, I am convinced, the Real Presence of God.

— Thomas Kelly

Religion loses its nerve when it ceases to believe that it expresses in some way truth about our relation to a reality beyond ourselves which ultimately concerns us.

— Dorothy Emmet

IN HIS BOOK, *Godless for God's Sake*, specifically addressed to members of the Religious Society of Friends, David Boulton defines theism as a 'lie':

> the 'lie' is not God, but the simplistic, literalist notion of God: the notion that 'he' or 'she' or 'it' exists independently of our human consciousness encoded in human language.[124]

This is what has come to be known as the 'non-realist' position, the view that there is no objectively existing God and indeed no objective reality at all to which we, as experiencing subjects, respond. What we think of as reality, and what we think of as God, it is insisted, are no more than mental constructs formed by human beings using human language. Non-realism, on this account, is a purely atheistic philosophy which is not only opposed to theism but to any form of mysticism which testifies to a higher good beyond human flourishing.

---

[124] *Godless*, p. 11.

In British theological circles it is associated with the name of Don Cupitt, the founder of the Sea of Faith Movement, but its chief relevance for us is that it provides the framework for Boulton's concept of a new non-theist theology suited to meeting "the daunting challenges of the 21st century".

Whilst we may continue to welcome atheists into our meetings, it would be a disaster for Quakerism if such a theology were to be widely accepted. The present chapter is written in the belief that there are more attractive alternatives which are philosophically interesting, better suited to meeting the challenges ahead and do not require us to think of theism as a 'lie' or even a mistake.

Alternatives to Sea of Faith Non-Realism

What distinguishes Don Cupitt's and David Boulton's non-realism from the alternative views I will be considering is that, like Marxism, it is a closed system. Once we have accepted the premise that the only basis we can have for claims about the external world is our own language-bounded experience, we are well and truly trapped within a cognitive and ideological system — one that requires us to 'challenge' and 'have the courage' to reject our most cherished religious beliefs. Paradoxically, non-realism claims to be liberating, absolving us from the 'old certainties' and enabling us to enter a new and more authentic life of freedom, while all the time it is claiming certainty in its own right, the certainty that there is no other intellectually respectable way of viewing the world and that there is no escape from its entrapping conclusions. One hopes that it will be welcome news to some of its more unwilling captives that this is simply not the case.

Because it is a general theory of knowledge, non-realism must be extended beyond theology and philosophy to every other branch of knowledge including the natural sciences. For this reason, it will be useful to consider how well it works in the scientific field before applying it to our thinking about God. If it is felt to be inadequate as a theory of knowledge in science, then we can assume it is unlikely to be of much value in theology either.

The two main alternatives to non-realism which I shall be considering in this chapter are realism and critical realism, neither of which excludes the possibility of God or conflicts with the suppositions underlying scientific enquiry.

Realism, or what is sometimes called 'naïve realism' or 'objectivism', holds that mind and the world are completely separate; objects exist independently of the mind of the person who perceives them. This seems to accord very well with our everyday experience and is the 'commonsense' view of the ordinary layman and also most scientists. Roy Bhaskar defines the "basic principle of a realist philosophy of science" as the belief "that perception gives us access to things and experimental activity access to structures that exist independently of us" — the very opposite of the philosophical position that underpins Boulton's derogatory statement about theism.[125]

John Searle (a leading realist philosopher and logician) doesn't regard realism as a theory of knowledge at all, but as a basic assumption underlying all our communication. He points out that in order to take part in the debate on realism and non-realism, we must already have taken realism for granted, and unless we do take it for granted, we cannot understand one another as we normally do. He uses the same type of argument to refute the non-realist claim that reality is socially constructed. Here it is in three easy steps:

1. To construct money, property and language, there have to be the raw materials.
2. Therefore, a socially constructed reality presupposes a non-socially constructed reality.
3. Therefore, there must be a non-socially constructed reality.

---

125 A. McGrath, *The Science of God: An Introduction to Scientific Theology* (London: T. & T. Clarke International, 2004), p. 141.

The non-realist, however, is likely to point out that our concept of 'raw materials' is itself a linguistic construct. It is impossible, s/he will insist, to go outside our language to gain access to something that is not in turn defined by language. To maintain otherwise is a mistake, or in Boulton's case, a 'lie' — there is no 'outside' to language. And, like it or not, this applies whether we are speaking of raw materials or of God.

So according to Boulton, God is no more "and gloriously no less" (as he is fond of saying) than a linguistic (that is, a human) concept. And yet, there is a third option which is less concerned with logic and more with process, and could be described as a kind of half-way house between these two opposing viewpoints.

Scientists who describe themselves as realists would probably extend the meaning of realism to include *critical realism* (which Bhaskar's definition allows). Critical realism acknowledges that perception not only gives us access to a reality that exists independently of us, as in Bhaskar's definition, but also affects the way in which information about that reality is received. Indeed, it is now a commonplace of quantum physics that the observer, by the simple act of observing, can affect and alter the phenomenon that is being observed. For the critical realist, therefore, there is a strong subjective element in our perception of the world, but the process is not *entirely* subjective in that the world also impacts on us and determines the *way* in which it can be known and *how far* it can be known. In other words, there is a reciprocity between the perceiver and the thing perceived which isn't available in rational terms to the non-realist. Both the realist and the critical realist, therefore, reject the non-realist view that "what we think of as reality is *no more than* a construct formed by human beings using human language". To think in that way, they suggest, would be to make reality entirely subjective and to ignore the way it impinges on us.

It is along this line of interaction between the perceiver and the thing perceived (some have called it a 'conversation') that the scientist tends to situate herself, and it is also the philosophical approach that is favoured by most theists. John Polkinghorne, an internationally known theoretical physicist and equally well known theologian, summarises his own position as follows:

> I believe that the advance of science is not just concerned with our ability to manipulate the physical world, but to gain knowledge of its actual nature. In a word, I am a realist. Of course, such knowledge is to a degree partial and corrigible. Our attainment is verisimilitude, not absolute truth. Our method is the creative interpretation of experience, not rigorous deduction from it. Thus I am a critical realist.[126]

In presenting their non-realist perspective, neither Don Cupitt nor David Boulton pays much attention to the alternative options I have sketched here. As a result the reader tends to be swept along by the force and eloquence of their arguments (and they *are* eloquent) without being offered anything in the way of choice. Both write as if non-realism is the only credible worldview and anyone who thinks otherwise is either lacking in intellectual rigour or being wilfully obtuse. This is despite the fact that non-realism has been rejected by some of the best minds of our generation. A Cambridge-led survey of philosophical opinion in 2013 found that although most British philosophers (with some notable exceptions) are atheists, the overwhelming majority also reject non-realism.[127]

Non-realism: is God (merely) a 'human construct'?

Boulton's declaration that theism is a lie is more than a personal opinion; it is a philosophical statement based on Cupitt's non-realist supposition that language creates reality and God is therefore a human construct beyond which we cannot go.[128] A form of extreme

---

126 *ibid.*, p. 143.

127 See below, p. 139

128 Boulton makes his debt to Cupitt's brand of poststructuralism explicit in *The Trouble with God*, pp. 196-201.

subjectivism which claims 'ultimate truth' in its own right while denying that any one 'truth' should be privileged over any other (a contradiction in itself) it has its roots in the poststructuralist theory which spread like wildfire through British and US universities in the 1980s. It was all part of the general trend that came to be known as postmodernism. There was probably not a single university student or young Friend who was not affected by it, and there can be little doubt that this has contributed to the ease with which non-realist ideas have penetrated the Religious Society of Friends.

Poststructuralism found its keenest supporters in the humanities and social sciences. Here the attack centred on metaphysics with its supposedly outdated concerns around questions of truth and value and the nature of ultimate reality. Inevitably, this brought theology and even philosophy into contempt. The new thinking was that "philosophy must not be 'taken seriously', that the traditional subjects of philosophy (morality as well as metaphysics) should be approached 'playfully', 'light-mindedly', and that only a 'metaphysical prig' believes in such things as 'truth' and 'reality'". [129] The academic community was divided down the middle and there was a tendency to take sides on the basis of political affiliation rather than on values of objectivity and unbiased truth, insofar as these are attainable.

Those on the left of politics were particularly attracted to the new ideas and found in deconstruction and cultural relativism, two offshoots of poststructuralism, intellectual support for their political ideas and particularly for their work with minority groups struggling to achieve greater social equality and acceptance. It is undeniable that this powerful combination produced considerable benefits for these groups, and thus for society, but cultural relativism also had its big drawbacks. In some cases it led to academics, if not excusing, at least writing dispassionately about such practices as honour killings, female infanticide and even genocide. Their concern was less with the victims of these practices than with avoiding the charge of imposing Western values on people who had already suffered enough from colonialism.

---

[129] Himmelfarb, *On Looking into the Abyss* (NY.: Alfred A. Knoff, 1994), p. xii.

In Britain it led to the authorities closing their eyes to forced marriages and female genital mutilation, 'sensitive' issues most certainly, but ones which led politicians and academics alike to ignore the existential experience of the young women victims who were left without a voice.

The other offshoot, deconstruction, praised by Terry Eagleton for its success in 'uncovering the power relationships hidden in texts', and by Don Cupitt for its usefulness in dismantling the 'meta-narratives' of religion, took the same 'playful' attitude to historical truth; but this too revealed its negative side when it culminated in the deconstruction of the Holocaust which so shocked Gertrude Himmelfarb.[130]

Fashions in intellectual life as elsewhere tend to be short-lived and cyclical. There are signs that the tide is now beginning to turn back in favour of metaphysics with the counter attack being led from within the ranks of the French left-wing intelligentsia in the person of Alain Badiou (praised by Terry Eagleton for putting "notions of truth and universality back on the agenda"), and in Germany, although more cautiously, by Jürgen Habermas. It is odd to see the very people who took such notions off the agenda, now putting them back again. We have yet to understand how this will ultimately play out, but whatever the eventual outcome, in Britain there has always been strong opposition to the non-realist strand in postmodernism and not only amongst classical philosophers. The most strenuous resistance has come from science, including, as we shall see, those scientists who share the non-realist's hostility to theism.[131]

Scientists on the whole want to believe there really is a world out there which it is the task of science to explore. Cupitt, as one would expect, denies this:

> I am insisting that there is no Cosmos, no ready-made and fully formed real world out there, quite independent of our minds and yet somehow

---

[130] *ibid.*, pp. xi, 149.

[131] See R. Dawkins, "Postmodernism Disrobed", *Nature* 394 (1998), pp. 141-3.

standing ready to be called upon to vouch for the accuracy of our scientific theories. [132]

Here we have the same non-realist argument used about the universe that we have seen Boulton using about God. Does it follow (for Boulton) that the universe is a lie? And would he say that "the lie is not the universe, but the simplistic, literalist notion of the universe: the notion, held by the overwhelming majority of scientists, that it exists independently of our human consciousness encoded in human language?" In other words, that it would still exist if the human race ceased to exist? What an oddly homocentric position he would then find himself in! And it gets worse — to be fully consistent he would have to say that just as the universe is a lie, so science itself is a lie — unless, of course, it is that rare thing, a science based on postmodernist principles.

Despite his insistence that there is no cosmos out there, it will be noted that Cupitt's formulation is full of qualifying phrases — no *ready-made*, no *fully formed*, *quite* independent. So does he believe there is *no* cosmos out there, or that there is a cosmos but we can know nothing about it? His approach to this question is curiously ambivalent. At first sight it would seem that he favours the latter position: "Anti-realism does not say that there is no world at all, but only that we cannot compare our view of the world with the way the world is absolutely, for we have no access to the way things are absolutely". But he then stops short, skirting round the implications of this statement which would immediately take him into critical realist territory. We will be looking at critical realism again later in the chapter but I think we can say with confidence that this is not where Cupitt wishes to take us. He is a non-realist through and through and we must therefore conclude that the phrases in question don't represent a modification of his argument but that he does really believe the whole of reality exists only in our minds.

132 Cupitt, *The Old Creed and the New*, p. 38.

There is nothing wrong with that in itself — a similar view was taken by the eighteenth-century philosopher, Bishop Berkeley. Berkeley believed that things exist only as ideas in some mind, but got round the philosophical impasse represented by non-realism by saying that material things continue in existence when we are not aware of them as ideas in the mind of God. Cupitt by contrast has taken a prior decision to leave God out of the equation. For him, as for Boulton, there is no reality that "exists independently of our human consciousness encoded in human language". Because if there is available to us any kind of *reliable* knowledge of an external world, even including the knowledge that it exists, his (and with it, Boulton's) thesis immediately loses all credibility. Once we concede that our subjective knowledge is knowledge of *something*, we are then free to use the same argument with regard to religious experience. And if it is further acknowledged that the world is not only there, waiting to be discovered, but impinges on our minds in ways that transcend our subjective construction of it, then the same can be argued in relation to God.

This Cupitt and David Boulton cannot allow. It is the reason why the slightest shred of objectivity has to be eliminated, why the qualifying phrases are not in the end integral to the argument but are there solely for their rhetorical effect. Cupitt's denial of the real existence of a ready-made universe has to be absolute because his denial of the transcendent reality of God has to be absolute. In Cupitt's universe there can be no wriggle room for persons of faith, no cosmic worm holes through which they can be allowed to escape. But despite insisting that his non-realism "is entirely compatible with a full commitment to modern knowledge as it is acquired by orthodox scientific method", his views have proved unattractive to the scientific community, even that part of it which is avowedly atheist. Indeed, there appears to be a high degree of antipathy between these two perspectives. Cupitt tells us that non-realists like himself "secretly regard science as being naive in its one-eyed objectivism", [133] while Richard Dawkins has made it abundantly clear that he has no time to waste on the views of non-realists when they are applied to the processes of scientific discovery or the objects of scientific investigation. So, for example, when Alan Sokal and Jean Bricmont, two US professors of physics, managed to get a spoof article on a non-realist approach to quantum gravity into a well-respected French postmodernist journal, Dawkins could scarcely contain his glee: "Sokal's paper must have seemed a gift to the editors because this was a *physicist* saying all the right-on things they wanted to hear, attacking the 'post-Enlightenment hegemony' and such uncool notions as the existence of the real world".[134] While this hardly amounts to a coherent argument, it is enough to warn us that in considering the value of Cupitt's 'objective nihilism' (his alternative term for 'non-realism') we should put firmly to one side any idea that his views are comfortably in line in with modern science.

As already noted, Cupitt likes to give his readers the impression that there is no escape from the non-realist position:

> There is only *our* knowledge, only *our* world, only *our* point of view, *outsidelessly* — which means that the whole idea of getting outside the preview cinema to look directly at the external world was a mistake, because there *is* no external 'real' world to get out into. Nobody ever has been, or ever will be, 'outside' the preview cinema. *It has no outside.*[135]

Scientists, however, point out that their theories have predictive value (the most famous example being the discovery of Neptune from prior mathematical calculation) which suggests that the universe transcends our subjective construction of it. This conclusion is also supported by the well-known fact that scientific experiments must be capable of being repeated by others using the same procedures and

---

[133] Cupitt, *Creation out of Nothing*, p. 110.
[134] Dawkins, *ibid.*
[135] Cupitt, *The Old Creed and the New*, p. 37.

producing the same results. Finally, it has been noted by Norman Sheppard in an article on the distinguished scientist and philosopher, Michael Polanyi, how scientific experimentation can throw up unexpected data which can lead research in quite new directions. Serendipity of this kind, he says, is "a good example of how nature itself continuously intervenes to control the direction of scientific progress". This reflects a critical realist viewpoint which holds that the distinctive identity of the object of scientific investigation shapes our understanding of it.

Polanyi himself said with regard to the scientifically-trained guesswork he called 'tacit knowledge' that it is "guided by the urge to make contact with a reality, which is felt to be there already to start with, waiting to be apprehended":

> That is why the egg of Columbus is the proverbial symbol of great discovery. It suggests that great discovery is the realisation of something obvious; a presence staring us in the face, waiting until we open our eyes. In this light it may appear perhaps more appropriate to regard discovery in the natural sciences as guided not so much by the potentiality of a scientific proposition as by an aspect of nature seeking realisation in our minds.[136]

---

[136] M. Polanyi, *Science, Faith and Society* (Burlington, VT.: Phoenix Books, 1964 [1946]), p. 35. According to Wikipedia, "an egg of Columbus or Columbus's egg refers to a brilliant idea or discovery that seems simple or easy after the fact." Note: attributing intentionality to nature, especially in its inorganic aspect, seems — if taken literally — to be at the very least counter-intuitive; but this remark of Polanyi is probably better understood as an elaborate 'as if' formulation to give greater force to his sense that nature is present to the scientist in ways that transcend symbolic representation and yet give form to the scientist's discoveries. The same point is made even more forcefully by Rowan Williams in *The Edge of Words: God and the Habits of Language* (The Gifford Lectures. London: Bloomsbury, 2014) pp. 20-21: "At the most abstract level, philosophers have spoken of the intelligible form of something; but this does not quite do justice to the perception that when an object is understood and spoken of — spoken of either 'literally' or 'metaphorically' — there is a convergence or confluence of action between object and subject. What is understood and spoken of is present as modifying the subject's activity, both limiting its options in certain ways and expanding its capacity in others". Or more ambitiously, remembering that we and our language are also a part of the material world: ""'what we need is a metaphysics that thinks of matter itself as invariably and

The language employed here will surely resonate with Friends: it has an almost mystical ring, bringing to mind 'the God who first seeks us'. Polanyi emphasised the role of judgement, faith and imagination in scientific discovery, setting them above logic and rationality. He was therefore fully aware of the 'subjective' element in science, although he refused to employ that term. Explaining why he called his major work 'Personal Knowledge', he referred first of all to "the personal participation of the knower in all acts of understanding" and then attested that "such knowing is indeed objective in the sense of establishing contact with a hidden reality; a contact that is defined as the condition for anticipating an indeterminate range of yet unknown (and perhaps yet inconceivable) true implications."[137]

It is the unfolding of these yet unknown but true implications that is the guarantor of whatever objectivity the discovery possesses. He is not concerned to establish the *absolute* objectivity of scientific knowledge but only that it is achieved through engagement with a reality that lies outside our subjectivity and is apprehended by the use of tacit as well as explicit knowledge and expertise. The results of such enquiry he called *reliable* knowledge to distinguish it from any claim to being absolutely objective. This position is nicely encapsulated in his statement that scientific discovery "must involve an intuitive perception of the real structure of natural phenomena".[138]

My concern here, however, is with theology where there is only one truly foundational type of evidence, namely, religious experience, which has a *very* strong subjective element. So what then is the value of Polanyi's paradigm in defending the reality of God? Only that in affirming the independent reality of the natural world, it affirms a reality which transcends our conceptual understanding of it. It penetrates the postmodern obfuscation that imprisons us within our

---

necessarily communicative — not as a sheer passivity moulded by our minds into intelligible structure" (ibid., p.xi).

137 Polanyi, *Personal Knowledge* (London: Routledge, 1998 [1958, 1962, 1974]), pp. vii-viii.

138 Polanyi, *Science Faith and Society*, p. 25.

own subjectivity — a nightmare perspective in which nothing fresh and real, no new revelation from 'outside' can break through into our lives. It follows that if the world investigated by science can be real, then logically so can the God known to the mystics. It is interesting that in Polanyi the methods of enquiry in science and 'experiential' religion are not without some resemblances, and indeed he points them out, comparing the assiduous mental preparation of the experimental scientist to "the prayerful search for God" which culminates in the mystic's experience of absolute Truth, comparable to the 'Eureka' moment of the successful scientist.

Scientists, it should now be clear, are rarely non-realists; they tend to be 'realists' or 'critical realists', or to hold to the kind of 'personalist' philosophy we have been discussing in relation to Polanyi. All of these posit the existence of a real world which is discovered (revealed) rather than 'constructed' but in the apprehension of which both subject and object are involved. A convenient if rather crude way of representing this might be in the form of a Venn diagram where realism is represented by two separate circles, non-realism by a single circle (with no outside) and critical realism (and personalism) by two overlapping circles.

Reading Cupitt, there are times when it seems he is attempting to reap all the advantages of non-realism while scooping up those of critical realism as well. In other words, there appears to be a contradiction in his thinking which may go unnoticed in the persuasive rhetoric he uses to advance his argument. While *insisting* that "there is no Cosmos out there . . . no external 'real' world to get out into", he says:

> Our perceptual and cognitive apparatus doesn't just mirror, or copy exactly, the external world. Our senses actively search the environment, scanning for and seeking out things important to us, selecting and interpreting data, fitting them together in patterns, checking out hypotheses, construing and constructing, and so continuously building and testing our world-picture.[139]

---

139 Cupitt, *The Old Creed and the New*, p. 36.

So it appears after all that there *is* an external 'real' world out there, a world that *does* transcend our subjective construction of it, only it is not *really* external to us in the sense that nothing *can* be "since our knowledge is always only human knowledge". Or to put it another way: although the world may transcend our subjective construction of it, we ourselves are unable to do so because we cannot get outside the language or system of signs we use to describe it. The more we think about it, the more we find ourselves going round in circles — circles of self-contradiction. How would we *know* that the world transcends our subjectivity when all we have *is* our subjectivity? As we saw John Searle argue earlier, in order to justify non-realism the non-realist has to pre-suppose the existence of the external reality which it is the whole point of non-realism to deny.

The danger for the non-realist is a fall into solipsism. What does he or she test the scientific hypothesis *against*? Surely as an 'objective nihilist' it has be nothing? But no, we test it against what the non-realist puts in place of the external world, our own subjective but collectively agreed world-picture. It follows that science involves testing one kind of fiction, the scientific hypothesis, against another kind of fiction, an external world that is constructed rather than discovered, and constructed out of nothing but our own agreed constructs:

> There is no cosmos out-there and there are no laws out-there: nothing is ready made. We gradually evolve among ourselves, and try to come to agreement about, our own current world picture. *We* make the world look the way it does to us — by which I mean that previous generations evolved the theory that leads us today to look at the world in the way we do.[140]

How then does anything new enter in? What is the point of "our senses actively searching the environment" — an environment that for

[140] *ibid.*, p. 80. Cupitt's emphasis.

the objective nihilist can be no more than a human concept, no more 'out-there' than the cosmos is held to be?

In the two passages I have quoted we find the same qualifying phrases, the same ambiguities, that we noted earlier; but now they seem to have a slightly different function. The idea that "our perceptual and cognitive apparatus doesn't just mirror, or copy exactly, the external world" presupposes the existence of an objective, external world, a proposition that has already been denied by the statement that there is no cosmos, no external world out there to get into. That our perceptual and cognitive apparatus doesn't copy the external world *exactly* again assumes that there is an external world but that our perceptual and cognitive apparatus distorts it, or that it has characteristics that are inaccessible to us (the standard Kantian position). 'Our senses actively scanning the environment' suggests once again that there *is* an environment and it is more than just the self-generated imaginings of an introspective world community of scientists, and moreover that the essentially new can be incorporated into existing knowledge by the application of the scientific method. There is little here that a critical realist of theist convictions would not accept. [141] It seems that for most of the time Cupitt wants to be seen as a *super* non-realist, that is, an 'objective nihilist', but when it is more convenient, when he is protesting his orthodox scientific credentials, he falls back on the position of a *cautious* non-realist, and perhaps even of a *de facto* critical realist. As we have seen in other contexts, ambiguity is not without its uses.

---

[141] In fact this is the position taken up by Rowan Williams — a theist by any standard. He writes: "We test our schemata, we criticise and enlarge and rework our representational structures, transforming both our relationships with each other and our capacity to negotiate with the environment. We claim to move from less to more adequate representation, not only — as Rorty and others suggest — from one imaginative experiment to another . . . . What we say is capable of being not only a representation but a misrepresentation; the elements of description may be assembled in ways that bear no relation to what has been encountered or engaged." Rowan Williams, *The Edge of Words,* pp. 44-5.

These are fundamental flaws in Cupitt's (and hence David Boulton's) argument. Similar points have been made by Alister McGrath, who like John Polkinghorne, mentioned earlier, has a scientific as well as a theological background.

> The problems with Cupitt's approach are probably best seen in the sections of *The Sea of Faith* which survey the radical changes that have come about in our understanding of the world as the result of Newtonian mechanics and Darwin's theory of evolution. These new insights have, he insists, transformed our religious situation, making it impossible to go back to earlier forms of belief. Yet Cupitt assumes that the reason we must abandon these earlier beliefs is that these scientific insights are *correct*. He assumes that Darwin's theory of evolution is more or less true, and that it offers a reliable account of the real world. As a result of this, Christianity has to rethink its ideas about human origins, and the place of humanity within nature. The blindingly obvious fact is that a form of scientific realism has been smuggled in here; indeed, without it, Cupitt would have to speak merely of arbitrary shifts in intellectual fashion, rather than permanent changes in our understanding of the world. To discredit theological realism, Cupitt is obliged to assume [the truth of] its historical or scientific counterparts. So it seems that all of our ideas are not free creations of the human mind after all. Cupitt's non-realism simply is not capable of dealing with the natural sciences.[142]

If Cupitt really is saying that there is an external world open to scientific investigation, even one that cannot be accessed except as a figment of our own language-ruled imaginations, that would be a very significant concession. For if the world can be assumed to exist in a way that is not language or mind dependent (in the sense that it would survive the extinction of human consciousness) then, contrary to Boulton's assertion that "the 'lie' is not God, but the notion that 'he' or 'she' or 'it' exists independently of our human consciousness . . .", the same could be argued for God. That leaves us with just the second part

[142] McGrath, *The Science of God*, pp. 155-6. My interpolation.

of Boulton's formulation, ". . . encoded in human language", without which the assertion that God is no more than a human concept can no longer be regarded as self-evident.

For Cupitt, language "goes all the way down". There is "no thinking which is not couched in some kind of language, and no apprehension of the world which is not language-like". Language is therefore inescapable. Boulton echoes these sentiments in words which reveal the extent of his reliance on his mentor. In *Real Like Daisies* he says:

> I would suggest that the most important insight to be had from these postmodern developments . . . is that our "experience", our "religious experience", is always encoded in words, in language. In the beginning was the word, not some wordless "experience". . . There is no such thing as wholly extra-linguistic experience, knowledge or truth. The very act of experiencing is language-built. Language goes all the way down. It's there in the great stick of rock of life wherever you cut it. There is no meaningfulness and no cognition without language.[143]

However, it is debatable that the relation between language and reality is quite as Cupitt or Boulton describes it. Later we will see how Rowan Williams in *The Edge of Words* maintains that (for example) the poet's dissatisfaction with our 'ordinary' language stems from the pressure of a non-linguistic apprehension of reality, a 'jolt' from that which lies outside us.[144] But quite apart from this, the idea that everything has to be mediated through language in order to be experienced, or that language creates the experience, has been convincingly refuted by Bryan Magee in his *Confessions of a Philosopher*.[145] Magee gives numerous examples of things directly experienced through the senses and grasped by the human mind

---

[143] Boulton, *Real Like Daisies or Real Like I Love You?* (Dent: Dales Historical Monographs, 2002), p. 39.

[144] See below, p.132

[145] Magee, *Confessions of a Philosopher* (London: Phoenix 1998 [1997]); see esp. his Chapter 5, "The Inadequacy of Linguistic Philosophy", pp. 93-114.

without the use of words. He argues that language just cannot represent our direct experience in all its complexity and depth and that to believe it can is actually impoverishing. Interestingly, he then goes on to say something that speaks directly to the Quaker condition. He points to direct *experience* as not only primary and of a higher order than language but as the source of the richly lived life — a view which not only endorses one of Quakerism's core beliefs but is the very opposite of Cupitt's and Boulton's 'objective nihilism':

> . . . this direct experience which is never adequately communicable in words is the only knowledge we ever fully have. *That* is our one and only true, unadulterated, direct and immediate form of knowledge of the world, wholly possessed, uniquely ours. People who are rich in that are rich in lived life. But the very putting of it into words translates it into something of the second order, something derived, watered down, abstracted, generalised, publicly sharable.

The passage is too long for me to quote in full here and I have therefore put it into an Appendix (A). But it is not difficult to find examples of our own which perhaps bear more directly on our experience as Quakers. Just to take the sense of taste, it should be obvious to everyone that we can never describe the taste of a delicious apple in words which exactly match the experience — there is a sense in which the taste is *ineffable*. Nevertheless, we can testify to the *reality* of the taste, and even convey some notion of what it is like — 'sharp', 'sweet', 'tingly' — and we can be fairly sure, though obviously we cannot prove it, that the taste is the same for others eating an apple from the same batch. This gives it a kind of objectivity, corresponding to (though of course not quite the same as) the scientist's peer review.

The parallel with religious experience is obvious. Ineffability according to William James is one of the hallmarks of the religious experience and sense perception, especially taste, is often used by mystics like Isaac Penington as a metaphor for the direct experience of God. Despite this, ineffability has never put mystics off the attempt to find words for their experiences, although no group could be more conscious of the yawning gap between their words and the excess of being which is the Divine essence itself.

Magee also makes the point, in terms which again flatly deny the claim that language "goes all the way down", that humans even *think* without language. He says, "I should have supposed this to be self-evident were it not for the fact that so many language-oriented academics of many kinds either deny it or proceed as if it were untrue." For example, what do we mean when we say, 'I don't know how to express this' or 'she has a very good way of putting things'? He quotes Noam Chomsky: "I'm sure that everyone who introspects will know at once that much of his thinking doesn't involve language"; and the Nobel Prize-winning geneticist, Jacques Monod: "I am sure every scientist must have noticed how his mental reflection, at the deeper level, is not verbal: it is an imagined experience, simulated with the aid of forms, of forces, of interactions which together barely compose an 'image' in the visual sense of the term . . . numerous observations prove that in man the cognitive functions, even the most complex ones, are not immediately linked with speech (nor with any other means of symbolic expression)".[146]

Monod's mention of numerous (presumably scientific) observations puts me in mind of my sister-in-law who had been diagnosed with Broca's aphasia, a condition characterised by an inability to use language in speech or writing. When she recovered and was able to talk about it she said she had known exactly what she wanted to say but didn't have the language to express it. Another example is the human ability to empathise without language. Empathy requires understanding of another's feelings and situation. Carolyn Zahn-Walker, a pioneer in empathy research, has shown that empathy emerges before language in human children, suggesting that it is not a language dependent trait.[147] Nor should we exempt animals. Animals

---

[146] *ibid.,* p. 100.

[147] See J. Balcombe, *Second Nature: the Inner Lives of Animals,* Palgrave Macmillan, 2010, p.131.

are generally thought not to possess language, yet many show an ability to perform intentional acts, that is, acts which are complex enough to require some degree of forethought and planning. [148] Crows, for instance, have been known to shape hooks from pieces of wire in order to get food out of a container or lift a latch to release another crow from a cage. So does language "go all the way down" in crows as well as in humans? From the poststructuralist perspective, it would seem so, which incidentally puts the poststructuralist in the anomalous position of being able to settle a longstanding scientific controversy by a process of simple deduction, without having to produce any evidence of a scientific kind!

Two other well-known figures who have contested the idea that nothing can be comprehended without language are Iris Murdoch and Karen Armstrong. Murdoch saw language as a 'content of thought' rather than the other way round, and believed (as I think most Quakers would) that it has a 'revelatory role'. "Language and thought are not co-extensive . . . it seems that a thought may be described as an experience into which words enter variously or not at all."[149] Karen Armstrong goes further; she rests her whole 'case for God' on the observation that it is "one of the peculiarities of the human mind . . . to have ideas and experiences that exceed our conceptual grasp", quoting the literary critic, George Steiner, in support: "When we listen critically to our stuttering attempts to express ourselves , we become aware of an inexpressible otherness. 'It is decisively the fact that language does have frontiers,' explains Steiner, 'that gives proof of a transcendent presence in the fabric of the world. It is just because we can go no further, because speech so marvellously fails us, that we experience the certitude of a divine meaning surpassing and enfolding ours'". [150]

---

[148] *ibid.*

[149] Murdoch in P. Conradi (ed.), *Existentialists and Mystics: Writings on Philosophy and Literature* (London: Chatto & Windus, 1997), pp. 35-6.

[150] Armstrong, *The Case for God* (London: The Bodley Head, 2009), p. 6.

Of course, Cupitt doesn't restrict himself to language. He points out that acts of perception also involve "our sensory and cognitive apparatus . . . and our interests" — indeed the whole person. But that is essentially to concede the argument. If we can have direct experience of the world through our senses and thinking processes without having to encode it in the language that "goes all the way down", then again the same argument holds with regard to the transcendent reality of God. Once the argument around language collapses, Cupitt's position — and with it, Boulton's — is fatally undermined. There is no second line of defence that cannot be met from within the mainstream traditions of classical philosophy and metaphysics. And so far as the current debate is concerned, we are back in critical realist territory where the questions may be the same but the answers likely to be more intuitive, more allusive, more finely balanced, and intellectually and spiritually more adequate.

A word on Wittgenstein (and Derrida)

For Cupitt, as for David Boulton, the whole point of denying the existence of the cosmos as in any sense "independent of human consciousness encoded in human language" is to be able to say that there is nothing beyond what can be thought and articulated; no dimension of radical otherness, no God; it is not enough to say that language cannot give us access to that other dimension, but that it cannot be said to exist at all. This attitude is fulsomely illustrated by Cupitt's treatment of Wittgenstein.

It is not surprising that such an important figure as Wittgenstein should crop up with such frequency in Cupitt's writings. He is one of the most influential voices in linguistic philosophy of the last century and it is highly desirable as a polemicist to have him lined up on your side. His philosophy, however, is extremely difficult to grasp even by those trained in the subject and the ordinary reader of Cupitt's work, as he or she comes across such references, is more likely to take them at face value than subject them to critical examination.

In *The Sea of Faith* Cupitt devotes a long section (fifteen pages) to Wittgenstein in which, predictably, he tailors Wittgenstein's philosophy to his own. With few qualifications, Wittgenstein emerges as essentially a positivist (accepting as fact only what can be scientifically or mathematically verified) and non-realist. For Wittgenstein, he says, "Language comes first, for it prescribes the shape of the various 'realities' amongst which we move, and not the other way round. Reality does not determine language: language determines reality".[151] In keeping with this approach, he represents Wittgenstein's refusal to believe in the God that is yet one more 'thing' in the universe as a denial (rather than an affirmation) of the transcendent. When Wittgenstein famously said, "What we cannot speak about we must pass over in silence", he meant, according to Cupitt, that there was nothing beyond the limits of language. However, that is by no means a widely held view among Wittgenstein scholars. As Wittgenstein's close friend, Paul Engelmann, explains:

> A whole generation of disciples was able to take Wittgenstein for a positivist because he has something of enormous importance in common with the positivists: he draws the line between what we can speak about and what we must be silent about just as they do. The difference is only that they have nothing to be silent about. Positivism holds — and this is its essence — that what we can speak about is all that matters in life. *Whereas Wittgenstein passionately believes that all that really matters in human life is precisely what, in his view, we must be silent about.* When he nevertheless takes immense pains to delimit the unimportant, it is not the coastline of that island which he is bent on surveying with such meticulous accuracy, but the boundary of the ocean.[152]

[151] Cupitt, *The Sea of Faith* (London: BBC Publications, 1984), p. 220. The section on Wittgenstein spans pp. 213-60.
[152] Quoted in T. Labron, *Wittgenstein and Theology* (Edinburgh: T. & T. Clark, 2009), p. 37.

George Steiner, makes a similar point in his book, *Real Presences*. He says that for the early Wittgenstein, "the existential realm 'on the other side of language', the categories of felt being to which only silence (or music) give access, are neither fictitious nor trivial. On the contrary. They are, indeed, the most important, life-transforming categories conceivable to man . . . kindred to certain kinds of reticent mysticism . . . For the *Tractatus* [Wittgenstein's first book], the truly 'human' being, the man or woman most open to the solicitations of the ethical and the spiritual, is he who keeps silent before the essential".[153]

And even the judgement that the mystical dimension is situated so far beyond language as to render his philosophy an attack on metaphysics turns out to be infinitely more complicated than previously thought. Alain Badiou (the Marxist challenger I referred to in the earlier part of this chapter) sees Wittgenstein's "ontological construction" as a radical effort to make possible "the sovereignty of the mystical element" in such a way that we have here "one of the rare contemporary attempts axiomatically to lay the grounds for a doctrine of substance and the world".

What Badiou is attempting to do is situate Wittgenstein, a so-called 'anti-philosopher', on a bridge between postmodernism and classical philosophy but closer to the classical philosophy end. He is reclaiming him (to some extent) for metaphysics. Thus he speaks of Wittgenstein's 'ontology' of the world and language as a mirror which reflects only part (the worldly part) of that 'being' which stands before it: "The point of being that is 'truest' is not captured in the specular relationship in which the ontology of the world and of language is constructed. It is obtained there where 'something', which is precisely not a thing, comes up as a *remainder* of this relationship." Jurgen Habermas too has talked about "an awareness of something missing" in opening a debate on the role of religion in 'post-secular' society. These are precisely the kind of high profile left-wing intellectuals of

[153] Steiner, *Real Presences* (London: Faber and Faber, 1989), pp. 102-3.

the 1968 era whom Cupitt has assumed to be natural supporters of his new "religion of outsidelessness".[154]

What of Wittgenstein's later philosophy? After all, didn't he repudiate the ideas contained in his first book, describing them as 'grave mistakes'? As usual, the picture is somewhat more complicated. Whereas the *Tractatus* had dealt with one function of language — its use in philosophical analysis — the *Philosophical Investigations* and *On Certainty* acknowledged there were other functions which he had ignored. It is in relation to these other functions that Wittgenstein introduces his idea of the 'language game'. This is a complex idea, the ramifications of which are too multifarious to explore in detail here. For the sake of brevity, I shall describe it as 'the use of a characteristic form of language within a rather loosely defined subject area'. One such area might be science, another religion. Wittgenstein wants to emphasise that in order to understand the language game we have to observe how it functions in people's lives. It is the *use* of language in a 'form of life' that reveals its meaning. But if the meaning of the language game depends on its social application, where does this leave God? Isn't this a form of non-realism?

It is true that Wittgenstein's philosophy at this point is susceptible to non-realist interpretation. He says, for example, that there is nothing outside the language game — it has no outside (words which appear to support Cupitt). However, we need to get this into perspective. There are two noteworthy objections. First, he is not flatly denying the existence of a reality outside the language game but rather insisting that it is a reality for us only insofar as it becomes part of the language game. And second, it is an acknowledged feature of the use of *religious* language that it refers beyond itself. For most people who practise a religion there has to be something beyond the words, beyond the language game, which gives the activity its purpose. For Wittgenstein, this something is the inexpressible — that before which we can only be silent. There is no reason to believe that in his later

154 *The Old Creed and the New*, p. 75. His actual words are "new beliefless religion of outsideless *life*".

philosophy Wittgenstein renounced this idea. As late as 1933, as he was gathering his ideas together for the *Philosophical Investigations*, he commented in one of his notebooks: "What is inexpressible (what I find mysterious and am not able to express) is the background against whatever I could express has its meaning". It is for this reason also that he believed the proper medium for philosophy was the aesthetic, and in particular poetry. As the Irish literary critic, Denis Donoghue, explains, "poetry is adequate only insofar as it beckons beyond itself . . . Particularly, as it beckons towards the realm of the inexpressible, that which, as Wittgenstein argued, functions as the ground for all that finds expression."[155]

In this sense, there *is* nothing beyond the words, because the inexpressible cannot be defined as a thing. But the fact that the 'something' is inexpressible doesn't mean that, for Wittgenstein, it is any the less real. His paradoxical grasp of *the inexpressible as the real* is vividly illustrated in an early letter to Engelmann: "this is how it is: if only you do not try to utter what is unutterable then *nothing* gets lost. But the unutterable will be — unutterably — *contained* in what has been uttered." They were discussing a poem, 'Count Eberhard's Hawthorn', by Ludwig Uhland, which they both agreed was "a wonder of objectivity" and "really magnificent": "Almost all other poems (including the good ones) attempt to express the inexpressible, here it is not attempted, and precisely because of that it is achieved."[156]

Wittgenstein's biographer, Ray Monk, tells us that his notebooks in later life abound with reflections on the necessity of faith. He pictured our civilisation as (Wittgenstein's own words) "cheaply wrapped in cellophane, and isolated from everything great, from God, as it were". Technological advances were "separating man from his origins, from what is lofty and eternal". He was convinced that the

155 See C. Knight, *Uncommon Readers* (Toronto: University of Toronto Press, 2003), p. 116.

156 R. Monk, *Ludwig Wittgenstein: The Duty of Genius* (London: Vintage Books, 1991 [1990]), pp. 150-1. The second quote is from Engelmann (with Wittgenstein agreeing).

coming apocalypse "was the consequence of replacing the spirit with the machine, of turning away from God and placing our trust in scientific 'progress'". Theory was dead. To breathe again, says Monk, "it was no use merely thinking correctly; one had to act — to, as it were, rip the cellophane away and reveal the living world behind it". And this required faith. "The passion of religious faith was the only thing capable of overcoming the deadness of theory".[157]

Cupitt acknowledges this side of Wittgenstein, but sees it as incidental to his core philosophy. Having claimed him as one of his own, he eventually dismisses him with the words, "My own belief is that his ideas about religion were too conservative and nostalgic. He was left with a kind of mystical inertia, inherited from Schopenhauer, which expressed the utmost admiration for the highest levels of religious achievement, but declared them to be indescribable and beyond the reach of ordinary mortals here below".[158] Inherited from Schopenhauer? Could it have been the mystical element in Wittgenstein that drew him to Schopenhauer in the first place? It should not be forgotten that Wittgenstein had undergone a profound mystical experience when he was a soldier on the Eastern Front during the First World War, so he could not have believed these states were entirely beyond the reach of 'ordinary mortals'. Cupitt himself describes Wittgenstein as "highly inner-directed". It seems that the unforgiveable failure of this thinker of genius, one of the most acute and original of modern philosophers, was that he was not in the end a fully fledged 'objective nihilist'.

Despite Cupitt's claim that Wittgenstein was a non-realist, it appears he was much more one on his own, a highly complex thinker whom it is impossible to categorise. It is difficult to place him anywhere on the spectrum between realism and non-realism, and I

---

157 *ibid.*, pp. 489-90. This doesn't mean that faith was an easy option for Wittgenstein. As Monk also points out (*ibid.*, p. 491) "he felt himself to share exactly the faults characteristic of our age, and to need the same remedy: faith and love . . . so he found he could not pray: 'it's as though my knees were stiff. I am afraid of dissolution (of my own dissolution), should I become soft'".
158 Cupitt, *The Sea of Faith*, p. 227.

would not want to emulate Cupitt's strategy by claiming him for critical realism — although he does seem to come nearest to that position! Labron tells us that for Wittgenstein, "language mediates our contact with a reality that is not reduced to language; however, that reality so mediated is not independent of language". He points out that Wittgenstein's later work never claims that language use creates reality. "Reality is larger, in a sense, than language".

After Wittgenstein, Cupitt's most admired contemporary philosopher is the French deconstructionist, Jacques Derrida, whose methods he acclaims as the most suited to liberate us from any 'nostalgia' we may feel for metaphysics and "the absurd idea that language can transcend language":

> The most intellectually-correct and consistent techniques for me to use would be those of Jacques Derrida. He is the modern Kierkegaard. As Kierkegaard had to use stratagems to subvert Hegelianism, so Derrida has to use stratagems to subvert the pretensions and the realist illusions of Western reason, and to coax us through to the new way of thinking. A similar deconstruction of all false, nostalgic, otherworldly and metaphysical styles in theology is now needed in order to purify religion. [159]

There is no doubt that Derrida's view of language and its relation to reality is at the root of much of Cupitt's thinking and generally supportive of it. But even in his case, there are subtleties and distinctions that allow for a different point of view. Stephen Ross White points out that it is from modern French philosophy that Cupitt derives such phrases as 'there is only the text', 'there is no outside', and 'language goes all the way down', but it seems that the French, including Derrida, are not always as radical in their conclusions as Cupitt would wish.[160] Derrida, in an interview with the philosopher Richard Kearney, denies that he scorns the idea that "language can

---

[159] Cupitt, *Only Human* (London: SCM Press, 1985), p. xii.
[160] Ross White, *Don Cupitt and the Future of Christian Doctrine* (London: SCM Press, 1994), pp. 198-9.

transcend language" and makes the point that reference (which we will be looking at more closely in the next section) is more complex than has been assumed. Despite subverting "the pretensions and realist illusions of Western reason" it appears that Derrida's non-realist credentials are open to question. Thus he complains loudly against those "who see my work as a declaration that there is nothing beyond language, that we are imprisoned in language; it is, in fact, saying the opposite". Derrida is not someone who can be accused of timidity in facing the implications of his own theory. He believes that his readers simply misunderstand and possibly misrepresent it. He continues:

> Every week I receive critical commentaries and studies on deconstruction which operate on the assumption that what they call 'post-structuralism' amounts to saying there is nothing beyond language, that we are submerged in words — and other stupidities of that sort. Certainly, deconstruction tries to show that the question of reference is more complex and problematic than traditional theories supposed. It even asks whether our term 'reference' is entirely adequate for designating the 'other'. The other, which is beyond language and which summons language, is perhaps not a 'referent' in the normal sense which linguists have attached to the term. But to distance oneself thus from the habitual structure of reference, to challenge or to complicate our common assumptions about it, does not amount to saying that there is *nothing* beyond language.[161]

Note the inversion: it is the 'other' that summons language, not language that summons the 'other'. For Derrida, God is the unnameable 'Thou' that can be 'spoken to' but not 'spoken of', and the language that is 'summoned' is (surprisingly) prayer. Since it is the transcendent 'other' that summons prayer, prayer is the language that transcends language. But in insisting that the 'other' cannot be 'spoken of', Derrida is left with the problem of reconciling reference with the absence of a referent. Nevertheless, his procedure is quite different from that of Cupitt; his exploration takes him into the area of 'negative

---

161 *ibid.*

theology', the *via negativa* of the mystics, although in his case it is an abstract, intellectual exercise rather than the intense intuitive yearning of a St John of the Cross.

A similar inversion is to be found in Derrida's pupil, the eminent postmodernist philosopher and theologian, Jean-Luc Marion, whose major work, *God Without Being*, was subjected to the same kind of criticism and misunderstanding as Derrida's own writing. As Marion acknowledged, the title of the book itself was largely responsible for this. He asks: "was it insinuating that the God 'without being' is not, or does not exist? Let me repeat now the answer I gave then: no, definitely not. God is, exists, and that is the least of things. At issue here is not the possibility of God's attaining to Being. But, quite the opposite, the possibility of Being's attaining to God."[162]

Marion takes Derrida's thought further in the direction of a Christian theism. His account is characterised by the same 'inverse intentionality' that we saw in Derrida, but in Marion it is more pronounced. The existence of the 'other' as well as its essential character are 'objectively' grounded in God's past and continuing revelation to us through love. It is this divine love or *Agape* that finds expression in the inspired passages of scripture, in mystical experience and conclusively in the incarnation and example of Christ. Our response to this love is to return it, directly in worship and indirectly through our actions and service to others; and in Marion's case, precisely because it is *response*, 'the language that transcends language' is praise.[163]

It should be clear by now that Cupitt's parading of Wittgenstein and Derrida as fellow non-realists is a gross over-simplification and a violation of the trust between writer and reader. The reader is entitled to a fair and reasonably objective exposition of opposing viewpoints so that he can make an informed choice between them. Obviously, if the

---

[162] Marion, *God without Being*, pp. xix-xx.

[163] This is neatly expressed by St Augustine: "So when do we 'jubilate'? When we praise what we cannot speak of". See Rowan Williams, *The Wound of Knowledge: Christian Spirituality from the New Testament to St John of the Cross* (London: Darton, Longman and Todd, 1979; 1990), p.90.

writer has taken a prior decision to rule out metaphysics, that limits the choice considerably, but in the case of Derrida we are looking at a postmodernist thinker of the first rank. To ignore, play down or sideline concerns which are of such importance to Derrida's thought without feeling the need to justify it to one's readers may seem surprising in someone of Cupitt's stature, but it is a common feature of his writing and one could cite many more examples. Janet Martin Soskice's comment would certainly be applicable to the method adopted by Cupitt:

> There seems to be an assumption that, because we are wise and atheists, anyone in the past whom we admire cannot have been too much affected by religion — that their faith is just a cultural appurtenance of as little importance to understanding their thought as their hairstyle. This isn't objectivity: it's a prejudice.[164]

And more than a prejudice, a tactic. Boulton, almost certainly taking his cue from Cupitt, is an even more prolific offender in this regard, enlisting (and in the process, distorting) the views of such iconic figures as William Blake, William James, Meister Eckhart, Paul Tillich and even Dionysius the Areopagite. The effect on the reader will be to reinforce the idea that there is no way out of the preview cinema when, on closer examination, there may be more swing doors than there are solid walls.

Metaphor and reference

It is ironic that Friends who wish to promote a diversity that embraces atheism, and who therefore choose to devalue theological distinctions as 'just words', so often point to the inadequacy of language to describe the ineffable. It is ironic not because they are wrong (they are not), but because to acknowledge the ineffable — to

164 Shortt, *ibid.*, p. 29.

say that there is an ineffable reality even though we can say nothing about it — is to acknowledge the very transcendence that atheism denies. Friends who take this approach cannot, without contradicting themselves, say that beliefs "don't matter", since they are depending on a belief — the reality of the ineffable, a very key belief — to make that assertion. And to say that we cannot speak about that which is beyond words simply because it *is* beyond words, and that this somehow makes room for the non-realist who believes there is *nothing* beyond words, is not only contradictory but ignores the power of words themselves.

We can all cite examples in literature of the power of words to evoke that which lies beyond the words, the reality without which the words are an empty sign. Take the well-known lines in Wordsworth's *Tintern Abbey*:

> And I have felt
> A presence that disturbs me with the joy
> Of elevated thoughts: a sense sublime
> Of something far more deeply interfused,
> Whose dwelling is the light of setting suns,
> And the round ocean and the living air,
> And the blue sky, and in the mind of man:
> A motion and a spirit, that impels
> All thinking things, all objects of all thought,
> And rolls through all things.

We either accept that the words give us an intimation of a reality that is there, stretching beyond the words themselves — or we dismiss that reality as an illusion and one of the finest poems in the English language as high-flown nonsense. Or take Thomas Traherne's eidetically Blakean vision: "*The corn was orient and immortal wheat, which never should be reaped, nor was ever sown. I thought it had stood from everlasting to everlasting*".[165] The very fact that we *know* that the experience he is describing refers to a reality of supreme value

[165] Traherne, *Centuries* (London: The Faith Press, 1960), p. 110.

(a state of felicity outside time?) and is not just the product of a deeply disturbed mind, reveals the power of language to *touch* on the ineffable in a way that can surprise us. [166] "We are gifted for a flash to see with his own bright, wonderful eyes, and thus behold the world no longer besmirched but as he knew how its Creator made it: all radiant for our delight".[167]

Even so great a mystic as Eckhart resorted to verbal imagery to draw attention to particular aspects of Divine being, as for example when he compared God's joy in the creation to a horse at full gallop in a lush, green meadow. As Oliver Davies, a leading Eckhart scholar, comments, "It is not only because of the wisdom which their words convey to us that we select certain mystics from the past, dub them 'great' and read their works in profusion, but also, and fundamentally, because they possessed literary gifts of a high order which allowed them to *make present* for us, their readers, something of that very experience which inspired them and their lives . . . Eckhart's writing stirs us as it does and communicates to us something of his transcendental vision; for Eckhart believed, after all, that 'words also have great power; we could work wonders with words. All words have their power from the first Word'.[168]

Despite Wittgenstein's apparent embargo, it is evident that some people *do* feel they can speak of the transcendent in meaningful terms. The language they tend to use is invariably figurative rather than direct description. Thus Eckhart, in the example given, uses analogy or simile, likening his sense of God's joy in creation to the *joie de vivre* of a virile young horse, undoubtedly a form of verbal description but not *direct* description as when we say 'the sky is blue'. In this case the aim is to take the listener beyond the words to the sense of sharing in the emotional impact of the experience — a kind of showing rather

---

[166] In her Introduction to Traherne, Hilda Vaughan says, "His was a mind so well balanced as to keep not only sanity, but sweetness, through the cruel spectacles and personal terrors of civil war and religious persecution." See *ibid.*, p. xiii.

[167] *ibid.*, p.xii.

[168] O. Davies, *Meister Eckhart: Mystical Theologian* (London: SPCK, 1991), pp. 179-80.

than telling. Language used in this way is more a form of reference, "the bearer of meaning rather than meaning itself".

The most potent form of reference is undoubtedly metaphor. When religious people refer to God as 'person' or 'energy' or 'Father', 'Mother', 'Lover' they are using metaphor. The question I will be asking is 'how legitimate is it to use metaphor in relation to the experience of God in our lives?' But first we need to establish what metaphor is not.

In *Real Like Daisies*, Boulton tells us that "liturgies in God-language" may be acceptable if "taken with lashings of metaphor and poetic licence". He means of course that as 'religious humanists' we are free to use God-language in religious settings provided we don't take it literally. But 'metaphorically' does not mean 'not literally', although metaphors are not to be taken literally. A metaphor has to be a metaphor *for* something.

The Catholic theologian, Janet Martin Soskice, defines metaphor as "that figure of speech whereby we speak about one thing in terms which are seen to be suggestive of another". She gives the example of a student referring to her course supervisor as 'that old battleaxe'. The student doesn't mean her course supervisor is literally a medieval instrument of war but nevertheless feels that 'battleaxe' is the right metaphor *for* her, and in using it is referring to something real about her character.[169] Soskice maintains that to carry conviction a metaphor must be 'reality depicting'. It is easy to see how this would be the case with her battleaxe metaphor, but not so much with Boulton's "lashings of metaphor". What, for a non-realist, are "liturgies in God-language" a metaphor *for*?

Nor can we allow the often trumpeted claim that God is a 'metaphor' for our 'highest ideals'. Used in this way, 'God' is simply another name for them. Indeed, we may wonder why our 'highest ideals' should *need* to be spoken of in terms of an entity that an atheist believes is without content and in fact doesn't exist, unless the idea is

---

169 Soskice, *Metaphor and Religious Language* (Oxford: Clarendon Press, 1985), p. 17.

to give them greater authority than they would otherwise possess. But if metaphor is to speak about one thing in terms suggestive of another, then that surely would be the wrong metaphor? It would imply that the ideals themselves were fictional — or even a lie — which would give them no authority at all.

Soskice points out that scientific discourse uses metaphors all the time and to some extent depends on them. We speak of subatomic *particles*, light *waves*, magnetic *fields*, *black holes*. The usefulness of these images is not confined to their explanatory power when dealing with the media (for example). They actively assist the scientist in visualising realities which can be understood but not represented directly. What Soskice is concerned to establish is the analogy with religion, and specifically with the theological concepts of reference and transcendence. When metaphor is used in science, she argues, what is being described with partial adequacy is *real* but may lie outside our observation and, indeed, our *powers* of observation as human beings:

> These projections [metaphors, models, theories] are useful not only for the descriptions of entities and relations not presently observable, but also for the discussion of entities and relations which we could not possibly observe but which, none the less, we might wish to say are real entities or states of affairs. They are the 'transcendentally real' objects of science.[170]

An example of a 'transcendentally real' object of science might be 'whatever it is that we call electricity'. Her argument is that we can introduce a term like electricity "prior to any certain or unrevisable knowledge of its essential properties."[171] We cannot define or refer to it directly but we *can* say "whatever produces these effects is electricity" or "electricity is that which is responsible for these effects". The analogy with theological enquiry should be obvious. We

---

[170] *ibid.*, p.115.
[171] *ibid.*, p.129.

know nothing and can know nothing about the essential nature of a transcendent God but can point through, and beyond, God's effects to the transcendent reality.[172]

However, there remains a difficulty. Soskice argues that metaphor, in both the scientific and religious cases, can be reality depicting "without pretending to be directly descriptive". We have seen how this may be possible in science — a 'black hole' is not exactly a hole, nor a sub-atomic particle necessarily a particle — but as there can be no equivalence between the 'transcendent realities' of science and the transcendent reality we call God, how does it work in the case of religious language? If we reject non-realist presuppositions, how is reference in religious language to be objectively grounded?

Her answer is that "the claim for 'objectivity' — 'objective reference' — is grounded in the sense I have of being confronted, of being acted upon, in the discernment I have of some claim impinging on me."[173] This is close to what Derrida and Marion, in their different ways, were quoted as saying earlier and is familiar territory for Friends; it is what we refer to as 'a leading', what *Quaker Faith & Practice* speaks of as 'divine guidance', 'the promptings of the Holy Spirit', worship as response. In the context we are discussing, it corresponds to Polanyi's reversal of the subject-object relationship when he refers to nature itself continuously intervening to guide the direction of scientific progress. Whereas traditional theology posits the human person as subject and God as 'object', it makes as much if not more sense for the theist to think of God as subject and then, if God is love, of us as the recipients or objects of that love. To put the question this way round, moreover, conforms to the experience of God's love as described in so much Quaker and other mystical writing as 'overwhelming' and 'enfolding'. It enables us to say, 'Whatever it is that caused this experience is God'.

---

[172] Soskice had "point through His effects, and beyond His effects, to Him". I have altered her wording to avoid genderising God, although Sosckice would see the anthropomorphism as itself a metaphor.

[173] *Ibid.*, p.146. She is here quoting the philosopher and theologian, Ian Ramsey.

The same is true when we use the metaphor of 'person' in relation to God. To experience God as love is necessarily to experience God in some sense as 'personal' for without the personal there can be neither love nor relationship. However, rather than attempt to define God in terms of our human love and personhood, which would be mere anthropomorphism, we can see the human as participating in God's personhood. On this reading, God is the origin of all that is best and highest in us — 'that of God'. In fact, this has always been the Christian teaching. Christianity teaches that the good that is in us, above all our love and concern for others, is essentially 'of God' in whose 'image' we are made.

I now want to return to the use of metaphor in poetry and the allegedly absurd notion that "language can transcend language". We have seen how Wittgenstein considered it a waste of time trying to express the inexpressible in language but conceded that Ludwig Uhland's poem, 'Count Eberhard's Hawthorn', had succeeded in doing this very thing by showing rather than telling. Uhland's poem actually leaves me cold (perhaps it needs to be read in the original German) but I can see what Wittgenstein is getting at when I read this *haiku* by the Zen poet, Basho:

In the dark forest
A berry drops.
The sound of water.

Wittgenstein might have described this too as a "wonder of objectivity". It is not a metaphor for anything; it is pure description. But what it describes is more than the image itself. Read it over, take a few moments to let it sink in. It contains all of time, the whole of the cosmos. It is a beautiful example of language referring beyond itself, transcending itself, for the words on their own are as simple and factual as the individual notes on a piano. As arranged by the poet, they have a wonderful, evocative power, but the reality they refer to can only be intimated, not itself described. In fact, one could say that the words owe their power not to the poet's skill and imagination in arranging them in that particular order but to the reality *which speaks through them*.

What we are seeing is a two-way process in which language, to borrow a term from chemistry, 'chelates' with the reality confronting it to form an image or metaphor. The metaphor isn't (as in Soskice's examples) just one of a number of possible metaphors but is, in a sense, 'forced' on the poet by the effort (never finally successful) to articulate the nature of the reality that presses on the poet's imagination. As the philosopher, Eric Voegelin explains:

> Symbols are the language phenomena engendered by the process of participatory experience. The language symbols expressing an experience are not inventions of an immanentist human consciousness, but are engendered in the process of participation itself . . . A symbol is neither a human conventional sign signifying a reality outside consciousness, nor is it, as in certain theological constructions, a word of God conveniently transmitted in the language that the recipient can understand; rather, it is engendered by the divine-human encounter and participates, therefore, as much in divine as in human reality.[174]

What this means is that our relationship with that which can be experienced but not expressed is better understood in critical realist rather than non-realist terms. To say that we believe in God as metaphor is not to *fictionalise* God, but to recognise that the metaphorical use of language in certain kinds of mystical writing, including some kinds of poetry, is a variation of the critical realist approach to reality where subject and object are combined, or as Julian of Norwich would say, 'oned'; but not combined, or 'oned', in a way that abolishes the reality of the object.

---

174 Quoted in J. O'Neill, *Towards a New Mystical Poetics of God in the Post-Mortem Age: From God as the Supreme Being to God as the One-And-Only Being* (D. Arts. Albany, NY.: State University of New York, 2009), p. 30. I am indebted to O'Neill, not only for the example of Japanese *haiku* reproduced here, but also for some of the insights relating to it.

The frontier between language and reality and its relation to religious faith has nowhere been more interestingly explored than in Rowan Williams' Gifford Lectures (November 2013), now published as *The Edge of Words.*[175]

Language, says Williams, "is 'bound' to stimuli that it does not originate", otherwise "we would have no conception of what constitutes a mistake or lie". One of Britain's most outstanding philosopher-theologians, he takes us beyond non-realist presuppositions, beyond Wittgenstein, to a metaphysic which acknowledges the power of language to 'represent' a reality on which it can never finally close: perhaps something intangible about the environment we live in, the effect on our imaginations of an exquisitely emotional piece of music, some deeper understanding or communication that eludes definition, but equally what is factual, tangible, even mundane. Whatever the level of utterance, language is always 'unfinished', the object of our perception never exhausted. Language may not go all the way down, but it is deeply intertwined with a reality whose life and being it shares and which discloses itself to our awareness in ways which simultaneously enrich language itself and extends our knowledge of the environment. It is not a case of there being a word for everything, a simple one-to-one correspondence with 'the things before us', but the search for a truthfulness which goes beyond simple replication. "There are moments when our speech is jolted into a register different from its normal one, and more specifically a register that is generative of fresh meaning".[176] In such moments we invent more effective language involving surprising figures of speech to 'represent' in *analogous* form certain features of a reality that is already there.

---

175 Williams, *Making Representations: Religious Faith and the Habits of Language*" (The Gifford Lectures. University of Edinburgh, 2013), published as *The Edge of Words* (see above, note 138). Unless otherwise indicated, quotes are taken from the lecture online at:
<https://itunes.apple.com/gb/itunes-u/gifford-lectures-audio/id396651186?mt=10> Abstracts, Lectures 1 & 2

176 Williams, *The Edge of Words*, p. 7.

Here again a key element is the heightened language of metaphor which is found in poetry and is an essential part of innovative theoretical science, and also — and not least — a recognisable feature of our everyday speech. The effort to stretch language to encompass that which lies beyond it is therefore integral to our experience as living, conscious beings — our *natural* response to a "world that both demands understanding and invites us into the awareness of an unconditioned intelligent energy". To think otherwise is to accept "the paradox that the human intellect is ordered to a reality it cannot know". In short, metaphor and analogy are deeply human ways of bringing into the orbit of the known a reality we do not (entirely) create.

He ends the lecture series with a consideration of how silence too may refer "and so puts all we say in a new, and questioning, light". He means of course the silence that is "more than an absence of sound or concept" but is itself "a mode of knowing", the silence of the person standing before a great work of art or of the contemplative "attuned to the reality that we invite to 'inhabit' us". The silence, in other words, that is the basis of Quaker worship, although he emphasises what Friends might do well not to ignore — the danger of using such a practice as "an excuse for giving up the challenges of truthful speech", as when we take refuge from the credal implications of our experience by claiming that it is always and entirely beyond words.

Conclusion

My aim in this chapter has not been to prove that the critical realist position is the correct one and non-realism is *wrong* — although I believe it *is* wrong since it is refuted by the religious experience of generations of Friends and others — but to show that the questions posed by non-realism are not unanswerable and do not oblige us to retreat from or even modify our faith positions. David Boulton's confident assertion in *Godless for God's Sake* that theism is a lie stands or falls by the weight we give to non-realism as the *only credible* option. From my standpoint it is enough to show that there are equally credible options which support religious belief and enable us to refer to without defining God. There are indeed many more such options than I have been able to touch on here — the field is littered with post-Wittgensteinian theories of language, some tending towards non-realism, but many others towards critical realism and the kind of personalist philosophy represented by Michael Polanyi.

The growth of non-realism in the Religious Society of Friends is something of an anomaly. It has found in liberal Quakerism its most fertile soil, but its progress outside the world of Quakerism has been slow indeed. There have to be philosophical and theological reasons for this. Why are we not seeing a flood of new members from the ranks of secularism or the churches into the Sea of Faith? We have noted the attitude of the scientific community to non-realism. The national survey carried out in 2013 showed that its appeal to academic philosophers, at least in Britain, is virtually non-existent. Considering the sheer exuberance of Cupitt's and Boulton's writings, their absolute confidence that non-realism is the key to a new "non-theist understanding of human spirituality" — an understanding which they believe provides solid ground from which to "face the daunting challenges of the 21st century" — one cannot help feeling a little surprised by this finding. And it should be enough to set the alarm bells ringing. What does it say about the future prospects for a non-theist Society of Friends?[177]

Of all philosophies non-realism seems the most antithetical to the ethos and concerns of Quakerism. Whereas Friends have traditionally described themselves as seekers and "humble learners in the school of Christ", Cupitt tells us that "our journey [his journey] has taught us to give up the notion of life as a journey, quest, search or pilgrimage, because it rests upon the objectivist illusion of a Truth out there". Whereas Friends place a high value on qualities such as personal integrity, truthfulness and plain speech, Cupitt sees the world

[177] This and related questions are discussed in R. Cathey, *God in Post-Liberal Perspective* (Aldershot: Ashgate, 2009), pp. 188-94.

"as being like a literary text, full of linguistic ploys and stratagems, and endlessly discussible", and he seems to be at least half in agreement with his realist critics when he says that they see the non-realist as one who believes among other things in "the play of appearances, plurality and deception".[178]

Non-realism makes belief or trust in the reality of God impossible and both Cupitt and Boulton appear to delight in cutting off every means of escape from its dismaying conclusions. It spells the end of Quakerism since it makes nonsense of prayer, discernment and the leadings of the Spirit — all of which must have a real reference if they are not to lose their essential point and be discarded. The Sea of Faith already has a significant presence in the Society through the Non-theist Friends Network. As it becomes stronger and more established it is possible that even silence will eventually be sidetracked. Cupitt has already expressed his views on silence, contrasting it — unfavourably of course — with the 'holiness of garrulity':

> . . . the notion of silence as a specially important and religiously-valuable region outside language and ontologically prior to it can now be seen to be a mistake, just another form of death wish. The most frivolous gossip is holier, wiser and deeper than silence. Socrates, the Buddha and Jesus are all remembered as chiefly *talkers*.

It is sheer nonsense to claim that non-realism or 'objective nihilism' can provide the basis for a 21st century theology for the Religious Society of Friends when its leading exponent in humanist circles is capable of a statement like this — and when there are so many other interesting and fruitful perspectives to choose from. Non-realism is not a philosophy that will stand the test of time and it is sad to see sections of our Religious Society in thrall to what appears to be more than a philosophical point of view, having in the Sea of Faith some of the features of a cult.

---

178 Cupitt, *Creation Out of Nothing*, pp. 109 -11.

Critical realism on the other hand leaves open the way to faith in God and preserves the insights and practices that have made Quakerism what it is. It is not the only philosophical option but its availability is enough to show that it *is* possible to get outside the preview cinema if we choose, that it *does* have an outside — unless, like Plato's cave dwellers, we prefer to remain chained to its walls, believing that the flickering and self-reflecting shadows on the screen are the only true reality.

Quakers believe there is that of God in every one. It must follow that there is that beyond language which of its own volition can break through the thick clouds of our subjectivity or be felt as a gentle, healing Presence in our innermost depths — "be still and know that I am God". Since non-realism, despite its claims, does not *disprove* the existence of God, and other perspectives are no less convincing or appealing, it would seem to make sense for most of us to choose what coincides with our intuition, with our hope, with our faith, with the varieties of our personal and shared religious experience, and not least with our study and enjoyment of Quaker historical texts — the riches of our past surging up from our still flourishing Christian roots — while always, of course, holding open the possibility that our particular *philosophical* formulations may be mistaken or incomplete.

What we should not concede without a struggle is our sense of the *givenness* of Divine love. To say that theism is a 'lie' is to say that the experience of God's love as gift is a lie, and that is a proposition which surely has no place in Quaker tradition.

9

Relativism — the denial of Truth

What happens to our passion for literature when any "text" qualifies as literature, when theory is elevated above poetry and the critic above the poet, and when literature, interpretation and theory alike are said to be indeterminate and infinitely malleable? What happens to our respect for philosophy — the "love of wisdom" as it once was — when we are told that philosophy has nothing to do with either wisdom or virtue, that what passes as metaphysics is really linguistics, that morality is a form of aesthetics, and the best thing we can do is not to take philosophy seriously? And what happens to our sense of the past when we are told that there is no past save that which the historian creates?

- Gertrude Himmelfarb

THOSE OF US who accept an experience of a God who is more like a person with whom we can have relationship than like an impersonal energy or force, might also want to say that in this relationship we experience God as the source of Goodness, Justice, Love and Truth. Some, like Edward Burrough, might go further and include qualities like meekness, temperance, peace and true freedom (which lies in being able to do the high and holy thing that gives us joy, with full co-operation from all our energies and passions, whether this be pursuit of scientific discovery, or art, or service to humanity). All these are qualities traditionally associated with the character of Jesus, which is why Christians have always seen Jesus as an icon of God.

There are of course problems in looking at this sad and broken world, and seeing it as the work of such a God. This is a vast question in theology, and one which has no fully satisfactory answer. I shall not deal with it here, but do intend to present a sample of the most interesting recent thinking on the subject in my chapter on theism. Here I want to concentrate solely on the difficulties of seeing God as the source of Truth, and, on the other hand, the dangers of relativising truth in such a way that we end up believing there are no overarching criteria that apply to individuals, communities and cultures. Once we have accepted the notion that all criteria of judgement are 'relative to perspective', it is a short step to denying that there is such a thing as religious truth or a God who exists independently of the conditioned human mind.

'Truth', in *Quaker Faith and Practice*, is described as a complex term "sometimes used for God, sometimes for the conviction that arises from worship, sometimes for the way of life". But beyond this, when Quakers talked about Truth (with a capital T) they meant revelation: what was revealed of God in the inspired passages of the Old Testament, in the life and teachings of Jesus Christ, in our own personal and corporate experience of the Inward Light — the "Divine Light within us [which] is the Light of Christ".[179] They would have known by heart the words of Jesus: "If you dwell within the revelation I have brought, you are indeed my disciples; you shall know the truth, and the truth will set you free" (John 8, 31). Truth was inseparable from the gospel of peace and the vision of love as the first mover. Truth and Divine Love were the conjoined twins that guided their efforts to be "builders with God".[180]

Truth in this sense is rejected by the non-theist for whom God has no objective existence and Christianity is one cultural product among many. For the non-theist, revelation has no extra-subjective authority, and truth (now lower case) is plural and contingent. In his

[179] *CFP*, p. 137.
[180] *ibid.*, pp. 103-07.

chapter, 'The Diversity of Truth', in *Real Like Daisies*, Boulton sets out the non-theist position as follows:

> . . . there is no absolute, unchanging religious truth, no Truth with a capital T. Truth, we have learnt, is itself diverse, and is to be made rather than found. Whatever seems to speak to our condition, to ring true, that is our truth for the time being, and will remain so until our condition changes, until new bells ring out new truths. We have a theology that no one view is absolutely "right", even the view we most cherish. Truth is relative and cultural. Of course it is. We now wonder how it could ever have been thought to be anything else.[181]

What is missing here is any supporting argument. It may be felt that none is needed. But the case for relativism is not as widely accepted as these words suggest. Relativism is the view that there is no absolute truth but all truth is relative to the individual or culture. It is a staple component of many university courses and is particularly strong in sociology and literary studies. But in Britain and the English-speaking world generally it has very little support among philosophers. It is estimated that only 1.2% of professional philosophers would describe themselves as relativists, with another 1.7% as sympathetic to relativism. The disparity is enormous and the figures are only slightly improved when the field is narrowed to ethics, with 13.2% describing themselves as moral non-realists (which implies a form of relativism) and 14.5% as sympathetic.[182] As relativism is above all a philosophy, these figures are not without significance. They lead one to ask, is Boulton's rhetoric justified, and is it not perhaps a little misleading to the reader who could be made to feel the impossibility of taking any other position? At the very least the figures suggest that in the eyes of

---

[181] *Real Like Daisies*, p. 37.

[182] D. Bourget and D. Chalmers, "What Do Philosophers Believe?", PhilPapers Online Research in Philosophy (Nov. 2013), pp. 30-6 at: <*philpapers.org/archive/BOUWDP*>. The survey also shows that atheists vastly outnumber theists (in the ratio 7:1), but that most atheist philosophers are scientific realists (materialists) who reject both non-realism and relativism.

academic philosophers the relativist position must have serious weaknesses.

Relativism is now well established in the Religious Society of Friends, and is the background belief of those non-theists who identify with humanism. Its influence is borne out by the comments one hears from time to time to the effect that "there is no truth but only truths", "we all have our own truth", "decide for thyself" (a postmodern rendering of "what canst thou say?" — now on an official Quaker poster) and "no one truth should be privileged over any other". Relativism holds that all value judgements, individual and cultural, are equivalent since there is no objective standard by which to choose between them. It thus gives intellectual support to the idea that diversity is a good in itself and should be celebrated and indeed *strengthened* (as the NFN's introductory leaflet has it). In spiritual matters, it recognises no authority other than individual preference. And this is true even of the one authority most Friends would recognise — the Inward Light. Already it has been reduced to the *Inner Light* which allows its source to be located in the human mind. We may expect that before long, like Truth, it will be deprived of its capitals and 'diversified'; for just as there is no Truth but only truths, so for the relativist there can be no Inner Light but only 'inner lights'. Relativism makes nonsense of the Quaker practice of discernment and the traditional method of testing concerns.

Despite being rejected by moral philosophers, relativism has been able to hold on in the Religious Society of Friends because the different 'truths' that Friends individually espouse are (on the whole) morally commensurate. There is very little *moral* difference between being a Christian and being a Universalist, whereas there is a considerable moral difference between being a community activist and a racist. In the one case, we can say, without giving too much offence, 'we all have our own truth', but to maintain that position in the second case would seem at the very least morally evasive. It would also be dishonest and illogical — dishonest because we don't *really* believe that racism is good for the racist, and illogical because, as relativists, we would have to give equal truth value to beliefs that contradict each other.[183]

The idea that all truth is relative to the individual is more than dishonest and illogical however; it can have serious social consequences. It can override even the *cultural* relativism which sees human society as setting the standards by which attitudes and actions are judged. Nietzsche, for example, maintained that the individual of genius and strength (the 'superman') creates his or her own morality without regard to the 'slavish mentality' of the masses, an idea which has proved immensely attractive to a long line of narcissistic and dangerous personalities — people like Hitler and the 'moors murderer', Ian Brady.

We may all have our different views about who would figure in history as an individual of genius and strength, but I think most people would agree that Dostoyevsky was one such person. In his analysis of the character of Alyosha in *The Brothers Karamazov*, Rowan Williams makes the point that Dostoyevsky "despite his intense commitment to the freedom of the will . . . cannot see any possible way of saying simultaneously that we create value and that we are obligated to it".[184] That, it seems to me, is the crux of the question. If as Boulton claims, "truth is made rather than found", then it can be re-made when circumstances make such a move inviting; and this applies as much to nation states as to individuals, even when, as in Britain, it seems that our agreed values are protected in law. We have only to think of the illegal activities of the Military Reaction Force in Northern Ireland during the Troubles and the horrors of 'extraordinary rendition'. Once we say that "truth is our truth for the time being" there is no reliable

[183] *The Penguin Dictionary of Philosophy* defines 'truth-relativism' as "the view that a belief or opinion cannot be said to be true simply, but only true relative to a species, a conceptual scheme, a social practice, a social group, or a person. To illustrate with the last-mentioned kind: whenever a person, X, says or thinks: 'p is true', this can only mean 'p is true for X'. This view has the absurd consequence that if A believes that *p is true* and B believes that *p is not true*, there is no contradiction between what A and B believe!

[184] Williams, *Dostoyevsky: Language, Faith and Fiction* (London: Continuum, 2008,), p. 235.

background truth, no way of holding to truth as a standard. Rowan Williams goes on to say of the truth we have merely *decided* to honour, "it cannot be defeated but still real, hidden but still present, paradoxically surviving the denials of history".

I think most people want to be able to say that there are *some* attitudes and actions that are objectively good or bad, honest or deceitful, kind or unkind, and not just good, bad etc. relative to culture or individual judgement. As Quakers we want to be able to say that certain things are wrong in all cultures and all circumstances, not just in the mind of this individual or that ethnic group. Torture, capital punishment, terrorism, slavery, the possession and use of nuclear weapons, huge expenditure on armaments and space programmes instead of the relief of poverty — these are categorically and *objectively* wrong and need to be condemned as such. Relativism prevents us from taking this absolutist stand. If we acknowledge no basis for objective Truth in philosophy, scripture or religious experience what final authority do we have? All we can say is that *in our opinion* torture, slavery etc are wrong, always having to add, in feeble parenthesis, that this is only from our own religious or cultural perspective. Since it follows that from the other's perspective such practices are perfectly admissible, the effect is to close down dialogue, leaving us (and relativism) "in a state of self-inflicted paralysis".[185]

By now it will be clear that any discussion of individual relativism soon passes over into a discussion of cultural relativism. The principles are exactly the same. Cultural relativism holds that value is determined by criteria generated within each culture independently. When we look at aspects of these cultures from outside we cannot evaluate them in any objective sense but only state what we prefer, recognising that our preferences are also culturally determined and have no overarching validity.

One of the advantages of cultural relativism, as perceived by its supporters, is that it promotes tolerance of other ways of life, avoiding

---

[185] See L. Kołakowski, *Metaphysical Horror* (London: Basil Blackwell, 1988), pp. 6-7.

the arrogance and cultural imperialism that sees our own way of life as the norm and even as the source of the superior standards that others should follow. This is probably why it has held such appeal for Universalists, who have seen it as a means to relativise Christianity, and for multiculturalists struggling to advance minority rights. However, there is a darker side to cultural relativism. Not all cultural practices are benign and relativism may inhibit us from speaking out against them. Thus we find relativists in the social sciences reserving judgement when faced with such practices as honour killings, female infanticide, female genital mutilation, judicial amputation and the persecution in traditional African societies of sexual minorities. Some have even refused to condemn inter-cultural genocide and have objected to the very idea of human rights on the ground that it is a trans-cultural concept imposed by the West.[186]

Even as they strive to avoid it, cultural relativists are often unconsciously ethnocentric in focusing only on *our* perception of other cultures rather than *their* perception of our culture. There is a sense in which we patronise other cultures by thinking of ourselves as the cultural imperialists and they as the victims of our supposed superiority. We see but we are not seen. So what happens when instead of us looking at the world outside, the world outside is looking at us? Does cultural relativism then give us immunity from criticism? This is the question raised with admirable clarity by Keith Ward:

> The impression of tolerance . . . is greatly misplaced. If all values are relative, then no-one has the right to criticise the values of my culture. I can continue to say that these values are 'right for me', and ignore all possible criticisms, which merely express the different values that other people think are right for them. Thus my values will be uncriticizable from outside; and there will be no question of them being 'incorrect' or 'mistaken' from some allegedly objective point of view. That may indeed seem tolerant, as long as my values do not interfere with the lives of other people. But suppose that my values

[186] See E. Amitai, "The End of Cross-Cultural Relativism" in *Alternatives, Social Transformation and Humane Governance* 22, 2 (1997), pp. 177-89.

> are that strength, power and domination of the weak are right; that my society should dominate all others and revel in power and strength of will. Such values are not unknown in our world . . . It is obvious, therefore, that relativism does not at all guarantee greater tolerance than the view that there are some objective values, some values true for all human beings as such. Relativists will only be tolerant if their own cultural values happen to be tolerant. Conversely, objectivists will be tolerant if the objective values in question include the value of tolerance. Relativism, as such, is no guarantee of tolerance.[187]

In arguing for the objective truth of *some* values that apply across cultures, Ward is saying that no culture, including our own, should be immune from criticism from outside, and how many people would disagree? One has only to think of Nazi Germany. If there are no objective standards, no trans-cultural criteria by which to make value judgements, on what basis can we condemn the régime's policies and actions? Not by criteria generated within the Third Reich itself — surely? And yet some relativists come very close to this position. Gertrude Himmelfarb in *Looking into the Abyss*, her polemic against postmodernist methods of doing history, shows how in denying the ideal of objectivity in the ordinary sense of unbiased truth, and viewing all of history as a social construct, we may soon find ourselves on the slippery road to belittling one of the great tragedies of all time, namely, the Holocaust. The danger lies precisely in the relativist and non-realist notion that denies the existence of historical facts in favour of 'interpretations' and sees no objective reason for 'privileging' one interpretation over another.

So, for example, Himmelfarb criticises the leading relativist philosopher, Richard Rorty, for allowing that "the wisdom of the novel" could encompass "a sense of how Hitler might be seen in the right and the Jews in the wrong". Not that Rorty believed that himself, but his 'playful', 'light-minded' approach to historical truth,

---

[187] Ward, *A Vision to Pursue: Beyond the Crisis in Christianity* (London: SCM Press, 1991), p. 180.

Himmelfarb argues, was a form of irresponsibility that allowed him to tender this as an idea worth considering.[188] Another example quoted by Himmelfarb is that of Paul De Man, the Yale professor and deconstructionist literary critic who after his death was discovered to have written pro-Nazi and anti-Semitic articles for a German newspaper during the Nazi era. However, it is not so much to De Man himself that Himmelfarb wants to draw our attention as to the approach taken by his relativist colleagues in trying to defend him, one of whom remarks "that although many facts about the affair have emerged, facts in themselves are meaningless. It is all a matter of interpretation, and each interpretation will probably reveal more about the interpreter than about De Man". The speaker is clearly unaware of the enormity of the crime — De Man's crime — that he is on the point of excusing. We have here an example of the irresponsible attitude to historical truth that in a more developed form is characteristic of the Holocaust denier.

It was Nietzsche who first said "there are no facts, only interpretations", an aphorism not so far removed from Boulton's insistence that "Truth . . . is to be made rather than found". They are both relativist and non-realist statements, although to be fair to Nietzsche his was probably intended more in a critical realist than a non-realist sense. The Holocaust, however, is one 'hard fact' that refuses to be 'interpreted away'. As Himmelfarb observes, "it is especially hard for postmodernists, who face the prospect of doing to the Holocaust what they do to all of history — relativising, problematising, ultimately aestheticising or fictionalising it". She cites the case of one relativist historian, Jane Caplan, who tries to face up to the problem, only to confess that the task is beyond her. It is worth noting the disparaging terms in which Caplan characterises the relativist philosophy which guides her own historical research:

> To put it bluntly, what can one usefully say about National Socialism as an ideology or a political movement and regime via theories that

[188] Himmelfarb, *On Looking into the Abyss,* pp. 16-17.

> appear to discount rationality as a mode of explanation, that resist the claims of truth, relativise and disseminate power, cannot assign responsibility clearly, and do not privilege (one) truth or morality over (multiple) interpretation? . . . It is one thing to embrace poststructuralism and postmodernism, to disseminate power, to decentre subjects, and all in all let a hundred kinds of meaning contend, when *Bleak House* or philology or even archaeology of knowledge are at issue. But should the rules of contention be different when it is a question, not simply of History, but of a recent history of lives, deaths, and suffering, and the concept of justice that seeks to draw some meaningful relation between these?[189]

Relativism is subject to all the problems I raised in relation to non-realism in Chapter 8. In fact the two approaches go hand in hand. Himmelfarb says of the relativist Richard Rorty, "Rorty would abolish philosophy by abolishing reality itself, which [he contends] is nothing more than the arbitrary construct of the philosopher". In Chapter 8 I posited a critical realist and personalist approach in response to Cupitt's and Boulton's similar contention. The danger, as I explained there, is a fall into solipsism. The critical realist approach overcomes this danger by including both subject and object in the act of cognition. Truth in science is both made *and* discovered, the objective reality which impinges on the scientist from outside affecting the way in which he frames the results of his researches. In the same way, for the historian, an interpretation is more than an interpretation of an interpretation of an interpretation . . . at some point we engage with a 'state of affairs'. As with the scientist, the 'facts' impinge on the historian and play a part, hopefully the key part, in shaping her interpretation. Caplan has had to admit this in relation to the one

---

[189] Caplan, "Postmodernism, Poststructuralism, and Deconstruction: Notes for Historians", *Central European History* (Sept-Dec., 1989), pp. 274, 278 and quoted in Himmelfarb, *ibid.*, p.143. On reading this, my friend James Hogg commented: "The idea of a continuum of conditions along which at some point postmodernism may be embraced but beyond which it is not applicable is interesting. Is the distinction one of ethically neutral entities and ethically involved entities? But how is this distinction made? Is a novel morally neutral?"

morally indisputable fact of the Holocaust and this one 'exception' is enough to undermine the entire case.

The actual objective truth of a situation may be unknowable. It is true, and in agreement with a critical realist approach, that to some extent all our conclusions are 'relative to perspective'. But we can still try to get as near to the objective truth as possible, bringing together all the different perspectives of those working in the field, together with the new facts that *we must assume* are objectively there to be interpreted as they are discovered. "Here lies the crucial distinction", says Himmelfarb, "between modernism and postmodernism, between the old relativistic relativism, one might say, and the new absolutistic version. Where modernism tolerates relativism, postmodernism celebrates it. Where modernism, aware of the obstacles in the way of objectivity, regards this as a challenge and makes a strenuous effort to attain as much objectivity and unbiased truth as possible, postmodernism takes the rejection of absolute truth as a deliverance from all truth and from the obligation to maintain any degree of objectivity".[190]

The really damaging flaw in the relativist argument, however, is that it doesn't stand up to logical scrutiny. The statement 'Truth is relative' is self-contradictory because the statement itself is in the form of an objective truth. Therefore at least one objective truth is possible. Or as John Byl puts it: "the dilemma of relativism is that it asserts a non-relative claim, which inevitably leads to its self-refutation".[191] This means that the argument for relativism is irrational. At this point, the only defence that the relativist can put up is that relativism doesn't recognise objective rationality.

---

[190] Himmelfarb, *ibid.*, p. 137.

[191] Byl, "Naturalism, Theism, and Objective Knowledge", *Journal of Interdisciplinary Studies* XIV (2002), pp. 69-90. Another way of framing this objection is to point out that if all truth is relative to perspective, then this must also apply to the truth of relativism. Relativism, therefore, cannot be *objectively* true, and to concede that it is only *relatively* true denies it universal application. It is tantamount to saying that relativism is true only for the community of relativists.

But even this way out is barred by Robin Attfield in his *Creation, Evolution and Meaning*, one of the most penetrating studies of these issues in recent years. In a section on Cupitt's non-realist 'perspectivism', he points out that Cupitt's claim that all truth is relative to perspective undermines itself, not because it takes the form of an objective truth, as in the argument presented above (although he doesn't deny this), but because in order to be coherent it must itself be relative — relative to perspectives that endorse perspectivism. However, it is one of the tenets of perpectivism that truths cannot transcend or cross perspectives. So either the claim that all truth is relative to perspective is 'self-stultifying' or there are exceptions to the rule which allow for the kind of reasoning that perspectivism rejects. This means that truth claims need not always be relative to perspective and we have room for the kind of 'rational realism' that permits us to accept the approximate truth of scientific theories. The same reasoning can then be applied to the relativist's objections to religious truth which would no longer constitute a barrier to faith.[192]

To some this will seem mere 'logic chopping', but it was an argument similar to the first argument that put an end to an earlier philosophical fashion that did much damage to religion, namely logical positivism, as its main British exponent, A.J. Ayer, eventually came to acknowledge. If something is illogical it will not last long, even if it is a form of thinking that doesn't recognise logic. Indeed the tide is already beginning to turn back in favour of metaphysics with some of the old faces in the postmodernist gallery (Terry Eagleton, Jürgen Habermas, Alain Badiou) brazenly switching sides, while a new generation of young academics waits impatiently in the wings, eager to throw off the yoke of their elders and make their own distinctive mark.

It may be worth considering then whether Boulton's enthusiastic endorsement of relativism — "Truth is relative and cultural. Of course

---

[192] Attfield, *Creation, Evolution and Meaning* (Aldershot; Ashgate, 2006), p. 45. I have paraphrased Attfield's argument to make it easier to follow for the general reader. In so doing I may have slightly altered his meaning and I therefore refer the reader to the original passage at the end of the section on Cupitt.

it is. We now wonder how it could ever have been thought to be anything else" — is premature if not altogether misplaced. It is surely ironic that a theory which denies that there is anything beyond language cannot find self-expression *in language* without self-contradiction. Again, why does relativism exempt logic and mathematics from its strictures, thereby allowing in a kind of eternal truth? Isn't that also contradictory? As Kołakowski wittily observes, if there is no truth worth searching out, nothing that transcends history and culture, "how did it happen that Galileo and Newton left Aristotelian physics in a shambles whereas Euclid's proofs are still valid?"[193]

None of these inconsistencies, nor any of the less acceptable consequences of relativism for the way human beings are seen to relate and behave towards one another, is given so much as a mention in *Real Like Daisies*. Instead, Boulton, relying as always on simple assertion, congratulates Cupitt on "the exuberant joy and delight with which he sees off the tyranny of 'one Truth' and embraces the provisional". He likens this postmodern *jouissance* to the very different spiritual joy of the early Friends who, he says, "like Cupitt, located ultimate authority within rather than without: the first step on the long road to relativism, which is the truth that makes us free". Leaving aside the a-historical nature of this assessment of early Friends as pioneers of relativism, we may ask in what way does relativism make us free? Free from any teaching that is held to be true for all time? For example, the teaching that it is right to love one's neighbour, that prefers social courtesy towards minorities to giving them needless offence? Not all truth is relative to culture , or where would this leave the theorems of Euclid? We cannot generalise and, in this field at least, admit exceptions.

In his Introduction to *Godless* (adopted by the NFN as 'Our Book'), Boulton is particularly scathing in his criticism of the "good and godly" in the Religious Society of Friends who attempt to defend theism against the accusation that it is the root cause of so much of the

---

193 Kołakowski, *ibid.*, p. 7.

religious conflict in the world. His point is that it is no use appealing to some truer version of theism when we have such different understandings of what constitutes truth. “This defence of ‘*true* religion’”, he says, “raises the big question of how we distinguish the true from the false, the good from the bad. ‘By their fruits ye shall know them’? But who judges which fruit is ripe, refreshing and life-giving, and which is past its sell-by date? By scripture? But whose scripture? By intuition? But what when your intuition and mine lead us in opposite directions?” What standard of truth can we bring to bear “when George Bush and Osama bin Laden both claim to be hearing the voice of God and doing his will? When Quakers and suicide bombers each claim to be following the leadings of the Spirit?” He refers us to the prayer found in Mohammad Atta’s luggage after he crashed the plane into the twin towers. “It could be the prayer of an evangelical Christian or a liberal Quaker”. And one has to agree that it is indeed a shockingly beautiful prayer which asks for forgiveness and guidance, although we have no way of knowing if Mohammad Atta composed it himself or copied it from some external source.

Of course, if we say that all perspectives are morally equivalent, it is true we do *not* have a way of distinguishing the true from the false, the good from the bad. And even Jesus’ advice to judge people not by what they say but by their “fruits” will not hold up by relativist standards since moral equivalence cannot tell us which fruits are to be valued and which discarded. On the other hand, if we acknowledge that there are some moral values we could describe as moral absolutes we don’t *need* to land ourselves in this ethical quagmire. Although directed at the theist, the questions posed by Boulton are really more of a problem for the non-theist because there is no guidance that relativism can offer.

In *The Trouble with God*, Boulton tries to persuade us that reason and imagination are a sufficient basis for a moral life: “if humankind is a moral and ethical species, it is because humankind is the species that reasons and imagines . . . we need no supernatural ground for acting reasonably and imaginatively in our dealings with others".[194] Reason and imagination, he says, enable us to feel the fortunes and misfortunes of others as our own, "so we may develop a natural impulse to feed the hungry and care for the destitute".[195] However, as we well know, there are other uses to which human beings have put reason and imagination. Reason and imagination are human faculties rather than ethical standards, and like intelligence and creativity, they can be put to the service of cruelty as much as caring for others. To conclude that human beings have no need of a supernatural (I prefer the word 'supra-natural') ground may therefore be premature. It takes intelligence, imagination, empathy and even creativity, to devise a torture like water-boarding, and its use is invariably justified by an appeal to reason. Combined with a relativism which offers no objective criterion for choosing one use of reason and imagination over another, how can we have any confidence that these highly adaptable capacities of the human mind can provide a secure foundation for a system of ethics, even within a single, isolated culture? Surely, it is because we have these faculties that we *need* a code of ethics that is independent of our preferences?

It is a curious feature of Boulton's discussion of humanist morality that he omits love and truth from his list of the virtues, giving precedence as we have seen to reason and imagination. Boulton acknowledges love, frequently quoting William Blake's "The Divine Image" (wrongly, it seems to me) to support his claim that we don't need God's love in order to love our fellow humans, but this is not the same as placing it at the heart of a public system of morals. He has explained where he stands in relation to truth: it is partial, provisional and 'made' and, in his view, none the worse for that. So if he recognises their intrinsic worth, why are love and truth absent from his discussion of "morality as a human creation"? The only reason I can think of is that neither quality fits easily into a relativist framework — love because it knows no cultural boundaries, and truth, as normally understood, because it is dependent on a presumption of objectivity

[194] *The Trouble with God*, p. 219.
[195] *ibid.*

going beyond individual or group preference. To have introduced them into the discussion, therefore, might have badly muddied the waters. But if this is so, we are left with the question, is a relativist ethics even *possible*?

I think most Quakers would agree that love and truth are absolute values that subsume a host of others. But here we have to be particularly careful not to conflate human love with God's love for us. Human love, on its own, invariably carries a taint of self-interest. The New Testament theologian, Rudolph Bultmann, said, "in reality, the love which is based on emotions of sympathy and affection, is self-love; for it is a love of preference, of choice, and the standard of preference or choice is the self".[196] We have also learnt from social anthropology about the biological and evolutionary roots of human love and its function in holding the family and the group together in order to survive. Human love can go along with hatred of 'them' as well as love of 'us'. Mohammad Atta and his co-terrorists may be a case in point. But that is not to relativise human love altogether. There is some evidence that altruistic feelings based on empathy can override the opportunity to escape from distressing situations, a finding that is contrary to the Hobbesian view that altruistic behaviour is only a form of disguised self-interest.[197] There appears to be something within us, "some particle of the dove kneaded into our frame along with elements of the wolf and serpent", that exceeds Bultmann's self-love — what Quakers might describe as "that of God".

The Greeks had a different word for this larger love that subsumed ordinary human love. The word was *Agape* which used to be translated as 'charity'. Ordinary human love as we have seen is

---

[196] Bultmann, *Jesus and the Word* (NY.: Scribner & Sons, 1934), p. 117. Luther's *Heidelberg Disputation* (1518) also contrasts human and divine love: "The love of God does not find, but creates, that which is pleasing to it. The love of man comes into being through that which is pleasing to it". See Volf, *Free of Charge: Giving and Forgiving in a Culture Stripped of Grace* (Grand Rapids, MI.: Zondervan, 2005), p. 38.

[197] C. Batson *et al*, "Is Empathetic Emotion a Source of Altruistic Motivation?", *Journal of Personality and Social Psychology* 40 (Feb. 1981), pp. 290-302.

limited, but 'charity' goes much further: it has no boundaries. Like God, whose being is 'Charity', it flows over and into all. 'Charity' has lost its first meaning in Christian circles and become merely giving to the needy. So again we need a new, much larger, word to contrast with and subsume ordinary human love.

Charity in this sense is the totally unselfish, all-inclusive love which in Jesus took the form of a self-giving commitment pursued to its end on the cross. It is an absolute value if and only if it is anchored in the nature of Reality, in the being of God. Otherwise it would be foolishness, as many onlookers thought it at the time. If it is so anchored, then it is the Absolute Truth which relativism denies. This is not to say that it is confined to Jesus. Another example of someone who displayed charity in this sense might be Maximilian Kolbe, a Franciscan monk who perished in Auschwitz after substituting himself for a fellow prisoner, and there are many others: Gandhi, Saint Francis, Father Damien, Jane Haining (known as the 'angel of Auschwitz'), Dorothy Stang, the US/Brazilian environmentalist. The Christian imperative to "love thy neighbour", that is, to love the 'out-group' as much as the 'in-group', according to Anders Nygren, is to be understood as "God's own Agape active in the human heart, or, in other words, the presence of the Holy Spirit".[198]

However, for love to be anchored in God, God must be in some way personal — an impersonal God would not be able to love. It follows that love as Absolute Truth is not a concept that sits well with non-theism which denies the personal nature of God. The non-theist and humanist must be content with the *relative* value of love and the philosophical/theological problems that come with it.

"Take heed, dear Friends, to the promptings of love and truth in your hearts. Trust them as the leadings of God whose Light shows us our darkness and brings us to new life" (QF&P, 1.02). These words encapsulate the Quaker understanding of love and truth and, I believe, provide the surest test by which to weigh the leadings of any group of

---

198 Nygren, *Agape and Eros: A Study of the Christian Idea of Love* (London: SPCK, 1932), p. viii.

people, whether Quakers or suicide bombers. Mohammad Atta's suicide note may read like a prayer, and a well composed prayer, but in his heart was there not hatred for those he was going to kill? "A man may say, 'I am in the light'; but if he hates his brother, he is still in the dark. Only the man who loves his brother dwells in light" (1, John 2: 9-11). So in answer to the question 'how do we choose between differing claims to be following the will of God?' I would suggest 'through faith in the practice of spiritual discernment and in the absolute character of the Divine Love we meet in Worship and recognise in the life of Jesus'. If our meetings are truly held in the Spirit, we can truly discern what Love requires of us. Without that faith we are left with an imperfect human love, objective only in the sense of being transcultural, or failing that, thrown back on the relativist position which leaves us with no final grounds for believing one course of action better than any other.

The relativist may still reply that Divine Love is an illusion since all our concepts are human concepts, and that this includes our understanding of whatever is assumed to impinge on our human awareness from 'outside'. However, as I have argued in Chapter 8, this would mean privileging a non-realist over a critical realist view of reality (a choice which the overwhelming majority of scientists and philosophers have rejected) and ignores the way in which, as John Milbank puts it, "our mode of knowing is continuously reshaped by what there is to be known".[199] In other words, there is a way in which reality 'comes at us', forcing us to change or adapt our theories (if we're scientists), to extend the scope and reach of language itself (if we're poets) and opening us to the transforming power of Divine Love (if we are mystics or contemplatives). Boulton regards any suggestion that we may have access to absolute truth in any form as "displaying the overweening arrogance of men playing God",[200] paradoxically

---

[199] See Shortt, *ibid.*, p. 106.

[200] Boulton, *ibid.*, p. 217. We have of course been here before. David Hume makes the same charge, specifically focusing on the Quakers, and with the same assumption that religious experience is to be understood in terms of human pride rather than response to the free gift of Love. "The *Quakers* are the most

appealing to a theistic instinct, the wish to avoid blasphemy. But is it overweening arrogance or playing God to seek the absolute truth that may have access to *us*? — to feel in our heart of hearts that it is God who is taking the initiative in making us aware of that *in experience* which we *know* to be more than subjective, an awareness for which we can take no credit upon ourselves?

For the secularist, the objective (trans-cultural) nature of love in its imperfect human form may be one element in shaping a non-relativist ethics. But for Quakers something more is required. In attempting to discern right from wrong in any given situation the early Quakers turned to the perfect character of Divine Love to provide an unshakeable foundation for their decision-making. This remains the basis of the Quaker method today. Not relativism, but the progressive revelation of God's love and purpose for us is the Truth that sets us free. Relativism denies that Truth and aims to extinguish it in a flood of partial and conflicting truths that have no authority beyond individual and group preference. "Be valiant for God's truth upon the earth", Fox proclaimed, "and spread it abroad in the daylight of Christ". In a very few years we have moved a considerable way from that call, until we are now almost entirely out of earshot. As we prepare for the next revision of *Quaker Faith and Practice*, the question is, how much further do we want to go?

---

egregious . . . as enthusiasm arises from a presumptuous pride and confidence, it thinks itself sufficiently qualified to *approach* the Divinity, without any human mediator. Its rapturous devotions are so fervent, that it even imagines itself *actually to approach* him by way of contemplation and inward converse. . . The fanatic consecrates himself, and bestows on his own person a sacred character, much superior to what forms and ceremonious institutions can confer on any other." See Hume, *Of Superstition and Enthusiasm* (1741) in R. Wollheim (ed.), *Hume on Religion* (London: Fontana, 1963), pp. 248-9.

10

Non-theism — walking the faultline

Defining religion in terms of the distinction immanent/ transcendent is a move tailor-made for our culture. This may be seen as parochial, incestuous, navel-gazing, but I would argue that this is a wise move, since we are trying to understand changes in a culture for which this distinction has become foundational.

— Charles Taylor

THE TERM 'NON-THEISM', first used in the mid-nineteenth century as a polite alternative to 'atheism', is generally held to refer to non-belief in a personal God — that is, a God with whom one can have relationship. Otherwise it has no fixed meaning. Itself a negative, it tends to be defined by the use of further negatives which can vary according to the convenience or motivation of the speaker. This makes it an exceptionally difficult concept to pin down.

In the present chapter I will try to clarify the ways in which 'non-theist' tends to be used in the Religious Society of Friends. Drawing on the ideas of Charles Taylor, acknowledged as one of the world's leading authorities on secularism, I will be making a distinction between the mystical and humanist strands in non-theism, thereby hoping to show that far from sharing a common identity or commitment, these two currents have different destinations and are pulling in quite opposite directions. Taking my cue from Taylor, I will argue that this is because they stand on different sides of a crucial cultural divide, that between an openness and *aspiration* towards the transcendent and an anti-theism which is inexorably *opposed* to the transcendent, however minimalist its claims.

Inevitably, I will be making frequent references to the writings of David Boulton and the aims and objectives of the two organisations he helped to found, namely the Sea of Faith Network and the Nontheist Friends Network UK (NFN). I will explore the links between these organisations and the proposition that the NFN is to all intents and purposes an arm of the Sea of Faith Network, sharing essentially the same humanist agenda and secular vision as the parent organisation. In this sense, it will be part of my case that non-theism *in its organised form* is a kind of Trojan horse, a means of establishing an alien belief system within the host organisation with the aim of eventually achieving dominance.

In addition, I will look at the consequences of non-theism for the Religious Society of Friends, focusing in particular on discernment and the 'Quaker method' — what historically we have called 'gospel order' — and also challenging the claim of one type of non-theism, namely 'radical religious humanism', to offer a Quakerism more suited to meeting the "daunting challenges of the 21st century".

A theological and cultural fault line

Charles Taylor, in his monumental study of secularism, *A Secular Age*, suggests that a major fault line in our western culture, if not *the* major fault line, is that between an 'exclusive humanism' and an 'aspiration towards the transcendent'. "We have moved from a world in which the place of fullness was understood unproblematically outside or 'beyond' human life, to a conflicted age in which this construal is challenged by others which place it (in a wide range of different ways) 'within' human life. This is what a lot of the important fights have been about more recently." The question confronting us, therefore, is "whether one should restrict one's goals to a purely human fulfilment, or open a transcendent perspective to something more than this".[201]

[201] Taylor, *A Secular Age*, pp. 15, 471.

By 'exclusive humanism' Taylor means a humanism which, however it presents itself, is at bottom "a hardline, materialistic atheism". Transcendence can be understood in a minimalist sense as the "something more than" to which Taylor here refers, or as extending through various stages to a fully fledged belief in the God of Abraham which is Taylor's own (strictly bracketed) position as a Roman Catholic. Non-theism in the Religious Society of Friends encompasses both exclusive humanism and belief in a transcendent reality understood in this minimalist sense, but not (by definition) belief in, or experience of, a 'personal' God with whom one can have relationship. This leads one to conclude that the fault line Taylor identifies as a key feature of the age runs not only through the Religious Society of Friends *but through the new Nontheist Friends Network itself.*

Indeed this is obvious when one considers some of the publications produced by leading non-theists in the Society. For example, when David Rush carried out his survey of non-theist Friends in 2002, he included in his sample "a large number of respondents [who] thought of God as, in one sense or another, Spirit, with a description that often includes vital energy or creative force". Among the examples he gave are the following:

- the sacred source indwelling all that is, both transcendent (and so unknowable) and immanent (of experience)
- the transcendent mystery that illumines the inner person with altruism, love and beauty
- in the orthodox Christian faith 'God' is described in anthropomorphic terms — as human, male, father. I prefer Gandhi's word 'Presence'.[202]

[202] Rush, "They Too Are Quakers: A Survey of 199 Non-theist Friends", *The Woodbrooke Journal* 11 (Winter 2002), pp. 13-14. Also at: <http://www.universalistfriends.org>.

How Friends holding such views could be included in a statistical survey of non-theist Friends without distorting the overall presentation and interpretation of the figures is an interesting question. All of these statements point to a transcendent reality which makes its presence known in the innermost reaches of the human heart and are not only consistent with theism but are actually much closer to theism than they are to an all-embracing humanism.

Where, for example, do they fit with the definition of 'non-theist' offered by David Boulton in his *Godless for God Sake*, a compendium of 27 supposedly non-theist voices: "We therefore use 'Quaker non-theist' . . . as a general term embracing Quaker atheists, Quaker agnostics, Quaker naturalists [that is, Quakers who believe there is nothing beyond nature] and Quaker humanists: all who find that their own way of being valiant for truth is to declare themselves Godless — for God's sake".[203] There is no reference here to Rush's 'sacred source' or 'transcendent mystery', even though many who describe themselves as non-theists today appear to hold similar views of the transcendent and the mystical. There is in fact much confusion around the meaning of the term 'non-theist' and it is clear that different groups of non-theists would find themselves on different sides of Taylor's crucial divide.

Boulton himself uses the term 'non-theist' in a variety of ways, not all in accordance with the definition quoted above. In some of his writing he uses it interchangeably with 'humanist'; sometimes to denote a weaker form of atheism; and sometimes to include a range of 'non-theistic' beliefs such as deism (actually an obsolete form of theism) or pantheism, and even beliefs that retain some of the essential features of theism, as in Rush's examples. As I have said, these different usages may conflict with the *Godless* definition and some with each other, but that doesn't seem to be a matter of any significance to the author who adapts his definition and use of the term as he goes along. In one breath, we find the term being used in an expanded sense to suggest a liberal mindset at ease with a broad

---

[203] *Godless*, p. 7.

theological diversity, and in the next in the much more restricted sense of a secular and essentially materialistic humanism — a humanism closed to any sense of the Divine. This can be very confusing for the reader, though the more aware reader will resist being swept along by the persuasive rhetoric and will be less likely to overlook the underlying contradictions.

It is used too when the context seems to require a softly-softly approach, when the words 'atheism' and 'humanism' on their own might sound harsh or militant. Thus one of the contributors to *Godless* confesses that she uses the term 'non-theist' "primarily because 'atheist' has such negative associations". After "getting off the fence" and "deciding to live as if there is no God", she wanted a label other than 'atheist' to reflect that choice. One can see her point, but it is a long way from what we usually think of as 'Quaker plain speech', and arguably it still leaves her somewhat on the fence.

It seems, then, that the term 'non-theist' has no clear meaning even for those who describe themselves as such. In fact it can mean almost anything one would like it to mean. For that reason it has been criticised as a 'weasel word' even within the ranks of the Sea of Faith itself.[204]

Although Boulton is of the opinion that 'labelling' our different theological positions is necessary if we are to have an intelligent exchange of ideas, there are clearly times when he considers it more helpful to keep things vague. In *The Trouble With God*, he tells us that the Sea of Faith Network, while having objectives which look humanist enough to most people, keeps its mission statement "sufficiently ambiguous and flexible to attract those who understand religious *systems* as man-made but see them as aspects of a transcendent divinity or cosmic benevolence".[205] This looks

---

204 S. Mitchell criticizes David Boulton's use of the "weasel word 'non-theist'". See his "*The Trouble with SoF*" in the Sea of Faith Network's journal *Sofia* 78 (July, 2006), *passim*.

205 *The Trouble with God*, p. 209. Although Boulton makes a distinction here between objectives and mission statement, I have been unable to find a distinct mission statement. In his booklet, *A Reasonable Faith,* he says it is the 'stated

suspiciously like a tactic. It suggests that the Sea of Faith, whatever else it may be, is a *campaigning* organisation whose aim is to draw in as many of the theologically uncommitted as possible, even at the cost of hiding the full extent of its own commitment to humanist principles. In other words, it is prepared to *dissemble*, if that is what it takes, to win over the middle ground. For the Sea of Faith, the advantage of this tactic is that it brings into the humanist orbit individuals who can then, presumably, be worked on to strengthen the humanist core. The disadvantage , however, is that the organisation can seem to be at cross-purposes with itself, falling victim to inconsistency and self-contradiction as it steers a wobbly course between its exclusively humanist aspirations and its broadly 'non-theist' public profile.

In another of Boulton's writings, *A Reasonable Faith*, it is the stated objects of the Sea of Faith that are said to be "intentionally ambiguous and provisional". [206] Here we have the first of our contradictions. The stated objects look perfectly straightforward; they are given as "to explore and promote religious faith as a human creation" — that is, to promote an exclusive humanism. If there is, as Boulton claims, an ambiguity here it is not immediately apparent and one cannot help wondering how such a description came to be attached to the stated objects in the first place. It is, admittedly, an open and frank description, but an openness about an intention to be less than frank with those it seeks to win over.

Note also the shift from 'religious systems' to 'religious faith', a detail, perhaps, but nevertheless significant. Most theists would agree that religious systems are human creations. However, this is not the same as saying that religious *faith* is a human creation, since faith from a theist standpoint is better understood in terms of response. The Quaker journalist and broadcaster, Gerald Priestland, wrote, "Religions are not constructed, they are apprehended. They were not

---

objects' that are "intentionally ambiguous and provisional" and justifies this (not very clearly) as a means of avoiding hierarchy and credalism. See *A Reasonable Faith: Introducing the Sea of Faith Network*, Internet edn. (2013), pp. 3, 5.

[206] Boulton, *ibid.*, p. 5.

realised by people saying 'What do we need and how can we give it a religious shape?' but by people who felt something had been given to them from an independent source and who strove to find a shape in it".[207]

Priestland's view is a critical realist one in keeping with the arguments presented from the theist side in my Chapter 8. Boulton claims that the Sea of Faith Network includes critical realists, but one gets the impression that they are there on sufferance, since he goes out of his way to emphasise that the "common denominator" that holds the membership together is the view that religion and religious faith are wholly human creations and "not the product of 'revelation' from some extra-human source".[208] This is just another example of the inconsistency that arises when the mission statement is designed to disguise the true purpose of the organisation. Where does it leave the critical realist members, not to mention those who see religious systems as "aspects of a transcendent divinity or cosmic benevolence"? Are they no longer welcome?

Despite the 'common denominator' that holds the membership together, Boulton admits that "by no means all Sea of Faith members . . . share the enthusiasm which some of us have for 'religious humanism' as a description of our 'position'".

> . . . some members take the commitment to "religious faith as a human creation" as loosely and poetically as they take the creeds, liturgies and other forms of God-talk: it's just a picturesque form of words, they seem to suggest, not to be taken literally or seriously. For them the Network is not primarily an organisation promoting the understanding that religion and its gods are wholly human creations, but an open

[207] Priestland, *The Case Against God*, (London: Collins, 1984), pp. 24-5. Although agreeing with Priestland's overall stance, I am not sure it is true to say rulers have not tried to give shape through a religious system: one has only to think of the origins of the Church of England or the motivations underlying Constantine's adoption of Christianity as the religion of imperial Rome.
[208] Boulton, *ibid.*, p.5.

> forum for the exploration of religious ideas in general and doctrinal doubts in particular, un-anchored by any commitment to anything.[209]

The common denominator is clearly not common to everyone. For some, the Network (the Sea of Faith) is no more than a forum for the exchange of interesting ideas about religion. Although the inevitable result of the organisation's recruitment policy, Boulton is not happy with this situation and feels that it marks a division in the Sea of Faith which could have *apocalyptic* consequences!

> This is a potential fault-line which may one day open up and swallow us whole: the Network as open forum full stop, or the Network as open forum promoting a particular view of religion — the view that, like music, politics, football and summer pudding, religion is a human creation. My own view is simple. If we go down the open-forum-full-stop road and back away from our commitment to promote the understanding that religious faith is a wholly human creation without even a sliver of extra-terrestrial input, we may end up with the need to invent a new network to explore and promote religious faith as a human creation! But this is not the place to pursue apocalyptic Network politics![210]

The first thing to note is the change of perspective. Here the diversity that was good for the Society of Friends — "variety is the spice of modern Quaker life" — is represented as not quite so good for the Sea of Faith. Those who were invited to join on the basis of a flexibility that included belief in a "transcendent divinity or cosmic benevolence" are now told that the organisation may have to wind up if they continue to believe in "even a sliver of extra-terrestrial input". One could ask a lot of mischievous questions here, not least whether the new network, established after the old diversified one had been "swallowed up", would require a credal statement as a condition of entry, or at least a more explicit commitment to the only "particular

[209] *Real Like Daisies*, p. 60.
[210] *ibid.*, pp. 60-1.

view of religion" that would be positively encouraged — for surely without some curb on admissions it could happen all over again? The Network could re-diversify and a new fault line open up with the same alarming possibilities as before. Interestingly, 'diversification' is one of the reasons Boulton gives for the decline and eventual demise of early twentieth century experiments in religious humanism[211], so perhaps it is not surprising that he should want to check any such tendency in a *modern* humanist organisation before it got out of hand.

Boulton informs us that it is "the genius of the [Sea of Faith] movement . . . not to commit to any *ism* or anything resembling a fixed ideology".[212] So where do we stand with regard to the statement that the *common denominator* is "the view that religion and religious faith are wholly human creations and not the product of 'revelation' from some extra-human source"? That strikes me as an *ism* — it is called human*ism*. It is just conceivable that one could hold to such a position without *formally* committing to it, but again that sounds more like a strategy than a principle. In any case, it is clear from the most cursory glance at the literature that the movement does have, if not a fixed, at least a *consistent* ideology which may be described in terms of a whole set of *isms*, such as religious human*ism*, non-real*ism*, objective nihil*ism*, etc. The common denominator in respect of all of these is that they reject any notion that there is a transcendent reality independent of us and on which we are dependent.

New recruits to the Sea of Faith who believe in a 'transcendent divinity' or 'cosmic benevolence' may therefore find themselves in for a shock. Boulton, in scattered references throughout his writing, makes it quite clear that 'radical religious humanism' is not a refuge for those "who simply can't make up their minds"; a half-way house for prevaricators "who want to have their theistic cake and eat it." Nor is it intended to provide "a useful staging-post in a personal journey from one kind of commitment to another . . . if that is all it is, it's no big

211 *The Trouble With God*, p. 191.
212 *ibid.*, p. 209.

deal".[213] But, then, for many of us it *is* a big deal! Boulton wants to keep people in one fixed place, but if we are on a spiritual journey we may need to go *through* that place to understand what it is about, and then we may need to make a decision whether to let go of the false images of God that are kept there. For some people it is only possible to grasp what the holy is when they are able to contrast it with their experience of the farthest reaches of the secular. For such people, religious humanism could very well be a staging post, a necessary step on a long journey towards the mystery that is God.[214]

There is very little room in Boulton's scheme of things for the religious 'seeker' (a word which after all sums up a large part of Quakerism). Despite the use of ambiguity as a tactic, his followers are left in no doubt as to the secular nature of what it is they are committing to — a humanism without even a sliver of transcendence. Thus he warns against any illusions that may cohere around the term 'religious'. 'Religious humanism', he writes, "is not the binary opposite of secular humanism". It is "wholly secular in the root meaning of the word: it is of this world and for this age, the only world we can know and the only age of which we can have any direct experience".[215]

Among the traditions Boulton would "reasonably expect those who avow a humanist perspective to *sweep away*" are belief in a creator, the soul, the supernatural world, theism, deism and 'theological modernism'.[216] Moreover, he warns us that "superstition

---

[213] *Real Like Daisies,* p. 63. One may feel there is a contradiction between wanting to keep the word 'religious' in a term like 'religious humanism' while advocating its omission (as some humanists do from time to time) from the name of the Society.

[214] My brother, Gerard Guiton, on reading this, told me a story about a regular attender at Meeting for Worship in Melbourne who over the years had dropped his Marxism but maintained his atheism. One Sunday during Worship he felt he had been silently "tapped on the shoulder" and told it was "okay to believe". "It was clearly a very tender and moving moment for him, as it was in the re-telling. Tears came into his eyes and we both fell into a deep gathered silence, a gathered silence in something clearly 'other', a gathered silence in God."

[215] *Real Like Daisies,* p. 64.

[216] *The Trouble with God,* p. 186. My italics.

and the kinds of mysticism that are better described as mystification need to be kept under constant criticism. *They are too dangerous to be ignored in the name of tolerance*".[217] Among the kinds of mysticism that might be "better described as mystification" he would no doubt include the sense of the presence of God in our Meetings for Worship, including our business meetings, for he says that while the sense is real, the presence is not real, and to think otherwise is the sheerest superstition, on a level with the holding of a séance.[218] The tenor of these remarks suggests a certain coldness towards the beliefs of all those Friends who are still theists, and should alert us to the far reaching nature of the changes that "boldly embracing" radical religious humanism would bring.

They show, moreover, that the velvet covering of ambiguity and flexibility which we saw earlier conceals a barely disguised iron purpose. In taking this stance, Boulton is making it absolutely clear to those who are merely flirting with radical religious humanism that more is required of them. He wants and expects a wholehearted commitment to what the term 'humanism' implies. Above all, it must be brought home to those of a mystical turn of mind that their so-called 'religious experiences' cannot be thought to confer any special or privileged knowledge. The message is clear: mystical religion will get short shrift in a future, humanist dominated Society of Friends. The only acceptable mysticism is one confined to "the secular world which we now inhabit", a mysticism without secure foundation because, in his view, as a non-realist, there is no ultimate transcendent principle on which it can stand.[219]

Boulton is right to identify transcendence as the key issue that divides the humanism of the Sea of Faith from both theism and non-humanist forms of non-theism. It is transcendence, dismissed (and derided) in the passage quoted earlier as 'extra-terrestrial input', that marks the "potential fault line" which he fears may one day open up

---

217 *ibid.*, p. 204. My italics.
218 *Real Like Daisies*, p. 51.
219 See *ibid.*, p. 43.

and swallow the entire Network unless something is done about it. Thus he locates the fault line along precisely the same plane as Charles Taylor. On the one side we have an openness to the transcendent and on the other its frontal denial in an all-pervading humanism. For this reason I shall refer to it henceforth as the Taylor-Boulton fault line. Giving it this name will remind us of the importance that both writers, from their different perspectives, attach to it. It is worth mentioning that David and Margaret Heathfield in an excellent article in *The Friends Quarterly*, which I would urge all Friends to read, also refer to a fault line running through the Society which they have called the "Faith — Non-Faith fault line".[220]

The Nontheist Friends Network

So far we have been discussing non-theism in relation to the Sea of Faith movement where the dominant creed is 'radical religious humanism'. It is now time to consider non-theism in relation to a much more urgent issue for Friends: the setting up of the 'Nontheist Friends Network UK' (NFN).

Non-theism in the Religious Society of Friends covers a much broader range of theological belief than the Sea of Faith's 'radical religious humanism' which is uniformly atheist — in theory anyway. With the Sea of Faith there was the problem of dealing with a few independently minded individuals who wanted all the intellectual excitement of the humanist salon without paying the price in terms of a fully declared commitment to humanist principles. In the case of the NFN there is the much trickier problem of how to win over a large group of people who occupy the middle ground of an established Religious Society without frightening them away prematurely. That is no easy task, and in trying to maintain a focus on the wholly humanist dimension, while at the same time appealing to a theologically diverse audience, some very nimble footwork will be required. One of the

[220] David and Margaret Heathfield, "In essentials, unity", *The Friends Quarterly* (April, 2012).

trickier steps to be mastered will be that around the definition of non-theism itself. We shall see how radically that is affected by the mood music and the intricate movements of the dancers!

The March 2012 Minute and Epistle of the NFN represents non-theism as "signifying a positive commitment to wholly human values", where 'wholly' signifies an unqualifiedly humanist perspective. In these words non-theism is *defined* as humanism, and this is confirmed by the wording of the founding document whose first aim is to "provide a supportive framework for Friends with an agnostic, humanist, atheist or related world-view, and those who experience religion as a wholly human creation". This definition of non-theism, if acted upon, would exclude from the NFN a large number of Friends who see themselves as non-theists but who do not fit the humanist profile: Universalists, pantheists, syncretists, Quagans, also those who believe that religious *systems* are human creations but who remain open to the transcendent, and those who are unsure what they believe — in fact all those categories for whom the Sea of Faith mission statement and objects were made intentionally ambiguous, flexible *and provisional*. But in fact none of these groups is excluded at all.

From this point on it all gets a bit muddled. The second and third aims refer to the *varieties* of non-theism and the NFN's task as strengthening the Religious Society of Friends' theological *diversity*. Since presumably some varieties of non-theism will be non-humanist, the scope of the term 'non-theism' now seems to be wider than in the Epistle. One moment it seems the NFN is a fully humanist organisation, defining non-theism *as* humanism, the next it is a broad-based Quaker organisation which happens to *include* humanism and defines non-theism as consisting of all shades of theological opinion with the one exception of theism.

The same confusion and self-contradiction crops up when we compare other public statements. Having declared in *Godless*, that there is "no unified or official 'non-theist Quaker view'. . . None of us speaks for all Quaker non-theists", Boulton then writes, *speaking for all Quaker non-theists* in an *official* report on the NFN inaugural conference: “Non-theism affirms an understanding of the Spirit as a human construct, our imagined projection of the ideal, the fictional protagonist in our cosmic story.” It appears, then, that we not only have a *unified* view after all, but non-theism is once again defined — *officially* — in humanist and non-realist terms! The goal remains the same, but the means of getting there are as flexible as ever.

A lot of this may seem to be merely nit-picking, but the point is to demonstrate the kind of muddled practice and methodology with which non-theists within the Society of Friends are attempting to challenge our longstanding theist tradition. Having opened ourselves to the secular, we are now having to deal with the kind of political manoeuvring we are familiar with in the corporate workplace. A key skill in this kind of setting is the ability to manage (some would say ‘manipulate’) change. This is particularly needed when one strategy, which has outlived its purpose, is replaced by another that is quite opposite. Pragmatism and principle are often in conflict, but here, as we shall see, pragmatism wins hands down.

Whereas not very long ago we were being severely castigated for wanting to “have our theistic cake and eat it” and told that theism is a lie and “our problem rather than our salvation”, now with the launch of the NFN we are assured that theism and non-theism can peacefully co-exist and are simply “two different ways of understanding God-language, but both affirmative — and, for Friends, neither excluding the other”. The NFN website goes further. Having showcased *Godless for God’s Sake* as ‘Our Book’ — the very book that contains the above derogatory evaluation of theism, the web page continues:

> We are not a pressure group trying to move Quakerism towards non-theism. We bless what our theist brothers and sisters bring to Quaker meetings and worship. All Friends have much to learn from each other. We hope to strengthen the Quaker tradition of welcoming people of diverse religious experience and to show by example that this can include non-theists.

The first and last sentences in this passage are themselves contradictory, and in my view misleading, since *strengthening* diversity in the Society (one of the aims clearly set out in the founding document) must involve *weakening* our allegiance to theism and will therefore almost certainly "move Quakerism towards non-theism". But that aside, what we are seeing here is a truly remarkable turnaround. From theism being "our problem" and the first of a number of belief systems to be 'swept away', theists are now to be *blessed* for what they bring to Meeting for Worship. What has changed to bring this about?

It could of course signal a complete change of heart, a harrowing realisation that the denunciation of theism in 'Our Book' was all a dreadful mistake. But it would be foolhardy and irresponsible not to consider other possibilities, *since nothing in 'Our Book' has actually been retracted.* There are two developments that coincide with this striking change of attitude: (1) the launch of the NFN itself in what might be regarded by its organisers as a theologically unsympathetic environment; and (2) the start of preparations for the next revision of *Quaker Faith & Practice*.

To take the first point first, the launch of the NFN: I am sure that the NFN steering committee recognises that the management of change requires the skill to keep everyone on board, at least until the desired change has been achieved. The last thing one wants when a project is at a vulnerable stage and bidding for wider acceptance is to provoke a backlash. At this time it is reassurance that is called for — calming fears while 'gently moving' the change agenda forward. If I am right about this, we can safely predict that from hereon we shall see a strategic emphasis on *co-existence*, alongside the now familiar appeal to joyfully celebrate a diversity that opens the door to yet further change.

And this brings me to my second point. Nothing is more certain to guarantee the future of non-theism in the Religious Society of Friends than its incorporation into *Quaker Faith & Practice*, which as well as being our book of discipline is now also our constitutional document. Once non-theism (providing cover for humanism) is accepted as a "permissible strand" in Quakerism *and given this status in our constitution*, there is nothing to stand in its way, there is no going back, and from that point on we can expect no let up in its demands. Whatever privileged place Christianity and theism have held in the Society will be inexorably deconstructed, and with every current of thought on an equal footing the drift towards a secular Society may become irreversible.

With the next revision now in the offing, we should not be surprised to find reassurance coming our way in floods. For example, responding to a letter from Carole Hamby in *The Friend* (9th August 2013), in which she voices her concern that some Friends may be planning to 'modernise' the language of *Quaker Faith & Practice* to avoid giving offence to non-theists, Boulton assures the reader that it is not the intention of the NFN to 'impose' non-theist language and write God out of the text but only to press for the incorporation of views that "challenge traditional understandings of 'God' and 'Spirit' as transcendental realities". Reassurance, yes, but with a lethal sting in the tail. The promise that 'the God word' is not under attack is scarcely reassuring when that which it signifies clearly is. Once that transcendent reality is denied, changes to the language will inevitably follow without needing to be 'imposed'. The "work in progress" undertaken jointly with John Lampen which requires us to use words that are "as inclusive as possible" would almost guarantee it.

The sticking point for Boulton is transcendence. The humanist who cannot tolerate "even a sliver of extra-terrestrial input" is unlikely to accept "the something more than" that Taylor posits as a minimalist definition of this important concept. It raises the question 'more than what?' and the obvious answer is 'more than the human', 'more than nature'. Immanence is less of a problem. It is welcomed by Boulton as "locating ultimate authority within rather than without" and as representing the first step towards a humanist understanding of truth. The traditional Christian view, however, is that immanence and transcendence are not mutually exclusive. The 'something more' could refer to both: '*including and beyond* the human', '*including and beyond* nature'. This is probably what the mainstream of British Quakerism believes even today. It coincides with the early Quaker insistence that in stressing the presence of God within they were not denying 'God without'; or as the Bhagavad Gita expresses it: "he who sees me in everything and everything in me, him I shall never forsake, nor shall he lose me". John Lampen, also referring to "the something more", says he finds it hard to understand how anyone could reject it and still feel at ease in a Friends Meeting.[221]

However, as Charles Taylor points out, there are different understandings of immanence. The default position, especially in intellectual and academic circles, is that immanence admits of no beyond. He calls this "the closed reading" of immanence, "the view that modernity must bring secularity in its train". He contrasts the closed reading with "the open reading" which leaves room for the transcendent, and argues that the 'immanent frame', properly understood, "allows for both readings, without compelling us to either".[222]

The even-handed tolerance and flexibility of the open reading is not available to the advocates of the closed reading, since their need is to shut down all other possibilities. This doesn't mean they are wrong. There may be nothing, Taylor concedes, beyond the immanent frame, but an important feature of his analysis is the need to dispel "the false aura of the obvious" that surrounds the closed reading and is (he says) a kind of "illusion" and even "disability".

From this perspective, non-theists fall into two main groups. On the one hand, there are those who are uneasy with the idea of a personal God but who would nevertheless see themselves as seekers or mystics in the Quaker tradition; and on the other, those who no longer see themselves as seekers in that sense, but have opted to *commit* themselves to non-theism as a final stopping point on their journey.

---

[221] J. Lampen, *Finding the Words: Quaker Experience and Language* (Stourbridge: The Hope Project, 2007), pp. 6-7.
[222] Taylor, *A Secular Age*, p.550.

The first group would be likely to opt for the open reading of immanence, and in most cases to accept Lampen's and Taylor's "something more", both as a foundation for their own belief and as a possible requirement for membership. I shall refer to these as 'seeker non-theists'. The second group, "accepting no final goals beyond human flourishing", have already opted for the closed reading. Having chosen to remain in this relatively fixed position, their spiritual seeking (in the traditional sense) has ceased. They recognise no credal boundaries where Quakerism is concerned, and would almost certainly reject the "something more" as credal and as opening a perspective to the transcendent. I shall refer to these as 'humanist non-theists'. Seeker non-theists are likely to opt for co-existence alongside others, including theists; humanist non-theists to campaign actively for a humanist version of non-theism with the intention of ultimately replacing theism as the dominant Quaker theology.

The Taylor-Boulton Fault Line

Theist seeker, mystic	Humanist: atheist, naturalist etc
Non-theist seeker, mystic	Non-theist as end position
Aspiration towards the transcendent	Frontal denial of the transcendent
Content to be accepted alongside others	Active campaigner with clear agenda
Open reading of immanence	Closed reading of immanence

Given these very different characteristics, there is an obvious question around the compatibility of the two groups and their different needs. Does the NFN have the capacity to meet both sets of needs simultaneously, and why would it want to? In the case of seeker non-theists (those who hold to the 'open reading of immanence') surely their needs would be better met in the mainstream? Friends have always included a large number of those whom we call 'seekers'. Indeed, we are all seekers, and (since God is infinite) that includes those who also think of themselves as finders. This being so, we may ask why has it become necessary to bring such Friends together in a separate organisation within an already existing organisation which is dedicated to that very activity? It is not as if theism, as found in the Society, were a phenomenon that other Friends find overwhelming or suffocating, or that theist Friends were seeking to push others out. Only two explanations seem possible. Either the underlying aim is to move non-theism as a whole into the centre ground, thereby (intentionally or not) isolating theists as a group, or the NFN exists simply as an organisation offering pastoral support to those who feel vulnerable because of their theological position.

But then, to take the second explanation first, why should seeker non-theists who hold to the open reading of immanence *need* the support of an NFN framework when we already have a very good support system in our elders and overseers? I am not suggesting that these Friends don't have personal and spiritual needs that may be difficult to meet within the existing structures, but is retreating behind the barrier of a special interest group, and one moreover that consists largely of humanists who would 'sweep away' every vestige of the object of their search, the best way to satisfy them? In so far as such Friends are open to the possibility of transcendence, 'the something more', they will have needs of an entirely different order to those of the second group, needs that I suggest would be better met in a theist orientated *Religious* Society than in one that is humanist and secular orientated. In view of the harm that would be wreaked on the Society if humanism were to get the upper hand, we might pray that such Friends will withdraw their support and conduct their seeking within a spiritual context which speaks to their condition more lovingly and with greater understanding.

Humanist non-theists, being more decided in their views, would seem even less in need of a supportive framework. Why should an atheist, a nihilist or non-realist in the Society of Friends be more in need of support than people holding similar views in the world at large? Friends who hold to these positions are hardly to be thought of as shrinking violets and you cannot help wondering what is going on when you hear plaintive references to 'my non-theism' or talk of 'coming out' as a non-theist. Non-theism is not a condition or way-of-being comparable to race, disability, gender or sexual orientation, so why should it warrant so much trepidation? It is an idea, a theological or philosophical concept, and while ideas or concepts can be creative or destructive, they do not usually, at least in Britain, confer victim status on those who voluntarily espouse them. So taking all this into account, what is the 'supportive framework' *for*? Is it really necessary for either group or does it serve a different need altogether?

I believe that the real need — the need which brought the NFN into existence in the first place — has less to do with providing support to a 'vulnerable' group, and much more to do with furthering the agenda of the Sea of Faith Network within the Society of Friends. The role of the NFN, I suggest, is to act as an arm of the Sea of Faith Network, amplifying the voice of non-theism in the Society and widening its influence with a view to realising Cupitt's and Boulton's dream of establishing "an avowedly religious humanist organisation" in Britain. The Sea of Faith Network, of course, *is* such an organisation but lacks the infrastructure, historical tradition and public respect that the Quaker name can offer. The wholesale conversion to humanism of the Religious Society of Friends, or even a breakaway section of it, would have a multiplying effect beyond anything that the Sea of Faith Network could achieve on its own. It would provide humanists with a ready-made infrastructure and launch pad from which to campaign more effectively within the wider society and in particular within the wider Christian Church.

Ultimately it will fail because any form of organised atheism is too bleak and comfortless to be borne for long and humanist organisations that are rooted in what were previously church communities have a poor survival record. However, in the meantime such movements can do untold damage and the Society of Friends would be fully justified in taking a minimum of precautions to ensure its continuation as that which it was always intended to be, a vehicle for the worship of God and the realisation through peaceful voluntary action of the Kingdom (or Covenant) of God.

The Society of Friends is not the only faith organisation which may have to take this kind of action. As Alister McGrath has pointed out, "Every movement based on core ideas or values has to determine its centre on the one hand and its boundaries on the other. What is the focus of the movement? And what are the limits of diversity within the movement?"[223] Friends have not so far been able to answer these questions adequately, inhibited to some extent by their reputation for liberal tolerance. However, a credal requirement for membership as minimal as the 'something more' or the 'open reading of immanence' would in no way detract from our liberal credentials and would be accepted by most thoughtful persons as rational and justified. It draws the line precisely where Charles Taylor, David and Margaret Heathfield, and David Boulton himself in his own way, have all located it. Indeed, such a requirement need not be seen as credal in any sense at all. All we would be looking for is an *attitude* of openness to the *possibility* of the Real Presence rather than an already established belief in it.

It seems that a number of Friends in Britain Yearly Meeting are now thinking along these lines. Dorothy Searle in an article in the *The Friend* entitled, 'What do non-theists not believe in?', says, "It's been suggested that there should be a minimum of belief for members of the Religious Society of Friends, and I agree. But that minimum needs to reflect consciousness of the Reality itself, consciousness that is already present or being striven for, not a particular image or belief system". It should be noted that she is talking here about a *minimum* of belief, and not even a belief, but a genuine desire for and seeking after "a Reality beyond a mundane human level of understanding".[224] Without that

---

[223] McGrath, *Heresy: A History of Defending the Truth* (London, SPCK, 2009), p. 33.

[224] Searle, *The Friend*, (2nd Sept., 2011), p. 14.

desire and striving, there would seem little point in anyone applying for membership, unless the intention is to change the fundamental nature of the thing they are joining. Even then, any exclusions would apply only to membership, not to attendance and worship. We would be 'welcoming the stranger' but not giving him/her control over our affairs.

In this chapter I have tried to clear away some of the confusion around the term 'non-theism' as used in Quaker circles. In particular I have made a distinction between two different kinds of non-theists whom I have called 'seeker non-theists' and 'humanist non-theists'. This is no arbitrary distinction but corresponds to the 'Taylor-Boulton fault line', the widening ontological crack that Boulton saw threatening to swallow up the Sea of Faith Network and Charles Taylor saw zig-zagging through our entire Western culture. While the debate in *The Friend* is usually represented as a dispute between theism and non-theism, the real division, as Taylor sees it, is that between a modest 'aspiration towards the transcendent' (the 'open reading of immanence') and its 'frontal denial' in an 'exclusive humanism' (the 'closed reading'). What we are seeing is not an argument over the wording of a creed so much as a fundamental difference in attitude and orientation, a difference possibly unrecognised as yet by the majority of those who now describe themselves as non-theists. Although not reflected in the way the debate has taken shape in current Quaker writing, it may be along this trajectory that any future revision to our admission criteria will have to be considered.

I have also in this chapter drawn attention to some highly questionable strategies that have been, and are being, used to bring both groups of non-theists under a single umbrella. I have suggested that the aim of these strategies is to attract the seeker group away from the theistically oriented mainstream which has traditionally been their spiritual home. Whereas in earlier years the unity of Friends was always to be found among theists and seekers ("in Christian love"), it now seems that the centre of gravity has shifted onto less stable foundations and the search for unity consequently deflected into a negotiated secular space — the fruits without the Spirit. While the groundwork has been prepared by decades of accommodation to the prevailing intellectual fashions, it is the conscious intervention of the two organisations set up to promote religion as a "wholly human creation" that here marks a decisive turn. In my next chapter I will discuss the charge that the Sea of Faith Network has created a bridgehead into Britain Yearly Meeting in the form of the Nontheist Friends Network. I will argue that the ultimate aim of both these organisations is to replace Quaker theism with an exclusive humanism which in the last resort is indistinguishable from any other progressive secular ideology. Such a move will herald the merging and disappearance of what we have known historically as 'Quakerism' into the unfolding diversity of the world at large.

11

Non-theism — disappearing into the secular

The devilry of modernity has its own magic: the theologian who sups with it will find his spoon getting shorter and shorter — until that last supper in which he is left alone at the table, with no spoon at all and with an empty plate.

— Peter Berger

Enriching or supplanting?

IN THE MAY 2012 issue of *The Friends Quarterly*, the editor, Tony Stoller, makes a startling observation. "British Quakerism", he says, "is at risk from what in political circles is termed 'entryism', where a small group of activists gain disproportionate influence over a much larger organisation, replacing its values with beliefs that are contrary to its own natural traditions. The flirtation with Buddhism and the dead-end of non-theism may be current examples, if they end up supplanting, rather than enriching."

This is a serious charge and it brought a swift response from David Boulton on behalf of the NFN. In an 'Endpiece' to the next issue of the journal he challenged Stoller's use of the term 'entryism'.

> The suggestion that the non-theist Friends' movement . . . may be comparable to the Trotskyite cells which sought to infiltrate the Labour Party in the 1980s is bizarre. The Militant Tendency's entryism was a tactic whereby extremists, hiding their real views, wormed their way into the party with the express intention of subverting its

democracy and seizing control . . . . Where non-theists have joined the Society from outside, they have made their views explicit as a matter of integrity, submitting themselves to the Society's discernment process. The contrast with entryism could hardly be greater.

Comparison with the Militant Tendency in the Labour Party may be bizarre; but the comparison is Boulton's, not Stoller's. Entryism can take different forms. The OED defines it as "the policy or practice of joining an organisation with the intention of subverting its aims and activities: organised infiltration"; but the Wikipedia definition suggests that infiltration, in the sense of dishonest concealment of one's real views, is only likely where the host organisation is resistant to the ideas being introduced. Trotsky, with whom the term originated, advised his followers in the nineteen thirties to enter the French Socialist Party *openly* and form their own revolutionary grouping from the leftward-leaning elements that were already there. There is no suggestion in Stoller's remarks that non-theist Friends hide their views, and as membership of the Society is open to non-theists of all shapes and sizes there would obviously be no need for them to do so.

Boulton makes the point that the majority of Friends who identify with non-theism are longstanding members of the Society, many of whom have served in a variety of ways in their local and area meetings. However, if entryism is a reality, this is just what one would expect. All entryism is to some extent 'home-grown'. The whole point of the exercise is to build the movement by gathering under one banner the disparate groupings that are already present in the host organisation. If the tactic is successful the new recruits will greatly outnumber the original entryists, and when, as usually happens, their activities lead to a split in the organisation, the entryists come away with a handsome net gain. Even better from the point of view of the entryists would be the complete takeover of the host organisation, but this seldom succeeds.

The real issue, as Stoller presents it, is not whether non-theism in the Society of Friends fits this or that description of entryism but whether it will "end up supplanting rather than enriching". On this last point, Boulton's Endpiece seeks to reassure. He tells us that "the newly-formed Non-theist Friends Network has repeatedly made clear that, far from seeking to turn Britain Yearly Meeting into yet another humanist or secularist organisation, its aim is to 'strengthen and celebrate theological and spiritual diversity' within the Society":

> As the Network's introductory leaflet puts it, 'Our various ways of being non-theist are simply various ways of being Quaker, and we celebrate the radical diversity of Quakerism, theist and non-theist'.

A fundamental flaw in the non-theist outlook is the failure to recognise that for Friends the diversity that is truly 'enriching' is not so much the diversity of secular or even religious *viewpoints* but our various individual responses to 'the things that are eternal', as shared especially in ministry. These personal responses are shaped by the diversity of *gifts* but they are responses to the same Spirit. They are the true diversity which it would seem odd and even inappropriate to 'celebrate', as they are more a matter of spiritual consciousness, a reaching inward to the Divine ground, than a display of tolerance towards a set of abstract and disharmonious opinions. But to return to the Endpiece, why the diversity of Quakerism should need further 'strengthening' or how that is to be achieved without displacing more tested theologies is not explained. Nor does Boulton reflect on the likelihood that such 'strengthening' would itself contribute to turning Britain Yearly Meeting into a more humanist or secularist organisation. And we might also ask: how do our *various* ways of being non-theist tie in with the serious minded commitment, insisted on elsewhere, to "wholly human" values?

Boulton welcomes the fact that many "who would not call themselves non-theists" nevertheless support "the continuing inclusion of non-theist Friends as one rich colour in the Quaker rainbow", and commends Jan Arriens, a theist and Universalist, for recognising "that the Nontheist Friends Network 'does not regard theism and non-theism as adversarial viewpoints'". That may well be Jan Arriens' view. But where does Boulton stand in this regard? What rich colour does he see *theism* as adding to the Quaker rainbow?

The difficulty I have with the Endpiece is reconciling it with Boulton's earlier published remarks — his assertion that theism, is a lie, "our problem, rather than our salvation", his depiction of "the good and godly in our religious societies and *our Religious Society*" (his emphasis) as naive believers unable to accept that God is dead, his refusal to countenance even the tiniest "sliver" of transcendence, and his condemnation of "those who want to have their theistic cake and eat it." These are clearly adversarial, anti-theist viewpoints, more 'supplanting', on balance, than 'enriching'.

It is true that in representing theism in these terms Boulton is speaking as a member of the Sea of Faith Network whereas in the Endpiece he is speaking as a member of the NFN which consists of both seeker and humanist non-theists. That of course makes being a spokesperson more difficult; one has to keep one's own views to some extent in the background. However, if that is the source of the discrepancy it is left to his readers to work it out for themselves: no explanation or apology is offered. One can only assume that if Boulton were speaking for his fellow humanists in the NFN, and not for non-theists in general, he would be saying something very different. Going on his previous remarks, which he has never retracted, he would have to say that the aim was indeed to turn Britain Yearly Meeting into a humanist or secularist organisation. And if he were being really candid he would add that this has been a longstanding project in which he has invested a good deal of his time and energy. Let us look at some of the thinking behind it.

The 2012 Minute and Epistle of the NFN, as we have seen, equates non-theism with "a serious commitment to wholly human values". It should come as no surprise therefore to learn that although the NFN arranged to have a theist and a humanist as keynote speakers at its inaugural conference in 2011, the humanist speaker was the very formidable Don Cupitt, widely regarded as the guru of the Sea of Faith movement.

In *Real Like Daisies*, Boulton informs us that every year since 1995, Cupitt had been calling for a "new this-worldly and democratic religious humanism"[225] (a 'religious' humanism that later in the book is described as 'wholly secular'). There had been some encouraging developments in this direction in the United States, where a number of synagogues had gone over to "a rigorously non-theistic version of the faith", but nothing equivalent in the United Kingdom, "no avowedly religious humanist organisation".[226] Then in the Introduction to *Godless for God's Sake*, published in 2006, and written exclusively for a Quaker audience, he announced that 'radical religious humanism' was a voice that "cannot now be silenced".[227] The question he and his co-thinkers were faced with was how to *amplify* that voice and "build a new secular spirituality" that would no longer be "confined to the fringes". But where to start?

> Where better to start than among Friends? Numerically small as we are, compared with the massed ranks of mainstream institutional religion, our beloved Society is uniquely placed to make a contribution. We have no creed. We never have, never do and never will insist that those who join us believe this or that — or if we do we betray our own tradition. We have no clerical hierarchies to enforce unanimity or conformity. We are not in bondage to the authority of scripture or a spiritual elite. We are seekers, cautious of those who loudly proclaim themselves finders. We claim to live adventurously and experimentally.[228]

It appears then that the Society of Friends is to be the crucible for this new experiment in humanist spirituality, perfect because of its small size, its tradition of not requiring a statement of belief as a condition of membership, its openness to ideas that are alien to its own traditions, and its non-authoritarian structures. We could add to this its

---

225 *Real Like Daisies*, p. 60.
226 *The Trouble with God* (Alresford: O Books, 2002), p. 177.
227 *Godless*, p. 15. A curious expression since no-one had attempted to silence it.
228 *ibid.*

penchant for re-writing its scripture every thirty years, for in the course of a talk at Hebden Bridge, also in 2006, Boulton commented on how his humanist colleagues in the mainstream churches couldn't believe his good fortune when he told them he belonged to a religious tradition that treated this as routine.

We can see here the lineaments of the future NFN, but even if it is allowed that the aim of the NFN is not to turn Britain Yearly Meeting into "yet another humanist or secularist organisation", can we truthfully make the same claim here? The fact that Cupitt had been calling year after year for a 'new this-worldly and democratic religious humanism', along with Boulton's enthusiastic reporting of those US synagogues which had gone over to a "rigorously non-theistic version of the faith" (note 'rigorously'), suggests something a lot more ambitious. Nevertheless, the question needs to be asked: if the aim is to amplify the voice of the 'new secular spirituality' in Britain Yearly Meeting so *that it is no longer confined to the fringes*, should this be interpreted as a plea to *share* the centre ground with theism rather than replace theism altogether?

Whatever reassurances are offered, I fear we have to say No. Not only is the whole tone of the Introduction to *Godless* as militantly *anti*-theist as anything one could find in the writings of the 'new atheists', but Boulton also makes a distinction there between those who "simply ask for nothing more than *acceptance* of non-theism as part of the diversity of modern liberal and creedless Quakerism", and those who "hope to see a non-theistic understanding of human spirituality gradually *replace* traditional theism"[229] — leaving us to guess (not a difficult task) which one of these he favours. There is an air of inconsequence about the way the options are presented, rather as if one were being asked to choose between the white and the dark continental chocolates, but of course they are very different. The first group is quietist and, yes, *possibly* enriching, the second indisputably supplanting — but it should be noted that neither option rules out the other and both are grist to the mill.

---

[229] *ibid.*, p. 1 (my emphasis).

There is almost nothing reassuring for theists in 'Our Book'. We are given only the comforting suggestion, and that barely noticeable, that the process will be *gradual* and that it is *traditional* theism that is targeted. The tone of the book, however, is anything but gradualist; it is ebullient, urgent, impatient. Boulton concludes his Introduction with a clarion call to his readers to take the plunge! commit! identify! as if to be 'Godless' carries with it a reforming zeal from which the theist by nature or temperament is excluded:

> There is so much to do! So much in our divided, warring world, our atavistic religion, our polluted politics, our unexamined ways of thinking that we need to *subvert*! Where shall we find the society of rebels, agitators and outsiders, the partisan recruits to the underground army of subversion whose loyalty is pledged to the republic of heaven on earth? Who will choose to be Godless — for God's sake?[230]

A gesture in the direction of that 'underground army' lying side by side in Quaker burial grounds up and down the country — theists and mystics all — who spent their lives working for the abolition of slavery, votes for women and a world without nuclear weapons — would have been welcome here. Today we have the Framework for Action which is open to all, theists and non-theists alike. Friends have always been subversive.

It may be thought that by limiting the theism that supposedly needs replacing to *traditional* theism, Boulton is leaving the door open to newer theologies of theism that take account of the kind of objections that humanists feel are important. Part of the problem is that Boulton is very selective about defining his terms. What does he mean by '*traditional* theism'? What *are* the kinds of mysticism that can be better described as mystification? And what kinds of mysticism would *not* be swept away by 'the avowed humanist'? How can I be sure that what he means by 'the supernatural world' is what I mean? These are important questions. For example, a humanist might find Quaker

[230] *Godless,* p.17

ministry mystifying and even 'dangerous' if it is interpreted as a divine leading — perhaps "too dangerous to be ignored in the name of tolerance".

The more one delves into the literature the more evident it is that at least one section of the NFN envisages a future for Britain Yearly Meeting that few of us would recognise as Quakerism and that would force many of our current members, including many of those I have called 'seeker non-theists', out of the Society altogether. Creative visualisation or 'imaging' was a popular training technique in the eighties and nineties, believed to be particularly effective in setting long terms goals. In a talk to Friends who were celebrating the centenary of the 1895 Manchester Conference, Boulton asked his audience to picture a 21st century Society of Friends that "had come to embrace 'an expressionist, humanist or non-realistic religious faith', confident in the understanding that 'all religious faith — Catholic and Moony, Hindu and Native American, Rastafarian and Quaker, conservative and liberal — is created in human culture and by human imagination, matured in human history and celebrated in human language and human community'; that 'religious values are wholly human'; and that 'we must learn to get along without an absolute referent'". Here there can be no misunderstanding. This is a vision of the Society's future that is humanistic, secular and dedicated to the 'closed reading of immanence'. It is a vision in which the new colour added to the Quaker rainbow has finally supplanted all the rest.

More recently, following the launch of the NFN, and in the lead-up to Yearly Meeting 2014, the dream has changed. The new vision is of a Society of Friends "where committed Christians, Universalists, Jews, Buddhists, theists, post-theists, non-theists and religious humanists joyfully accept their theological and ideological differences, sharing their truths, listening to and respecting each other, and finding heresy only in any form of dogmatic assertion."[231] Tolerance of committed Christians and theists has now succeeded intolerance of all that an "an avowed humanist would sweep away". There is only the

---

[231] Boulton, *Quaker Voices* (July, 2014), p. 6.

uncertainty of what is meant by the prohibition on "any form of dogmatic assertion" — another undefined expression. Clarifying what one means by these kind of terms is essential to any intelligent wider discussion of the issues. Since committed Christians and theists are likely to advocate belief in a transcendent (and immanent) God as an article of faith, the insertion of this last clause is puzzling, and one might question whether the prohibition would apply equally to the assertion of a 'religious' belief in a 'No God'? "I have a dream!" Boulton writes. But what has happened to the dream announced at the centenary of the Manchester Conference — the 'wholly humanist' dream? Has it been put on the back burner until the times are more auspicious, or is this a permanent change in which we can confidently place our trust?

In *The Trouble with God*, we are told that Cupitt has argued consistently for the view that "the last stage in the historical evolution of religion is universal religious humanism, and the last ethic is humanitarianism". This is certainly an uncompromising, panoramic and ambitious claim, but in Cupitt's case we can take some comfort from the knowledge that it is all a long way in the future. After all, the Church of England to which he belongs is a vast organisation, and despite its current difficulties is well provided with able theologians, philosophers, scientists and historians who can be relied upon to slow the process up or overturn it altogether. Boulton's task, as he himself has indicated, is altogether more manageable. We are a small organisation, highly permeable, not so well defended intellectually and (as already noted) given to re-writing our 'scripture' every thirty years. The whole thing could be over, done and dusted within a decade or two — we have only to look at the fate of the US Unitarians!

The story of this hapless community is one which Boulton found so "entertaining" that it appears in at least two of his books, although, he admits (one senses a chuckle), it might not seem quite so entertaining if you happen to be a Unitarian! He tells the story not in his own words but in those of the humanist historian and propagandist, Nicolas Walter:

> Having discarded the second and third persons of the Trinity, they discarded the first person too, replacing supernaturalism and theism with naturalism and humanism. Although they ceased to believe in God, they continued to call themselves religious, and mostly to count themselves as Unitarians, but increasingly to adopt the term *Humanism*. Between the two world wars, about one-tenth of the Unitarian denomination became Humanists, and there was a danger of a schism between "God Men" and "No God Men"; but first the Humanists began to leave, and then the "God Men" began to adopt Humanism as well.[232]

It took only 10% of the Unitarian membership to espouse humanism for the church to go into freefall. It is not known how many Friends and attenders would actually describe themselves as 'non-theist', but with only 58% professing to believe in God, and 14.5% declaring themselves to be convinced non-believers, the dangers are obvious. Not all the remaining 27% would position themselves on the humanist side of the Taylor-Boulton fault line, but if only a few were to cross that line, and as we have seen, the number of believers is falling year by year, the Society would certainly, in Tony Stoller's words, be "at risk". We may feel heartened by the sense of unity and the depth of worship at Yearly Meeting in 2015, but these figures tell their own story. "Boldly embracing non-theism", Boulton warns, "would certainly change the Society. It would be foolish to pretend otherwise. And change can be uncomfortable, especially for those who love the Society as it is, with all its funny ways . . .". Let us look now at some of these 'funny ways' and how 'boldly embracing non-theism' may cause them to disappear.

Non-theism and 'the Quaker Way'

Not voting in our business meetings undoubtedly qualifies as one of our 'funnier ways' as we are the only Christian denomination that

---

[232] *The Trouble With God*, p. 180. For 'entertaining', see *Real Like Daisies*, p. 62.

has this prohibition. Yet it is more than a mere idiosyncracy, being integral to our faith and the way in which it came into being. This is clearly illustrated in the following passage from *Quaker Faith and Practice*:

> Our method of conducting our meetings for church affairs is an experience which has been tested over three hundred years. In days of hot contest and bitter controversy the early Friends, knit together by the glorious experience of the Holy Spirit's guidance in all their affairs, came into a simple understanding of how their corporate decisions should be made. (*QFP*, §3.04)

Rather than being guided by human judgement alone, we have placed our trust in the power of the Spirit to lead us forward and set us on the right path, a process we know as 'discernment'. Key to this is our corporate experience of worship which involves waiting on God in the silence:

> In our meetings for worship we seek through the stillness to know God's will for ourselves and for the gathered group. Our meetings for church affairs, in which we conduct our business, are also meetings for worship based on silence, and they carry the same expectation that God's guidance can be discerned if we are truly listening together and to each other, and are not blinkered by preconceived opinions. It is this belief that God's will can be recognised through the discipline of silent waiting which distinguishes our decision-making process from the secular idea of consensus. We have a common purpose in seeking God's will through waiting and listening, believing that every activity of life should be subject to divine guidance. (*QFP,* §3.02)

Ben Pink Dandelion, in his little booklet, 'Celebrating the Quaker Way', defines discernment as "deciding what is of God and what is not". He says, "in a faith which claims God speaks to us directly, knowing what is of God is crucial and we require reliable access to that experience for guidance in daily life".[233]

Another reason for not voting is that for Quakers it is repugnant to impose the will of the majority on a minority. The majority may well be wrong, and the minority, even a minority of one, may be more reflective of a deeper spiritual truth than the majority, however well articulated their views. And a further reason is that we wish to avoid a situation where the more dominant voices prevail simply because they are more dominant. However, it would be wrong to suppose that these additional considerations are based primarily on secular values, such as democracy and social equality. We may be democratic to our fingertips, but we are not, in this context at least, concerned with either democracy or equality (values which one might argue are better protected by the vote) but with recognising in a spirit of love and trust what Love requires of us.

A valuable insight into the nature of the Quaker business method, from a Quaker-Christian point of view, is provided by Jill Segger, director of Ekklesia, a well known think tank on beliefs and values in public life. In 'Thought for the Week' in *The Friend*, she writes: "The Quaker business method is both antithesis and antidote to the prevalent political, professional and personal manner of decision making, which so often leaves bitterness in its wake. Where there is no lobbying and no voting, the confident cannot gain advantage over the diffident and the unforeseen stands on an equal footing with the expected. The voice that is instrumental in encapsulating the Spirit may be the least eloquent or articulate in terms of worldly debate. Here are the radical inversions so central to the teaching of Jesus and which have served us well for three and a half centuries, from Meeting for Sufferings to the ordering of the affairs of the smallest Local Meeting".[234]

A radically different view is offered by Stephen Burkeman in his reply to Segger's article a fortnight later. Burkeman points out that the

---

[233] Dandelion, *Celebrating the Quaker Way* (London: Quaker Books, 2009), p. 19.
[234] Segger, "The Quaker Business Method", *The Friend* (9th Dec., 2011), p. 3.

Quaker business method was a product of its time and predated our modern knowledge of individual and group psychology. Far from bolstering the unconfident, it exposes them to the tyranny of the group or conversely allows the more confident and articulate individuals to manipulate the group. He also suggests that it puts undue power into the hands of those experienced Friends who, being more familiar with Quaker ways, can quash dissent. "Unless one believes that, when they do, the quashing is by definition divinely inspired, then surely one must accept that this is potentially violent to the human spirit."[235] There could be no sharper contrast: on the one side, a meeting of hearts and minds in the fellowship of the Spirit, on the other, very modern concerns about manipulation and abuse of power.

Leaving aside Burkeman's own position (which is not given in his letter), Friends who take this view tend to identify with non-theism or some form of atheism. From their standpoint there is no other logical way of looking at the question. What possible reason could they have for not supposing that the same motivations that Segger drew attention to in the public arena would not predominate here too? To the non-theist or atheist, the notion of divine guidance is at best irrelevant and at worst a pietistic cover for those seeking dominance and control, all the more effective for being encrusted with three hundred and fifty years of carefully observed tradition. Indeed, holding these views, it would be difficult not to feel it one's moral duty to campaign actively *against* the Quaker business method and all it stands for. The discussion throws into sharp relief the rift or fault line between these two incompatible (even if we say, for the sake of diplomacy, 'non-adversarial') positions. If there is no God and therefore no divine guidance, then *without question* we should reject the Quaker business method and replace it with the vote. It would be unacceptable to think otherwise.

Yet I wonder if it has occurred to non-theist Friends that in bringing a contrary (and alien) belief system to bear on our decision-making process, they may be helping to create the very problems they

---

[235] Burkeman, *The Friend* (23rd/30th Dec., 2011), p. 22.

maintain are inherent in the process itself? For where there is no 'unity in essentials', and such radical differences in belief and experience, it will be increasingly difficult for the group to settle down to that deep place where "all may feel the power of God's love drawing us together and leading us". So the stage is set for all the old egoisms, alliances, rivalries and group interests to get to work beneath the surface in a way that would have been inconceivable in the not-so-distant past when mutual and absolute trust were qualities expected of everyone. Nor is it any use to say that all love is the same — what I call 'God's love', others may call 'wholly human love', for why should we trust our everyday human loves more in a Quaker business meeting than in, say, a board meeting of a charity like Oxfam? What leads us to think that Quaker secularism would be more spiritual or profound or worthy of our trust than any other secularism? Without a belief in the power of God's love to bring us into unity, there is no reason why we should be less subject to the human desire to manipulate and control than any other corporate entity.

Of course, if you don't believe in, or experience, the unifying power of Divine love, you must accept that the Quaker business method as practised over the past three hundred and fifty years has been a gigantic delusion, that generation after generation of Quakers have been living a delusion, and those of us who follow the Quaker way today are living a delusion too. The question of voting then arises. If it is not God's will that we are discerning but the will of the more dominant individuals in the group, then it can be argued that the only fair alternative is the vote.

The Quaker business method depends not only on belief in, or a relationship with, God, but in a God who is in some way personal. In another of his books, Pink Dandelion says: "When a majority of Quakers no longer believe in a God with a will, or a God at all, the traditional view that meetings for worship or church affairs sought to 'seek the will of God' would be wholly anachronistic. The erstwhile heretical question, "Why not vote?" would then be a legitimate query."[236]

It follows that campaigning for, or even *asserting,* non-theism in the Society is to call into question our traditional method of discernment (which is more than a method) and to replace it with another, perhaps like that outlined by Sarah Richards, a non-theist and mathematician. Although it involves something of a digression, I believe it is worth looking at Richards' proposal in detail as it illustrates some of the ways in which non-theist reconstructions of our discernment process, while designed to allay anxiety and overcome division, can facilitate the pragmatism and secular drift that now threatens the very basis of our religious life.

Richards likens 'waiting on the will of God' (our discernment process) to belief in a mathematical concept such as 'i' (the square root of -1) which she says does not really exist but is nonetheless mathematically important. Hence, she finds it "quite natural that there should be some concept, such as 'the will of God', which exists in the same way as the square root of minus one: it has no real existence" but nevertheless is useful as a concept which can yield helpful results. She also suggests that the "set of principles and values, which would comprise all the Quaker testimonies, as well as . . . human attributes such as compassion, love, fairness and so on' are what 'theists think of as the 'will of God'".[237]

Richards' pragmatic approach does no more than re-state the problems around discernment that we have already discussed. One can accept the functionality of the non-existent or imaginary number as grounded in mathematics, but what are her grounds for faith in the 'non-existent' will? If the discussion is about grounding values in "a way that works", what gives that way legitimacy in the absence of either a mathematical reference point or an actually existing Divine will? It may be argued that pragmatism is self-legitimating, making

---

236 Dandelion (ed.), *The Creation of Quaker Theory*, p. 231.
237 Richards, 'Quaker Discernment: A Non-Theist View' at: <http://www.non-theist-quakers.org.uk/nfn-articles.php>.

questions like these irrelevant, but the drift towards the pragmatic can only erode the foundations of our Testimonies which are observed and put into practice regardless of their effectiveness in terms of *Realpolitik*.

Although Richards doesn't use the word 'pragmatism', this is clearly what her 'way that works' is pointing towards. In choosing this path, she is giving discernment a philosophical basis that many would question. It is always unsafe for a religious group to nail its colours to the mast of a specific secular philosophy since all such philosophies are eventually superseded, but pragmatism is one of the worst from the point of view of religious truth. The Cambridge philosopher, G. E. Moore, for example, believed that pragmatism identified true beliefs with useful ones but pointed out that ideas of usefulness change over time. If Richards is advocating a philosophical basis for discernment that allows us to create our own values, what is to stop us creating new 'pragmatic' values when circumstances change? As Rowan Williams asked, why should we feel bound (he uses the word 'obligated') to values we ourselves create?[238]

Richards' method of discernment fails because it leaves the Testimonies and other Quaker 'principles and values' open to amendment on the basis of a secular judgement which can then only be fairly exercised by means of the vote. Alternatively it sets them in stone as an agreed standard from which we are afraid to deviate lest we sow division. Richards believes her system will work because Quaker principles and values are among the 'best', but then asks herself the question: "best in whose view, though, on what scale of judgement?" That indeed is the crucial question, yet surprisingly she leaves it unanswered. Why should the Quaker testimonies or the teachings of Jesus, the Buddha or Gandhi, or any other teachings from a religious source, be considered the 'best' if there is no absolute or

---

[238] Williams, *Dostoyevsky,* p. 235. His actual words are: "What makes Dostoyevsky so emphatically not a voluntarist at the end of the day, despite his intense commitment to the freedom of the will, is that he cannot see any possible way of saying simultaneously that we create value and that we are obligated to it."

universal standard by which they can be judged? Why not the teachings and values of Nietzsche, Foucault, Polly Toynbee or Sam Harris? After all, good secular arguments can be advanced against any or all of our Testimonies. Just to take the Peace Testimony, without that absolute standard or Inner Guide, what is there to prevent a slide towards the pragmatic, the rational weighing of all the factors involved in a particular international situation? Yet the Peace Testimony is clear and, in the best sense of the word, *dogmatic*: "The spirit of Christ, by which we are guided, is not changeable, so as once to command us from a thing as evil and again to move unto it".

If I have represented Richards' point of view correctly, what she is saying is that the non-theist's imagined will of God is just as effective, and effective *in the same way*, as the theist's will of God because in both cases they are actuated by the same 'divine' attributes of love, compassion, etc. Love is love, so why fall out over how we interpret it? If we are all obeying the promptings of love and truth in our hearts, does it matter if we trust them as the leadings of a real or a fictional God? Although there is some truth in this, there is a danger in so easily equating human with divine love, not because they are intrinsically different but because they are of a different order. Human love, the love between members of a voluntary service such as Oxfam, or the human compassion that prompts a group of likeminded people to take joint action in the cause of justice, can lead us in quite different directions as we consider what is best in a given situation. Here the pragmatic may take precedence over the traditional method of discernment and the formulation of what Quakers call a 'concern'. From a Quaker theist standpoint, the term 'will of God' means something more than acting within an awareness of our highest ideals, even those incorporated in our Testimonies. From the very start of the Quaker movement it has meant arriving at our decisions through the discipline of waiting on God inwardly and surrendering our egos to the Love which can teach and *transform*.

I am not arguing that non-theists don't have a place in the Society. As we have seen, many such Friends are sincere seekers who cannot with integrity (at this moment and perhaps ever) say they believe, or place their trust, in God. But others have made it clear they have no wish to be treated as 'seekers', having found to their complete satisfaction that the experience of being 'truly human' is all that is required to lead a good life. It is these Friends on the humanist side of the fault line who call into question the Quaker method itself and undermine its legitimacy — as indeed, holding these views, they should.

But in order to uphold the Quaker method, is it necessary to believe or place one's faith in a *personal* God? What about "aligning ourselves" with a "force for good" in the universe — something quite different from the God of theism? Well, for a start we would have to re-write (or eliminate) so many of those wonderful passages on discernment in *Quaker Faith and Practice* which would mean altering the very spirit they breathe. But let us look at what a supposed "force for good" implies. If we mean something more than the other forces in the universe — such as gravity and dark matter — and the word 'good' seems to suggest that we do — then there are a number of consequences. 'Good' is a moral, not a scientific term. It implies that there is moral purpose in the universe. However, we can't have a moral purpose on its own. To make sense it needs a moral agent. Good also implies love, and we can't have love without a lover and a beloved. And these — the moral and the loving — require some form of conscious way of being. The lover must know that It loves and what It loves, otherwise love is impossible. A "force for good" cannot therefore be impersonal — like a stone, or the force of gravity. In some way it must include the personal. Without the element of the personal, however difficult it is to conceive of that in relation to God, we are reduced to bringing our own wills into alignment with *an impersonal* force which logically and by definition can be neither moral nor loving.[239]

[239] Some idea of what this can mean is suggested by Keith Ward in the chapter on 'the personal ground of being' in his book, *God: a Guide for the Perplexed* (London: One World, 2003). Among others, he refers to the philosopher Schopenhauer who

To judge by the declarations of faith in 'Our Book', it is precisely in this area that non-theists have most difficulty in knowing what they really believe. For example, in one such case God is identified with the physical universe and we are told that the universe has a 'direction'.[240] However, there is no suggestion as to what 'direction' means in this context. Is it a *moral* direction or are we referring to the scientific *fact* that the entire universe (and therefore also 'God') is heading towards a state of entropy? The writer appears to be unsure on this point. She says, "I'm not sure that the universe cares. It seems more likely the universe is neutral, simply doing what it's doing", but then adds, "when we go along with the universe, things go better for us."[241] Although this sounds more positive, there is clearly no intentionality in it. The universe/God remains impersonal. I will come back to this question of the personhood of God in my next chapter.

Similar problems to those discussed earlier in relation to divine and human love, and the trust we can afford to each, occur with terms like 'connectedness' and 'connectivity' which some non-theist Friends want to substitute for the sense of dependence on God. Of course in the gathered meeting there is a sense of connectedness, but the traditional Quaker view is that this sense of connectedness, which can sometimes go very deep, is centred in our experience of the reality of God. If it is no more than the connectedness between human individuals who differ as personalities — and in power, presence and authority — then we are back to where we started in that earlier

---

"saw the whole universe as the tragic appearance of a blind striving of the will, a striving which leads inevitably to conflict, unhappiness and suffering"; and to Nietzsche "who looked forward to the advent of the superman, who would completely reject Christian values such as mercy and submissiveness, and incarnate in himself the pure will to power, in a life serene and pitiless, strong and free". In Nietzsche, as in Schopenhauer, God is understood as "the universal Will which is beyond good and evil, and for which ceaseless striving without a moral goal is the only reality." Ward warns: "This is what happens when the vision of transcendent Goodness is lost, and one sees only the struggle and suffering and the will to power of the universe itself as the final reality".

240 *Godless*, pp. 26-7.

241 *ibid.*

discussion. Why should we assume that our merely human connectedness will be any more effective in a Quaker business meeting than in any other corporate setting, if that is all we have to rely on? And when it turns out that relying solely on this we are no more successful than other groups of well-meaning people in restraining our individual egos, how long will it be before we replace mysticism with rationalism and opt for the vote?

By leaving God out of the equation, we risk losing yet more of our traditional practices. For example, the practice of standing when we speak in our business meetings. We stand not so that everyone can see us, or so we can hold forth better, but because we are ministering in the presence and (we hope) under the inspiration and guidance of the Spirit, setting aside our own egos and preferences — or at least trying to. The business meeting, it is often pointed out, is itself a Meeting for Worship. We would also lose the sense of being prayerfully upheld — so important to the clerk as she or he is drafting a minute. Nor would we have the same loyalty to the decision made, particularly if it reflected a view opposed to the one we voted for. The way would be open to lobbying and attempts to overturn a decision by means of a subsequent vote. Lastly, we would be acting 'in our own strength' and could not expect the empowerment and consistency of effort which comes with faith. Ultimately, we would be no different from any other charity — Oxfam again springs to mind.

The Quaker business method is just one of the 'funny ways' that "boldly embracing non-theism" would fundamentally change or cause to disappear from Quaker life. There are others which I don't have space for here, but that is the crucial one. The vote in Quakerism would be a vote against our traditional trust in God, and calls for its institution on this or that pretext are disingenuous. It would spell the end of the Religious Society of Friends as we know it, and on grounds which, compared to the deep and profoundly spiritual reasons for opposing it, are flimsy to say the least. Friends don't vote, but for very positive reasons — not because they wish to dominate or control but because of their trust in God and *hence* in one another. We don't have to choose between these different loyalties. With the Quaker process of discernment we have it all — connectedness with one another and unity in God.

> We are not for names, nor men, nor titles of Government, nor are we for this party nor against the other . . . but we are for justice and mercy and truth and peace and true freedom, that these may be exalted in our nation, and that goodness, righteousness, meekness, temperance, peace and unity with God, and with one another, that these things may abound.
>
> — Edward Burrough, 1659 (*QFP*, §23.1)

What has 'religious humanism' to offer?

The British Quaker Survey 2013 describes non-theist Friends as the least likely to self-describe as Christian, the least likely to pray, the least likely to serve as Clerk, the least likely to apply for membership, the more likely to see Meeting for Worship in terms of thinking, the more likely to see the Quaker Business Method in terms of consensus and not as seeking the will of God, and the more likely to believe that violence can be morally justified. From a Quaker point of view there is little here that is positive, little that non-theism, as such, has to offer the Society. But if that is the situation as it stands at present, what would a future non-theist, and more, specifically, *humanist* non-theist, Society of Friends look like?

By 1995 the failure to establish an "avowedly religious humanist organisation in Britain" was giving leading figures in the Sea of Faith Movement serious cause for concern. One might have thought that the Sea of Faith organisation itself met this requirement but clearly the leadership was now hoping for something more ambitious, more visionary. So, as a kind of thought-experiment, let us suppose that their hopes are met in full and that they have succeeded in creating such an organisation out of the physical remains of the Religious Society of Friends. We are immediately faced with two questions: (1) how viable will such a project be in the longer term? and (2) what can it offer the secular world that the secular world doesn't already have in abundance?

The answer to the first question is, Not really viable at all. We are told in *The Trouble With God* that since the 1950's the history of "modernist or realist religious humanism . . . has been one of slow decline and *diversification.*"[242] Boulton goes on to express the hope that this outmoded brand of humanism will soon be replaced by a radical religious humanism which is *post*-modernist and *non*-realist. But the unanswered question then is: 'Why should postmodernism and non-realism do any better?' Postmodernism is more likely to act as a spur to diversification, and non-realism, even if widely accepted, has no binding power in itself. In any case, is it not the declared aim of the NFN to *strengthen* Quaker diversity? Strengthening diversity can only lead to further 'diversification', and since Boulton promotes diversity as providing the perfect conditions for *growing* the new humanism, it would seem there is no more hope of longer term success this time round than there was in the 1950s.

Turning to the second question, a major problem facing all humanism is that it is obliged to define itself negatively and reductively in relation to religion but cannot do so without at the same time dissolving itself in the wider culture. What is special about religion is reduced to the secular and the ordinary. Boulton himself provides the perfect examples. Prayer, he says, is no more than "talking to ourselves", seeking the will of God is "simply looking for the best course, in the best interest of all", asking for forgiveness and following the light of our conscience is only to express "our desire to be better people", working for the Kingdom is "taking action to make the world a better place".[243] When all the religious categories have been dismantled in this way what is there left of religion in 'religious

242 *The Trouble With God*, p. 191. My emphasis.

243 See *Real Like Daisies*, pp. 65-6.

humanism' to distinguish it from any other humanism or secular thinking generally? What is to stop us from disappearing into the mainstream? It is rather like the problem facing the Labour Party. How do we defeat the Tories if the only strategy we have is to become more like them?

Boulton argues that it is the religious colouring itself that makes religious humanism an attractive option. We like the prayers, the hymns, the art, the music, the liturgy . . . but reject what they stand for. So we continue to pray, to seek the will of God, to ask for forgiveness, etc. but only as a form of 'make-believe'. We know it's objectively false, but we can enjoy it in much the same way as we would a novel, a film or a soap opera. "This seems to me a telling insight into what may be happening when I, for instance, *attend and thereby participate* in a Quaker meeting for worship, or an Anglican or Catholic wedding or funeral service, or when I sing "Credo in unum Deum" in a Dent village choir performance of a Mozart mass".[244]

There are however a number of problems with this future scenario. Quite apart from the practical questions around the maintenance of a paid hierarchy and funding for church repairs — all for the benefit of a small nucleus of well educated disbelievers — there are deeper questions around our emotional responses to sacred music and art if what is being asked is that we detach ourselves entirely from the context in which they were created. Really to listen to sacred music opens up spiritual landscapes beyond anything words can utter and in which we totally participate rather than merely 'attend'. 'Suspending our disbelief' as we surrender to the heights and depths of Mozart's or Fauré's *Requiem* just won't hack it. To really understand and enjoy the emotional complexity and imaginative reach of such music — the transcendent coming to us as it did originally to the composers — we must be at least open to the possibility that the impulse which inspired them has some basis in reality. Art, sacred art, has the same effect. In the Greek Orthodox tradition, says Metropolitan Kallistos Ware, the icon "shows us God's closeness, his

[244] *The Trouble with God*, p. 213. My emphasis.

total involvement, his vulnerability. In the world but not of it, the icon bears witness to the nearness yet otherness of the Eternal. It introduces us to a world of mystery, yet at the same time we discover that this mystery is not far away, but is hidden within each one of us, closer to us than our own heart."[245] This is quite a good description of what takes place in Meeting for Worship when (to invert Boulton's phrase) we "participate and thereby attend".

Another difficulty is that a Quaker Meeting for Worship and an Anglican or Catholic mass are entirely different phenomena — at least where the externals of religion are concerned. One can understand a 'religious' humanist with, let us say, an Anglican background, wishing to preserve something of the beauty of church language, ritual, music, architecture and so on, because the Anglican Church has built up a treasury of these things over the centuries, and the humanist no less than the believer has come to cherish them; but what would be left of Quakerism to pick over once the inner reality and meaning of the faith had been removed? Our meeting houses are simple affairs, not very different in many cases from other houses in the same street. We sit on ordinary chairs or rough benches. We have no distracting images or pictures (despite having a wealth of artistic talent among our members). We have no liturgy other than our silent meetings. An Anglican service emptied of any profound or spiritual meaning might conceivably retain a nostalgic or historical interest for the few remaining 'Christian atheists' but how likely is it that a predominantly humanist Society of Friends would achieve even that level of commitment? How long before our silent meetings became lively discussion groups; before the discussion groups themselves broke up as different sub-groups went their different ways? What in fact would a religious humanist find in Meeting for Worship that would make him or her *want* to retain the religious form once the religious content had been 'disavowed'? My personal feeling is 'not very much'. Boulton's

---

245 Ware, "Preface" in Williams, *Ponder These Things: Praying with Icons of the Virgin Mary* (Norwich: The Canterbury Press), 2002, p. x.

own attitude to Meeting for Worship, I imagine, is fairly representative of humanist non-theists in general:

> I am not myself much at home with current Quaker-speak, with its "gathered meetings" and "centring down". I must confess that, while I treasure the memory of wonderful meetings empowered by the spirit (the wholly human spirit), it is rare that the experience matches the intensity of listening to great music (or singing in a choir), enjoying an inspired performance of Shakespeare, or sitting in a darkened cinema to watch *Priest* or *Wilde* or *Shine*. Our Sunday morning meetings are invaluable, but I believe it is what we do with the remaining 167 hours of the week which determines whether we are "in the life".[246]

The more I think about what Boulton is saying here the more convinced I am that the Religious Society of Friends is not safe in humanist hands. Humanist non-theism and the kind of pantheism that is itself a religious colouring for atheism are as dangerous to the future of Quakerism as Tory custodianship to the NHS. Indeed more so, for there would almost certainly be a speedy descent into anarchy:

> Some religious humanists will want to express their humanism within an existing religious tradition, others will want to separate themselves from traditional religious institutions. Some will want to devise non-theistic liturgies, some will be happy with liturgies in traditional God-language taken with lashings of metaphor and poetic licence, some won't want any liturgies or rituals at all, thank you very much.[247]

As Boulton says: "We know that we made it all, so we can unmake and remake it" (the definition of an idol is of something we make ourselves which we believe can help or save us). However, it is not the unfettered freedom to do as we like that is at issue here but the

---

[246] *Real Like Daisies*, p. 57.

[247] *ibid.*, pp. 63-4.

consequences for the future of the Society and its gift to the world at large. Even if it were possible to maintain some degree of unity in the face of such a confusing array of choices, Quaker simplicity provides very little of substance for the religious humanist to make or re-make. Once the spiritual heart of the meeting has been destroyed and the simple ritual of a circle of chairs and a bowl of flowers reduced to a charade, what further reason, religious or secular, should the Society have for existing? The answer, of course, is none; there is no future for Quakerism in a Quaker religious humanism — which is the same as saying there is no future for Quakerism in a humanistically-oriented non-theism. Modern humanistic non-theism has little that is positive to offer; it follows a *via negativa* of its own, defining itself not by what it is but by what it is not; and when it does attempt to define itself in positive terms it merges with the secular and gradually disappears from view.

For Boulton, faith in the real presence of the Holy Spirit is on a par with the kind of comic-strip superstitions he describes as "misty-mystical, gaseous, aromatic, Eastern . . ." In language that is bordering on the derisive he tells us that "for humanists, religious or secular, transcendental spiritualities will have little appeal" — they are "at best meaningless and at worst dangerous".[248] There is no reason to believe, despite the over-riding requirement to ensure the continued acceptance of the NFN, that his views on this particular point have changed; for what is radical about radical religious humanism is its *total* negation of that which theism affirms.

In my next and final chapter I will try to open a window to the other side of the Taylor-Boulton faultline where theists and some non-theists share in a fellowship that finds self-sacrificial love and ultimate meaning in the very transcendence that the humanist represents as absurd, authoritarian and cruel. For these are not complementary or mutually interpenetrative truths. Here we are dealing with polarities of interpretation and feeling that one would normally expect to find in two free-standing, quite separate institutions. No-one has traced this

[248] See, for example, *The Trouble with God*, p. 214.

fundamental rift in our culture more sensitively, more fairly and with greater scholarly insight than Charles Taylor:

> Exclusive humanism closes the transcendent window, as though there were nothing beyond. More, as though it weren't an irrepressible need of the human heart to open that window, and first look, and then go beyond. As though this need were the result of a mistake, an erroneous world-view, bad conditioning, or worse, some pathology. Two radically different perspectives on the human condition.[249]

---

[249] Taylor, *A Secular Age*, p. 638.

12

Theism — the sovereignty of Love

i thank You God for most this amazing
day: for the leaping greenly spirits of trees
and a blue true dream of sky; and for everything
which is natural which is infinite which is yes
(i who have died am alive again today,
and this is the sun's birthday; this is the birth
day of life and of love and wings: and of the gay
great happening illimitably earth)
how should tasting touching hearing seeing
breathing any — lifted from the no
of all nothing — human merely being
doubt unimaginable You?
(now the ears of my ears awake and
now the eyes of my eyes are opened)

— *e.e. cummings*

ON THE BLURB of Michael Hampson's book, *God Without God*, we read: "the God the atheist denies is not the God that people of true faith affirm. Take away the God defined by the atheist — the arbitrary wrathful king — and the western spiritual tradition not only survives, it flourishes". The "arbitrary, wrathful king" is exactly how David Boulton defines God in *The Trouble With God*. There he conjures up the picture of "an omniscient and omnipotent being cracking his metaphysical whip, commanding this and forbidding that, rewarding here, punishing there" — an image which had come to seem "terrifying or disgusting, neurotic and spiritually alienating."[250] Since he presents no alternative understandings of God and theism, either here or in the two books written specifically for a Quaker audience, we have to assume that the monster thus portrayed is the God whom he believes theist Friends are in the habit of worshipping — or perhaps the God from whom he feels they need to be rescued. In *Godless for God's Sake*, he goes further and imagines a God who is responsible for all the present troubles in the world; who by virtue of his function as Transcendent and Ultimate Authority justifies oppression and terror; who is the source of self-righteous, dogmatic, cultural arrogance, who is, moreover, a disapproving and monstrously controlling parent who "knows what is best for us; [so] that we obey or disobey . . . at our peril". "That's theism", he says, "and it's high time we recognised it for what it is: our problem, rather than our salvation".[251]

Boulton would later perform a complete volte face and say that theism and non-theism "need not be adversarial viewpoints but may be seen as different ways of seeking, finding and expressing meaning and purpose" and that it enriches the Society to celebrate a radical diversity that allows both sets of belief to exist side by side. In the previous chapter we considered whether this was a genuine change of heart or tactical reassurance at a time when the new Non-theist Friends Network was needing to establish itself. Words like 'seeking', 'finding', 'meaning' and 'purpose' may have a calming effect on Friends' nerves but what do they really concede in this context? What does such reassurance really amount to? A genuine change of heart would set out its reasons and discriminate between the different theisms. Instead, *Godless for God's Sake*, with its blanket condemnation of theism *per se*, continues to be promoted by the NFN as 'Our Book' and in my own Area Meeting is treated as a spiritual text for study, reflection and outreach.

[250] *The Trouble with God*, p. 196.
[251] *Godless for God's Sake*, pp. 10-11.

The Sovereignty of Love

There are, of course, other models of theistic belief that are neither cruel nor frightening nor spiritually alienating. Where Boulton refers to a politically dangerous and intellectually oppressive 'Ultimate Authority' and Hampson to 'the arbitrary, wrathful king', the fourteenth century mystic, Julian of Norwich, refers to the Sovereignty of Love. It was natural for someone living at that time to draw on the notion of kingship to express the sovereignty of a quality valued above all others. If Love is the supreme value, then God is the supreme being since God is perfect Love. But this is a different kind of 'supremacy', one without the negative associations that in our present-day culture cling to our ideas about inequality and power. For a start, such a 'king' or 'sovereign' could not be arbitrary or wrathful:

> Hence to the soul that seeth so far forth into the high marvellous goodness of God as to see that we are endlessly oned to him in love, nothing could be more impossible than that God should be wroth. For wrath and friendship are two contraries. He that layeth and destroyeth our wrath, and maketh us meek and mild — we must needs believe that he is ever, in the same love, meek and mild; which is contrary to wrath. [252]

Despite the social context in which she is writing, all of Julian's effort goes into expressing the revelation of God's *love* rather than defining God in relation to some earthly hierarchy. This can be seen in the way she makes free with titles, sometimes calling Christ 'our Lord' and sometimes 'Mother', and similarly with the Holy Spirit which at different times takes on the mantle of the Christ and the Father. In the well-known twelfth Revelation, she abandons all names and titles to emphasise the mystery that is 'it':

---

[252] From the 49th chapter of *The Revelations of Divine Love of Julian of Norwich* (tr. J. Walsh. London: Burns & Oates, 1961), p. 129.

Oftentimes our Lord said:

> I it am, I it am; I it am that is highest; I it am that thou lovest; I it am that thou likest; I it am that thou servest; I it am that thou longest; I it am that thou desireth; I it am that thou meanest; I it am that is all; I it am that Holy Church preacheth and teacheth thee; I it am that shewed myself to thee here.
>
> The number of his words passeth beyond my wits, and all my understanding, and all my powers; and they are the highest, as I see it. For therein is comprehended — I cannot tell what: except that the joy I saw in the shewing of them passeth all that heart can think or soul could desire.

She describes the Trinity as the interaction of three "properties in God" — life, love and light — all seen "in one goodness", reminding us that church dogmas are themselves ways of seeing, and are better not discarded but interpreted afresh for each generation. If I had to summarise her theology and her theism it would be with reference to her threefold understanding of Charity: "Charity unmade is God: charity made is our soul in God: charity given is the virtue. And that is a gracious gift, in the working of which we love God for himself and ourselves in God and all that God loveth, for God."

The dictatorship of a human king, therefore, is not to be compared with the over-mastering power of Love. For who would not willingly submit to "Charity unmade" if it led to "charity made" and then to "charity given" — that is, social action and kindness to others? What Julian is describing is the sacrament of the Eucharist which was never abandoned by Friends but 'internalised' in the shared silence of our meetings. If we are to interpret her words for our own time, they would mean that the reality of God is not to be understood in terms of an 'Ultimate Authority' in a hierarchy of authorities, but in the soul loving itself in God and spreading that love to others in the worshipping group and beyond. *That is theism*, or more properly 'theistic mysticism', and if 'salvation' means 'making whole', it is also our salvation. Nor is it in any sense 'our problem' — if there is a problem with this form of theism it is how to prevent ourselves placing obstacles in its way and in effect refusing the gift of life, love and light that is offered to us.

God as Energy and God as Person

Theism, says Dean Inge, means belief in God. But, he adds, "there is no unanimity about the attributes of God." [253] In other words, one can be a theist and believe a whole number of things about God. William James makes the same point in *The Will to Believe*, but maintains that there are still some attributes that must be regarded as essential. "First", he says, "it is essential that God be conceived as the deepest power in the universe; and, second, he must be conceived under the form of a mental personality." Moreover, the aspect of personality must be thought of as "lying outside our own and other than us, — a power not ourselves". He would therefore have disagreed with Cupitt's 'expressivist' view of God which sees God as included in love — our human love — rather than the other way round. He was aware that in mystical experience God was to be found within us, but maintained that that did not make God and the human subject one.[254]

But what of 'personality'? James understood that without the aspect of personality, without consciousness or purpose, there could be no mutual recognition or 'consanguinity', no mystical 'union', no love. God would be reduced to an impersonal energy or force which had as much to do with us humans as the energy given off by a distant star. Rachel Britton puts it well in her article "God as Energy and God as Person":

> It is no good saying vaguely that the God-force "is positive". In relation to impersonal energies, that has no meaning except in the

[253] Inge, 'Theism', *Philosophy* 23, 84 (1948), p. 38.

[254] See James, *The Will to Believe* (NY: Dover Publications, 1956 [1897]), p. 135.

sense that one end of a battery "is positive". No force is in all circumstances good for us. All can be destructive as well as beneficial. Where they are of benefit, there is no intention in it. We may have a relationship, a response to, such forces, but they have no relationship or response to us. If these were the only valid metaphors for God, we would be in precisely the same state of desolation in the universe as if there were no God at all. We would be random happenings swept by powerful forces which neither know nor care about us.[255]

When words like Light, Fire, Power, Energy and Force are used as metaphors for God, they can have great value: "they suggest vastness and universality as opposed to calling up an image of something as small and bounded as ourselves. They give the soul room to breathe". But, she insists, we need personal language too: "if ever we feel, in Meeting for Worship or in our own private experience, that our deepest longings are in some way met and answered, or even something given us to draw us in a certain direction, then the metaphor of the personal acquires value":

> . . . our experience of God is not all about awe and worship of the immensely Other. It is also an experience of being summoned and led, being welcomed and fulfilled, of meeting and merging with the divine in our own depths which we must in some way have a likeness to. All this aspect of experience can only be represented in personal terms.

Britton is at pains to emphasise that God is not a person like us — and certainly not a great Person in the sky; but the person, she says, "is the richest metaphor we have for God, because only the person is conscious, is self-aware, only the person can know and love persons, can discern truth or have purposes". Without that sense of the Ultimate Reality being "the source of our desire to love, to be just, to heal rather than afflict, then we could trust no testimonies [but] only look at the world and despair".

---

255 Britton, from a talk to Colchester Friends (unpublished). See Appendix B for the complete text..

So both the impersonal and the personal are metaphors, metaphors for something real. The question then arises, if that Ultimate Reality is *ineffable* how can metaphor of any kind say anything about it? I guess her reply to this would be that the metaphors in question are not arbitrary or poetic inventions but *responses* to the activity of the Spirit which can be known and felt deep within us. Metaphor and analogy, as I suggested in Chapter 8, are some of the ways in which language can engage with and illuminate that which lies beyond it. The importance of this insight has been highlighted by Rowan Williams in the Gifford Lectures (November 2013), now published as *The Edge of Words.*[256]

Experience and transcendence

In *Real Like Daisies*, Boulton hails William James as one who along with Darwin and others "dealt mortal blow after blow to the old transcendence model."[257] So far as James is concerned, the exact opposite appears to be the case (and even with Darwin the question is by no means settled[258]). In his book, *The Will to Believe*, James' insistence on the duality of God and humankind (and therefore the creation) presses the case for transcendence further than many modern theologians who have attempted to reconcile the supra-natural with monism would wish to take it. As we have seen, although he believed that in contemplation it was possible to have an authentic experience of God, he refused to believe that the experience made God and the human subject one:

---

[256] See above, pp. 131-3

[257] *Real Like Daisies*, pp. 15, 40. The idea that transcendence is an *outdated* concept is a nonsense. It is only thought to be so within a particular construction of European history since the Enlightenment, such as that propounded by Cupitt in *The Sea of Faith*.

[258] See, for example, J. David Pleins, *The Evolving God: Charles Darwin on the Naturalness of Religion* (New York and London: Bloomsbury, 2013), pp.107-10.

> This consciousness of self-surrender, of absolute practical union between one's self and the divine object of one's contemplation, is a totally different thing from any sort of substantial identity. Still the object God and the subject I are two. Still I simply come upon him, and find his existence given to me; and the climax of my practical union with what is given, forms at the same time the climax of my perception that as a numerical fact of existence I am something radically other than the Divinity with whose effulgence I am filled.[259]

It is true that James was not always as clear as this. His attitude towards the transcendent was complex, personal and exploratory. Boulton presents him as a resolute defender of what I earlier called 'the closed reading of immanence' when in fact he was an enthusiastic champion of the 'open reading'. In his 'Postscript' to the *Varieties of Religious Experience*, written some years later, he gives credence to the idea that "beyond each man and *in a fashion continuous with him* there exists a larger power which is friendly to him and to his ideals."[260] 'Beyond' and 'continuous': the boundary is unclear, and he was never quite able to resolve it. But he was not an atheist, and certainly not a non-realist. As he says in his lectures on pragmatism, "when I tell you that I have written a book on men's religious experience, which on the whole has been regarded as making for the reality of God, you will perhaps exempt my own pragmatism from the charge of being an atheistic system."[261] Although in these lectures he does attack Platonic and Hegelian ideas of the Absolute, these are

---

[259] James, *ibid.*, p. 135.

[260] James, *The Varieties of Religious Experience,* p. 525 (my emphasis). In fairness to Boulton, it ought to be mentioned that James, also in the 'Postscript', questions the notion of "one all-inclusive God" — but only in order to make room for the dualistic concept of a *possible* polytheism. With regard to non-realism, he explicitly rejects the suggestion that he denies "the existence of realities outside the thinker" or ignores the part the real object plays in deciding what ideas are true. See *Letters*, 2, p. 295.

[261] James, *Pragmatism* (ed. Bruce Kuklick. Indianapolis: Hackett Publishing, 1981 [1907]), p. 133.

certainly not the words of someone intent on hammering each and every manifestation of the transcendent.

When we speak of God's transcendence we mean God's reality considered apart from the material universe which nevertheless bears the imprint of the Creator and in that sense may be thought of as 'divine'. The 'opposite' term, 'immanence' — not a true opposite — may be thought of as God's Presence in the creation or, in Christian doctrine, as the action of the Holy Spirit within us. For a pantheist, however, it represents the identity of God with the universe itself; and for a non-theist like Boulton it is the only possible way to think about God — as an entity which has no existence outside the human mind. For Boulton, as I have argued throughout this book, transcendence is the key sticking point. It is a concept that he attacks at every turn, including its most minimal expression as 'the something more', if we mean by this more than the 'wholly human'. Any attempt at compromise with a non-theism which involves the idea of that 'something more' is bound to be rejected.

In his essay on theism, Inge points out that "immanence, as opposed to [complete] identification [of God with nature], *implies* transcendence". Most theists today would agree that God must be perceived as both transcendent *and* immanent; both are necessary if God is to be in any sense knowable, but here I want to emphasise the importance of transcendence in particular as being fundamental to any definition of theism and the *sine qua non* of religious mysticism.

Because Friends speak of the 'Inner Light' and 'God within', it is often assumed that the Quaker way of thinking about God involves a denial of God's transcendence.[262] Nothing could be further from the truth. Early Friends like Robert Barclay went out of their way to correct any such misunderstanding: "Because we have earnestly

---

[262] Boulton ascribes this belief even to George Fox, with a rather flippant reference to Fox's "radical understanding of God as more inner light than outer superman", a claim which can only be sustained by an anachronistic application of the term 'radical'. See Patrick Nugent, "Response to Papers on Theism (Just a Little) and Non-Theism (Much More)", in *Quaker Religious Thought* 118 (Jan., 2012), *passim.*

desired people to sense the presence of God in and near themselves, they have maliciously inferred that we deny God, except that of him that is within us. But what we have really been trying to tell them is that their notion of God as being beyond the clouds will be of little use to them if they cannot also find him near them". But in whatever way Friends choose to think about these issues today, when we look at their descriptions of personal or corporate religious experience we find that the transcendent is taken for granted. Many of these descriptions speak of being 'held' or 'enfolded' in love. Here is Diana Lampen's experience.

> At the very lowest, darkest moment of my life, as I sat by the broken body of my mother, who was dying after a car accident, when I cried out from the depths of my anguish and helplessness, I had the deepest, most profound experience of my life. It was of both us being held in a love beyond measure; of a peace 'beyond all understanding'; of a sense of joy and a certainty that 'all is well'.[263]

A humanist, while no doubt sympathising with the writer's situation, will be inclined to dismiss this as a delusion brought on by desperate need. Others will be more positive and accepting since it will have a number of features in common with experiences they know about from other sources or may have undergone themselves. Here, I want to focus on just one of these features. The sense of being 'held' or 'enveloped' is an important part of the experience as it suggests a transcendent dimension which is denied by the religious sceptic. One can only be 'held' or 'enveloped' by someone or something which in some sense is outside or beyond oneself. What is interesting is that it is not always the case that the person undergoing the experience, the person being 'held', has a particular or obvious need of being comforted, and when essentially the same experience requires multiple explanations in order to dismiss it as a delusion, one may feel that

---

[263] D. Lampen, "A Mystery", *The Friend* (29th March, 2013), p. 3.

something is being missed.[264] To illustrate this I have selected three further examples of theistic mystical experience, one Catholic and two Quaker, each coming from a distinctly different standpoint. The first is from the Catholic theologian, Janet Martin Soskice, in conversation with Rupert Shortt, a religious affairs editor on the *Times Literary Supplement*.

> I'm somewhat timid about saying this, but I am one of those people who then had quite a dramatic religious experience which led to conversion. It didn't seem to come from anywhere — I hadn't been talking to anyone or knowingly thinking about it — but it seemed to me powerfully that it was an experience of God . . . *It was like being wrapped in an enormous loving mystery*: I had a terrific sense of presence . . . but a presence to whom I could speak. We have a notion, we learn it from Bible stories in our children's illustrated Bibles, that God speaks to people, but what's startling is feeling you're in the presence of a God to whom you need to speak back. But it wasn't with words. I didn't hear words. I didn't see anything . . . but somehow the sense of being addressed was very strong and something to which I felt I could respond.[265]

The second example is from an account by Elizabeth Barnett, a Quaker; it describes what happened to her as she lay recovering in a hospital bed, after giving birth to her first child — and before anyone should even think it, *without* medication:

> I knew (as if I were seeing and physically feeling it) that we are all inherently and inextricably connected to each other. That so called 'universal brotherhood' (or sisterhood) is not merely an ethical objective, but an absolute reality. That 'love thy neighbour' is not just a moral precept we should try to live by, but a fundamental principle

264 An opposite, but no less valid point, is made by John Stuart Mill; "Objections which apply equally to all evidence are valid against none". Quoted in D. Elton Trueblood, *The Trustworthiness of Religious Experience* (London: George Allen & Unwin, 1939), p.25.

265 Shortt, *ibid.*, p. 25. My italics.

> of creation, the ignoring of which is just as destructive to our essential being as the ignoring of the principle of gravity can be to our physical existence. It was as if I felt in my physical being that connected-ness, that one-ness with all others and all that is, which if I think about it today I cannot even begin to imagine. Yet for a precious and golden moment I knew it with the certainty of my own breathing. *And beyond all that is — infinitely greater than, yet surrounding and permeating — was the spirit of God.* So that if I were asked to give my definition of God now, I would say that God is my address. God is that *within which* I live and move and have my being, and where I can meet all others in recognition and safety.[266]

My third and last example describes what Friends often refer to as a 'gathered' or 'covered' meeting. The truly gathered meeting has never been common, but it is nowadays such a rare event that it is possible that the majority of Friends and attenders have never experienced one. The following account is taken from Richenda Scott's 1964 Swarthmore Lecture:

> . . . the stirrings of a new and deeper life are felt stealing across the consciousness, *laying hold of us, enfolding us*, until we find, in wonder and joy and adoration, that it can unite us with the source of its being in God. The spoken words of ministry or prayer arising from the depths of such worship are fresh and spontaneous, bearing the fragrance of the newly-picked flower which has not passed through other men's hands, stamped with the authenticity of that which has been seen and known. *The veil between the worshipper and worshipped is drawn aside, and we are taken anew into the mystery of God's love and self-giving to us*; in that revelation we are broken and re-made, cleansed and renewed. Yet, in the moment of communion we do not stand alone before God. We are then most vividly aware of the one divine life flowing through all and in all, drawing us together in a unity which runs below and beyond all divisions or strife of opinion,

266 H. Gillman and A. Heron (eds.), *Searching the Depths: Essays on being a Quaker Today* (London: Quaker Home Service, 1996), pp. 12-13. My italics.

enlarging and enriching the individual vision as we share the full realization of God's presence with us.[267]

What all three accounts have in common is that, like Diana Lampen's, they are reported from an essentially theistic standpoint. In each case, God is experienced as a transcendent ('enfolding') presence, and at the same time as active within our deepest selves — active in ways which are positively and enduringly transforming. Soskice's experience brings out the personal nature of the relationship with God, the 'I — Thou' of Martin Buber, the Jewish theologian who emphasised the importance of the relation between self and personal other and its radical difference from that between self and impersonal object ('I — it'). Barnett's experience extends that vision outward, so that personhood (the 'I — Thou' of 'love thy neighbour') is understood as "a fundamental principle of creation" linking all of humankind and, through the personhood of God, all that is.[268]

So what of the third example, the gathered meeting? Here it is the group, not the individual alone, which 'stands before God'. One could say that the gathered meeting is the gold standard of Quaker worship. If the 'humble learner in the school of Christ' is seeking anything at all, it is surely that "new and deeper life" which "can unite us with the source of its being in God." The difference between this and the previous accounts is that the gentler experience of the 'still

---

[267] R. Scott, *Tradition and Experience*, pp. 19-20. My italics.

[268] It is a vision that links her to the medieval mystic, Nicholas de Cusa, now being rediscovered as theology's response to the current global ecological crisis. In de Cusa, transcendence and immanence are intimately linked: it is God's self-manifestation in nature that produces immanence and God's presence that characterises the relation between God and nature. This is seen as offering a more promising vision of the world than much contemporary 'stewardship theology', and as well as meeting the charge that Christianity is essentially hierarchical in its attitude to nature, goes some way towards meeting the concerns of feminist critics by de-emphasising the mind-body dichotomy which is said to be at the root of traditional Christian attitudes to sexuality. It is anxieties like these that have pushed forward the anti-Christian and non-theist agenda and yet the solutions are much closer to hand than we sometimes realise.

small voice of calm' in the gathered or 'covered' meeting is available to all, provided there is a sufficient core of Friends present who are spiritually experienced and able to carry the meeting with them 'into a deep place'. As *Quaker Faith and Practice* says (2.67), "to some are granted deeper spiritual discoveries and revelations than to others, but to all, waiting in expectancy, at moments and in some measure is given a sense of the living touch of God."

I have chosen these three descriptions of individual and corporate religious experience not because they are representative of religious experience in general (I suspect they are comparatively rare) but in order to point to the 'otherness' of the experience, the strong sense of an enfolding or sustaining Presence that has always accompanied them. It is this sense of Presence that is the basis of Quaker theism, however it may be represented in the writings of those who would dismiss it as a delusion. It is not confined to Quakers, of course, nor to these more dramatic moments in people's spiritual lives. Referring to the millions of men and women throughout history who have experienced God as a secret, gentle Presence, D. Elton Trueblood, in his Swarthmore lecture (1939), says "in prayer and worship, whether at stated times or in the midst of everyday duties, they have been acutely conscious of Another who has sustained them in life's darkest as well as life's brightest moments".[269] It is the strong or gentle Presence of that Other making itself known in the subjective inner experience, in the depths of the soul, that vindicates belief in God as "a present reality, the Divine Companion".

It is of course possible to 'explain away' any mental phenomenon as illusion, even the most convincing. It is quite possible to have what is called a 'peak experience', for example of the kind described as a feeling of oneness with nature, and interpret it in purely psychological or even neurological language. It is possible — the philosopher A.J. Ayer is a case in point — to have an experience that is felt to be a direct experience of God and yet interpret it in the same positivistic manner, having no other than a materialist framework *in*

[269] Trueblood, p.12.

which to interpret it. Barnett's experience could be explained as a natural reaction to hormonal changes following childbirth, George Fox's as the expression of a 'psychopathic' personality, the crowds on Firbank Fell as an example of mass hysteria; and so on, until all are accounted for by one means or another.

Much of literature and art could be dismissed with the same bleak gesture. That there is a tendency in many literary critics to 'explain away' rather than 'mediate' the visions that so inspired their subjects has been noted by, among others, A.C. Bradley. Here is Bradley commenting on a passage from Wordsworth's *The Prelude*:

> The visionary feeling here has a peculiar tone; but always, openly or covertly, it is the intimation of something illimitable, over-arching or breaking into the customary 'reality'. Its character varies; and so sometimes at its touch the soul, suddenly conscious of its own infinity, melts in rapture into that infinite being; while at other times the 'mortal nature' stands dumb, incapable of thought, or shrinking from some presence.

He then says, "this feeling is so essential to many of Wordsworth's most characteristic poems that it may almost be called their soul; and failure to understand them frequently arises from obtuseness to it".[270] The point is that Bradley believes Wordsworth is onto something — something *real*. How can we be so powerfully affected by the visionary quality of the poem if we are not engaging with a reality that in our hearts we recognise as lying beyond our everyday awareness? This is the case with all good art. Two painters paint the same landscape. One reproduces the scene in front of him with great skill and photographic exactitude, but the other has captured not just the quality and tone of the light, and with it the mood of that particular hour of the day, but something much deeper, something that reaches beyond appearance — a sense of presence, the pulsations from

---

[270] Bradley, *Oxford Lectures on Poetry* (London: Macmillan, 1923), p. 134.

distant woods, the very *soul* of the landscape, which is felt to be connected to a mystery even larger.

If this is characteristic of the best in literature and art, and has parallels with other ways of knowing in philosophy, theology and the sciences, then it cannot be dismissed as delusional, nor as simply conjured up from the poet's or the artist's 'imagination' — as if imagination were not a power which penetrates to the reality of things (it was Shelley who said "a poem is the very image of life expressed in its eternal truth"). Earlier we saw how Polanyi thought of scientific discovery "as guided not so much by the potentiality of a scientific proposition as by an aspect of nature seeking realisation in our minds". In the same way, we see Bradley pointing beyond the mundane to "something illimitable . . . breaking into the customary reality" and being captured — as a potency or presence — in language; while the theologian and saint are alerting us to the 'initiating action of God', the pure act unencumbered by interpretation that leaves us "speechless" (without and beyond words). If this convergence means anything, it is surely that an idea which opens so many different doors is not a projection or fantasy but a true perception in which we can place all our trust.

But can we say with any certainty that this transcendent, empowering and unconditional Love is 'God'? Can we really identify the experience as an experience of God without having some prior notion of God — a notion of God which is itself constitutive of the experience? The non-theist will say 'No', the 'No' coming with varying degrees of emphasis depending on the beliefs of the non-theist. For Boulton, it will be a very decisive No since this is a God who is felt to exist "independently of our human consciousness encoded in human language", the God he defined as a 'lie'. As a non-realist he would say that our presuppositions about God are *wholly* constitutive of the experience, differing in this from the critical realist who would say they are only partly so — that for both the scientist and the religious seeker the reality we experience can alter our prior conception of it. The more mystical non-theist, on the other hand, will see Love ('cosmic love') as an impersonal force, but will then be left with the problem of explaining how one can have 'Love' and purpose without consciousness. There is indeed little difference between that position and atheism, for as seekers we may well be open to the possibility of transcendence, but unless we subscribe to the notion of "the supernatural in nature" (an oxymoron) we must accept the verdict of Kołakowski: "Naturalistic pantheism or the attempt to shift on to Nature certain divine properties — purpose-orientated change, providential wisdom, creativity . . . hardly differs, save in phraseology, from an outright atheism (to say that the world is God amounts to saying there is no God, as Hobbes aptly remarked)".[271]

To illustrate the dilemma confronting the *mystical* non-theist or pantheist we need look no further than the article by Harvey Gillman on the meaning of 'Spirit' which appeared in *The Friend* (7th November, 2014). One of a series of sensitive meditations on commonly used Christian and Quaker words, it soon gets enmeshed in the trickier issues around ontology. Gillman suggests that we need an alternative for the word 'God' which for him has unwelcome overtones of transcendence, not to mention patriarchy. The alternative he proposes is 'Spirit', a word which can be interpreted 'playfully' in a number of different ways and is therefore likely to have wide appeal. However, the danger with the word Spirit, he says, "is that it is sometimes used dualistically, as when we consider it to be in opposition with the physical". His solution is to treat the physical too as Spirit: "a more holistic perspective might be to consider matter as a form of divine energy (perhaps an unorthodox expression of Albert Einstein's e=mc2 where energy, mass and light are set in an equation)". Of course, if everything is Spirit there is no dualism. Nor is there a need for transcendence, since Spirit cannot transcend Spirit. But not only is God, on this account, reduced to a mathematical formula, albeit a highly prestigious one, but (applying Kołakowski's formulation) a Spirit that is synonymous with the universe would be open to the same scientific investigation and subject to the same

[271] Kołakowski, *Religion* (Glasgow: Fontana, 1982), pp. 110, 112.

ultimate fate as that which we usually think of as the *physical* universe — for which it is really no more than another name. Such a Spirit would be finite in space and time. What is this but straightforward scientific materialism? Why clothe it in religious-sounding language?

Of course one could opt for *panentheism* and say that the physical universe is an expression of the divine but that the divine is 'more than' the physical universe rather than exactly congruent with it. This would be consistent with theism but would leave Gillman with the question (awkward for someone who rejects transcendence) 'more in what sense?' Would it be more of the same — which would simply mean extending the universe in size, or 'more' in the sense of 'other'? If the latter, we are left with the same problems around transcendence as before.[272] However unwelcome the word 'transcendence', it would seem to be unavoidable unless we can find a substitute which retains the same essential meaning but carries fewer undesirable connotations.

Whether we call the experience of transcendent Love 'God' or something else hardly matters. It is as much within the tradition of Christianity to think of God as the 'incomprehensible mystery' beyond naming as it is to refer to God as 'God'. The fifth century theologian, Dionysius the Areopagite urges us in *The Divine Names* not to speak of the Ineffable and Unknown "with the persuasive words of human wisdom" and so to "refrain from speaking or forming any conception whatever of the super-essential and hidden God". [273] Despite this, or in order to explain it further, he makes a distinction between God's *undifferentiated* nature which is beyond the reach of the human mind, being approached only through the practice of 'mystical unknowing', and God's *differentiated* nature by which is made manifest the Divine

---

272 His references to dualism and transcendence suggests that Gillman is thinking along pantheistic rather than panentheistic lines. In panentheism, the universe is an expression of the divine but the divine is ontologically separate from and 'more than' the universe.

273 See Dionysius the Areopagite, *The Divine Names* (tr. The Editors of the Shrine of Wisdom. Fintry Brook: The Shrine of Wisdom, 1957), p. 9. The term 'super-essential' is defined by the translators as "beyond the reach of that which is particular". Yet, they add, "through mystical *agnosia* or unknowing, the particular can be transcended".

'emanations' or attributes of Love, Goodness, Truth, Wisdom, Power, etc. In that sense, God is *more* than Love, the 'more' belonging to the *undifferentiated* nature which cannot be known in a conceptual sense since it transcends all knowledge, but can be experienced in union with God — as Dionysius says "after the manner of the angels, since it is through the stilling of all the activities of the mind that the union of the Godlike minds with the super-eminently Divine Light takes place".[274]

Here we have the two essential components of mystical religion, the understanding of God as both Mystery and Divine Love. Not God as Love without remainder, but God as the Mystery of the *source* of Love — a concept which will be familiar to Friends through the writings of the early Quakers, in particular Isaac Penington for whom (as we have seen) the things of the spirit could not be known but "in union with them [and] in the receiving of them".[275] Doubtless too this was what Eckhart meant when he spoke of "the God beyond God" and made his famous pronouncement that "man's last and highest parting occurs when, for God's sake, he takes leave of God". He was referring of course to what Dionysius called 'the mystical *agnosia*', and the long line of mystics who came after him, 'the *via negativa*', the self-emptying of the soul — and not, as Boulton suggests, an embryonic non-theism. For whatever we might understand by the 'nothing' (no-thing) that Eckhart applied to his experience of the Godhead it came to him by way of a consistent and dynamic theism.[276]

In a talk at Huddersfield in 2011, Boulton referred to the God he did not believe in as 'a being', 'an entity', and to theists as those who 'externalise' their understanding of God. Most modern theologians would also reject a concept of God as a discrete 'entity' since it would

---

274 *ibid.*, p. 13.

275 Penington, *A Question, ibid.*

276 See B. Lanzetta, "Three Categories of Nothingness in Eckhart, *The Journal of Religion* 72, 2 (April 1992), pp. 248-68. Boulton interprets Eckhart as saying that the price of truth is self-denial in matters material, intellectual and spiritual (*Godless*, p. 6). Eckhart, however, was referring to Truth as the goal of religious contemplation not philosophical truth. The substratum of his theology was theist and Trinitarian.

make God a part of the creation, not transcending it but existing in space and time — and therefore one more 'object' in the universe to be explored alongside other objects. A God, in other words, that would be subject to the same second law of thermodynamics as the rest of the known universe. It is, as we have seen, difficult to speak about God at all, but the Christian existentialists, Karl Jaspers, Gabriel Marcel and more recently John Macquarrie, all speak of God not as 'a being' but as the source and condition of being, as Being itself. It is true that traditional theism placed undue emphasis on God's transcendence, but all of these theologians see God as both transcendent and immanent in the creation. Gabriel Marcel, for example, explicitly rejects Kant's argument that the transcendent is unknowable because it is *beyond* experience and speaks instead of the transcendent *within* experience. Unless it is possible to have an experience *of* the transcendent, he argues, the word can have no meaning, and he justifies his position by distinguishing between the unknowable which is based on a metaphysical 'problem' (such as Kant's *'the thing in itself'*) and the transcendent *mystery* which is intuited and encountered in the depth of our being.[277]

Here we Quakers should take heart; it should give us some confidence in our theology to know that a religious movement consisting more of artisans than scholars anticipated the conclusions of these sophisticated thinkers by more than three hundred years. Whether they got their ideas from Jacob Boehme (whom Fox may have read), or later in the 1660s from the Cambridge Platonists, whose ideas were so similar to their own, it was through the Light of the Christ *within*, as they found it in the example of Jesus and their own personal experience, that they claimed to arrive at the Truth. Thus Isaac Penington tells us: "God is the fountain of beings and natures, the inward substance of all that appears".[278] He saw God (the Christ)

---

[277] See P. Rowntree Clifford, *Interpreting Human Experience: A Philosophical Prologue to Theology* (London: Collins, 1971), p. 19.

[278] Quoted in Beth Allen, *Ground and Spring: Foundations of Quaker Discipleship* (London: Quaker Peace and Social Witness, 2007), p. 43. Beth Allen's more

as present in Jesus and in each of us 'in our measure' but "not confined to be nowhere else but there." In other words, within us (immanent) and 'without' us (transcendent). The late Lorna Marsden, whose thinking was very close to Penington's, expresses the same thought in modern language:

> All truly spiritual experience of whatever century and whatever region of the world has a universal and shared relevance. A profound inner unity binds together the common impetus towards transcendence. This movement necessitates also the recognition of that accompanying immanence by which what we have called the divine becomes visible to us in the forms of the world and in the human soul. This we name Incarnation. For this, the true disposition of the heart prepares us. [279]

For today's theists, whether Quaker, Anglican or Roman Catholic, transcendence and immanence are not some kind of polar opposites. What the early Quakers took for granted is now part of mainstream thinking and religious practice. As Keith Ward, an Anglican, says, "God is the spiritual basis of all reality, which can be discovered by us, hidden deep within our own selves."[280]

I have not touched on the postmodernist theologians like Jean-Luc Marion and Emmanuel Levinas who are pushing the boundaries beyond Being to the notion of a God free of all the categories of being.[281] For these thinkers the God of metaphysics is a mere concept; but God's self-disclosure as Love is the supreme reality, beyond 'ontological difference', beyond the 'constraints of Being', but accepted (or retreated from) as pure gift. The impossibility or extreme difficulty of thinking outside 'ontological difference' is admitted (in

---

extended account of theism contains many of the ideas expressed here but in far more Friendly language, and is strongly recommended.

279 Marsden, *ibid.*, p. viii.

280 Keith Ward, *Holding Fast to God*, p. 9.

281 See Marion, *ibid.*; also E. Levinas, *Of God Who Comes to Mind* (tr. B. Bergo. Stanford, CA.: Stanford University Press, 1998).

fact insisted upon),[282] for this way of thinking takes us to the very limits of human thought, as when we try to imagine infinity or how sub-atomic particles can emerge from 'nothing'. The conceptual difficulty is reflected in the language which may often seem unduly obscure — but no more than, say, 'the large scale structure of space time' might seem to the non-mathematician or non-physicist. What these philosopher-theologians are trying to do is systematise ideas that have been around for some time (the idea that the 'Good' is 'beyond being' has been attributed to Plato) and reconcile them with the fashionable emphasis on monism as the only acceptable framework in which to think about God. Much easier to access are the insights of a mystic like Thomas Merton: "In the end the contemplative suffers the anguish of realising that he no longer knows what God is . . . this is a great gain, because God is not a 'what,', not a 'thing'. That is precisely one of the essential characteristics of contemplative experience. It sees that there is no 'what' that can be called God. There is 'no such thing' as God because God is neither a 'what' nor a 'thing but a pure 'Who'. He [sic] is the "Thou" before whom our inmost "I" springs into awareness".[283]

Theism, says William James, "at a single stroke . . . changes the dead blank *it* of the world into a living *thou*, with whom the whole man may have dealings."[284] Both Thomas Merton and William James would find themselves in full agreement with the title Boulton chose for one of his books, "Real like Daisies, or Real like I Love You?", but not with the way it is interpreted by Boulton. The title, as he acknowledges, was actually supplied by Janet Scott, a Quaker, a theist and a trained theologian, and it is ironic that it should be used (or misused) for a book which has the declared aim of promoting an atheistic spirituality. In Merton's case, he foresaw the misunderstanding that his statement "there is no such thing as God"

[282] Marion, *ibid.*, p. 45.
[283] Merton, *Seeds of Contemplation* (Wheathampstead: Anthony Clarke, 1972), pp. 10-11.
[284] James, *The Will to Believe*, p. 127.

might give rise to and added in a footnote: "This should not be taken to mean that man has no valid concept of the divine nature. Yet in contemplation abstract notions of the divine essence no longer play an important part since they are replaced by a concrete intuition, based on love".[285]

So, in religious terms, 'beyond being' is the frontier at which the conceptual makes way for the mystical, when the only true knowledge of God is that *revealed* to us by the Spirit (1.Cor. 2:9 ff.) and words like 'reality', 'being' and 'existence' have to be placed in inverted commas — not because they have been emptied of meaning but because they call into question the very transcendence denied by the humanist. When postmodern theologians say 'God does not exist' they mean something very different from their humanist counterparts who are likely to leap on such formulations as evidence of an unadmitted atheism. This is exactly how Boulton presents Paul Tillich and Dietrich Bonhoeffer in *Real Like Daisies*, comparing them to Dionysius the Areopagite who had said God is "not one of the things that are" (without of course explaining the theology behind this).[286] Similarly, in his talk at Huddersfield, he turned for support to Karen Armstrong, referring specifically to her book, *The Case for God.* But what Karen Armstrong is concerned to uphold is not the unreality of God but that same notion of divine transcendence that Boulton sees as the source of so much that is wrong with the world. She writes: "Jewish, Christian and Muslim theologians have insisted for centuries that God does not exist and that there is 'nothing' out there; in making

---

[285] *ibid*, p. 11.

[286] *Real Like Daisies*, p. 15. US theologian and Quaker Patrick Nugent comments ("Response to Papers on Theism (Just a Little) and Non-Theism (Much More)", *Quaker Religious Thought* 118 (Jan., 2012); "to insert Dietrich Bonhoeffer into a list of non-theist heroes on account of his "religionless Christianity" simply cannot be sustained by even the shallowest attention to his actual writing. What Bonhoeffer objected to was the state church's capitulation to state power; he was interested in pure Christian faith without an ecclesiastical structure tied to the state's purse-strings. Bonhoeffer is called "neo-orthodox" in company with Karl Barth and Emile Brunner, far more obstinately Christocentric than even many liberals can comfortably accept".

these assertions their aim was not to deny the reality of God but to safeguard God's transcendence. But in our talkative and opinionated society, we seem to have lost sight of this important tradition, which could solve many of our current religious problems".[287] She could not have spelt it out more clearly. Unless we are humanists or philosophical materialists believing that God is no more than a human construct, to say that our *experience* of God is beyond words, beyond naming, beyond conceptualisation is to uphold God's transcendence: "what lies beyond man's word is eloquent of God".[288]

Nothing but a human projection?

Among the thinkers most frequently cited in Boulton's talks to Friends and in his writings is the nineteenth century philosopher, Ludwig Feuerbach, whom he commends for his claim that "in talking about God, humanity was in fact talking about itself: in worshipping God, humanity worshipped a projection of its own needs and desires".[289] It is well-known that Feuerbach saw this tendency to project value onto 'God' as a form of 'alienation'. What this means is that human beings ascribe their ideas of perfection to an imaginary non-human entity towards whom they then direct the love and concern that is more properly due to their fellow creatures. "We impoverish ourselves", Feuerbach said, "for the sake of an illusion."

That this has become an integral part of non-theist thinking is clear from the following extract from 'Meeting Points', the newsletter of my own Area Meeting:

> At its simplest, Quaker non-theism stands for all the attributes of truth, integrity, justice and loving-kindness that a liberal theology would ascribe to God, but understands "God" not as an actual Supernatural Being revealing himself to us, or guiding us, but as (at best) a useful

[287] Armstrong, *The Case for God,* p. 8.
[288] *ibid.*
[289] See, for example, *The Trouble with God* , p. 140.

> fiction, an entirely human construction embodying entirely human aspirations. So, if there are many images of God — including those represented by the extreme fundamentalists of many faiths — they are all reflections of ourselves. There is no Reality beyond and outside these images.[290]

The writer evidently feels that in equating non-theism with non-realism he is speaking for all non-theists — an assumption which, as we saw in Chapter 10, is problematic. However, if we concede that our experience of God (in whatever form it takes) is an illusion, then it is obvious that we have to accept the reductionist view that God is no more than a projection of our own ideals of truth, love, goodness, justice, etc. For Quakers this means that God is no more than a projection of our Testimonies, and the Testimonies in that case no more than an expression of our corporate ideals at specific moments in history. There are then few safeguards left to ensure that they are not further relativised as our personal and corporate ideals gradually undergo change.

But what if we don't accept non-realism with its claim to be a watertight system and are not ready to make this concession? Non-realists often speak as if their conclusions should be self-evident. But as we have seen their views are not popular even among philosophers. There is, as it happens, another way of thinking about projection theory.

Christianity teaches that the good that is in us, including above all our loving-kindness and concern for others, is essentially 'of God' in whose image we are made. So in a sense we are projecting back to God what a loving and self-giving God has already gifted to us. This is not to dismiss Feuerbach altogether, since it is evidently true that projection does occur. To take one of Boulton's own examples, the Islamic terrorists who flew their planes into the twin towers were almost certainly projecting onto God their own murderous intentions,

---

290 *Meeting Points* (Brighouse and West Yorkshire Area Meeting Newsletter), 176 (Jan.-Feb. 2014), p. 12.

as is the Islamic State (ISIS) today, even if at another level they see themselves as serving the cause of political and social justice. Of course this is not a phenomenon peculiar to a minority of Muslims. Numerous and even worse examples could be cited from the history of European religious conflict. The sixteenth century Massacre of St Bartholomew's Eve, when the Huguenots were dragged out of their homes and butchered in the streets of Paris, is one such event that springs to mind. Northern Ireland is another.

But projection, whether of good or bad qualities, is far less likely to be a factor where there has been a direct experience of God — "not the declaration of the fountain", as Robert Barclay said, but "the fountain itself". Such experiences can take many forms, but the metaphor of the fountain, a commonplace among early Friends, is apposite. It carries with it the notion of excess — an excess of *presence* and the outpouring of an overwhelming all-inclusive love that exceeds anything we could imagine or express out of our own finite being. If the accounts that have been left to us bear any authority at all, there is just *no room* in these experiences for any kind of projection from the self. Moreover, if as Feuerbach claimed, God is a projection of our own needs and desires, why is it that the projection, far from reflecting those desires, is so often in direct conflict with them, so that we shrink from the demands the experience makes on us? A passive reflection of our desires is not likely to be transformative.

There is not space here to deal in any detail with the Freudian version of projection theory. Suffice it to say that the idea that theists are looking for an ideal father to replace their actual biological father who has been found wanting is no longer tenable in either a 'scientific' or therapeutic sense. On the contrary, there is a growing body of empirical evidence which points to the therapeutic benefits of spiritual experience in mental health care. This directly contradicts Freud's view of religious belief as an obstacle to improving the patient's mental health and is one of many factors which undermine the very foundation of his theories. An excellent discussion of Feuerbach and his influence on Freud may be found in Alister McGrath's, *The*

Twilight of Atheism (2004) where he observes that by 1998 there had been "a collapse of confidence in Freud's judgements concerning religion at the level of popular culture, this conclusion having been reached at least a decade earlier in professional circles".

God on trial — the problem of evil

In my attempt to explore theism in a Quaker context I left out the most difficult attribute to justify, namely, God's omnipotence. For many non-theists, this is the crux of the question. They cannot give their trust to a God of Love who is held to be all-powerful and at the same time allows so much evil and suffering in the world.

Boulton's Huddersfield talk began with a reference to the Japanese earthquake of 2011 which, as it had just happened, was on everyone's mind. He asked (not his exact words, but near enough): "how can God be both all powerful and all loving, since if he couldn't prevent a natural disaster such as that, he can't be all powerful, and if he could have prevented it but chose not to, he can't be all loving?" This is an age old theological conundrum and the attempt to answer it in a way that 'justifies the ways of God to men' even has its own name: theodicy.

However, there is no need to give up the idea of God if we concede that there may be a sense in which God is *not* all powerful. In fact it has always been accepted that there are limitations to 'omnipotence'. Thomas Aquinas in the fifteenth century pointed out that God could not do what is manifestly impossible. For example, God could not create a square circle. Other actions which are held to be impossible to God include the act of suicide and acts of cruelty (these last being the very ones called into question by theodicy). We can now take this a step further. One of Richard Dawkins key concepts is that conscious life could *only* emerge through a process of natural selection and natural selection also produces predators and parasites — the Ichneumon wasp which lays its eggs inside a living host being a particularly nasty example of the latter. Dawkins, like Boulton, sees this as evidence that an all powerful and all loving creator God could not exist.[291] But if we agree with Dawkins that natural selection is the *only* way that conscious life can emerge, then all other proposed ways of creating it are impossible, and we have already agreed that God cannot do what is impossible. While creature suffering, therefore, exists, and on an immense scale, we do not have to agree that it is intended by God. We can think of God as bearing that suffering as the price that has to be paid for the sake of the good which it allows, the existence and flourishing of all the beautiful forms of nature, the appearance of conscious human life, and through that the emergence of love itself in the creation.[292]

The same reasoning applies to natural disasters such as earthquakes. The Quaker theologian, peace activist and scientist, George Ellis (co-author with Stephen Hawking of *The Large Scale Structure of Space Time*), is one of a group of 'kenotic' theologians who stress God's self-giving *vulnerability* — infinite power restrained "in complete subordination to love." Ellis uses this idea to provide a model of divine action as self-limiting, non-authoritarian, non-coercive and directed towards the freedom and integrity of creatures in a universe which is 'finely tuned' to produce intelligent life. Earthquake is seen as one of many phenomena which are not willed by God but are inherent to material being and a by-product of the regular laws of physics which make an intelligence-and-freedom-producing universe possible. Without earthquakes and volcanic eruptions, the emergence of life on this planet, scientists tell us, would have been impossible, and God cannot do what is impossible.[293] Another way of looking at

---

[291] See Dawkins, *River Out of Eden* (NY: Basic Books, 1995), pp. 111-55.

[292] There is a fascinating discussion of these and related ideas in Attfield, *ibid.*, pp. 67-166. See also Ward, *God: A Guide for the Perplexed*, pp. 219-24.

[293] A good introduction to ideas in kenotic theology is J. Polkinghorne (ed.), *The Work of Love: Creation and Kenosis* (London: SPCK, 2001). For the chapter by George Ellis, see pp. 107-26.

this might be to say that God is limited by necessity — the necessity lying in the very nature of the physical world.[294]

So far we have been discussing natural evil. We now come to the question of *moral* evil. Here several different arguments have been advanced, the two main ones being the 'free will defence' as developed and brought up to date by the US philosopher of religion, Alvin Plantinga, and John Hick's 'soul-making defence' based on the teaching of Irenaeus, one of the early Church Fathers.[295] It is not possible to explore either of these in detail in the space available but I will try to summarise the main points for and against. The free will defence holds that it is logically impossible for God to create a world in which people are free moral agents but who are then not free to make morally reprehensible choices. Although some of these choices will have unimaginably evil consequences, the possession and exercise of free will is held to be of such value that it outweighs all the evils that result from its misuse. Without free will it is possible that God could have created a world in which humans would be programmed to perform only good acts but such acts would then have no moral worth. It follows that a loving God could not have created a world in which humans could be both free and potentially good without it also containing unavoidable evil.

Opponents of the free will defence argue that an omnipotent God (omnipotent although constrained by inner necessity) *could* have created a world of free persons who nevertheless do no evil if God had intervened, whenever the occasion arose, between the intention and the act. So, for example, a potential murderer would point the gun at his intended victim only to find that his bodily movements became

---

[294] Keith Ward explains the concept of necessity in relation to the being of God in *ibid.* pp. 125-9, where he says "there will be necessities in the nature of God which we cannot hope to understand from our finite viewpoint, but which may constrain the sorts of universe God can create". See also pp. 221-4.

[295] Alvin Plantinga, God, Freedom, and Evil (Michigan: Eerdmans Pulishing Co., 1977, pp.29 fff. Plantinga's views in general are orthodox and I only mention his version of the free will theodicy here because it is the most comprehensive so far. I do not subscribe to those aspects of it which include doctrines such as the atonement.

uncoordinated just when he was about to pull the trigger, or alternatively God could cause the mechanism to jam. [296] This argument is so absurd that it seems a waste of effort to point out the obvious drawbacks, however entertaining it might be to speculate about the possible knock-on effects for academic subject areas like history.

A second objection is that God could have endowed humans from the start with a fully-fledged 'morally enlightened intellect' "by means of which the correct moral principles and their proper application are as self-evident as are the basic principles of logic."[297] This is not quite as absurd as the first objection, but absurd nevertheless. It allows for no experience, no history, no development, no victory. There would be no place in such a world for a Sophocles or a Shakespeare. T.S. Eliot would never have written *Murder in the Cathedral*, Lord Byron would never have heard of Cain, let alone have based a drama on him. Such a world is more likely to be the brainchild of a Woody Allen than a creator God. I am not suggesting that the free will theodicy is invincible; but it is clear that despite Boulton's confident brandishing of the ace in the pack, the debate around these issues is not yet settled.

The second of the two main theodicies is the 'soul-making' or as he later came to call it 'person-making' theodicy proposed by John Hick which suggests that God may have permitted moral evil to exist so that humans could undergo moral development and growth "and finally be brought to the perfection intended for [them] by [their] Maker".[298] Some critics have dismissed this as yet another version of the free will theodicy although I imagine Plantinga and Hick might regard them as complementary.[299]

---

[296] See S. Boer, "The Irrelevance of the Free Will Defence", *Analysis* 38, 2 (March 1978), p. 111.

[297] This is an argument offered by R. Schoenig, "The Free Will Theodicy", *Religious Studies* 34, 4 (1998), p. 459.

[298] Hick, *Evil and the God of Love* (London: Fontana, 1968), p. 220.

[299] Hick, however, rejects the free will theodicy in its Augustinian form.

Hick has written a whole book on this subject, *Evil and the God of Love*. One significant challenge to his thesis is D.Z. Phillips's claim that 'soul-making' "promotes an indulgent concern with one's self . . . it seems to be both a logical and moral truth that to seek one's character development is to lose it". [300] But surely Phillips is missing the point here? What is under discussion is not *our* aim to develop *our* moral character but God's aim to provide the conditions which would make moral development possible. Even his claim that it is always self-defeating to strive for one's own moral development is open to question. What is wrong with someone, acutely aware of their moral failings, wanting to be a better person? What is wrong in wanting to blossom as an individual? Phillips assumes that the focus of such concern will be the opportunity to improve our standing as moral beings rather than alleviate the suffering around us. But this is a deeply pessimistic view of human motivation which owes any persuasive power it has to the seventeenth century philosopher, Thomas Hobbes. While it is probably true of all of us for some of the time, it denies the Quaker doctrine of 'that of God in us' and seems completely out of keeping with the traditional Christian attitude to suffering which involves empathy and loving response. Considered from this point of view, it is probably less of a danger to the theist than to the nonrealist for whom the goal of *disinterestedness* has taken the place of Christian love and who ultimately has no point of reference beyond the boundaries of the self.[301]

Phillips is on stronger ground when he considers *God's* purpose as represented in the soul-making theodicy. By providing the conditions for 'soul-making', he asks, isn't God allowing one person's moral and spiritual development to be dependent on another's suffering, and isn't that in itself immoral? Hick's answer is Yes to the

---

[300] Quoted from N. Trakakis, "Theodicy: The Solution to the Problem of Evil, or Part of the Problem?", *Sophia*, 47 (2008), p. 172.

[301] Hick clearly regarded Phillips as a non-realist despite Phillips's strenuous denials. See Hick, "D.Z. Phillips on God and Evil", *Religious Studies* 43 (2007), pp. 439-40. For a fascinating discussion of disinterestedness in relation to non-realism, see Williams in Higton (ed.), *Wrestling with Angels*, pp. 228-254.

first question and No to the second: we have to accept the interdependence of suffering and love as the only way in which beings endowed with free will can grow away from self-centredness towards love of the other and the Real (God). The basic question then is, "Was God justified in creating finite free beings in the first place?" Hick's reply to this is that 'soul-making' is a creative process that continues beyond this life and that ultimately all will enjoy "a common good which will be unending and therefore unlimited, and which will be seen by its participants as justifying all that has been endured along the way to it". He bases this hope, or expectation, on the Christian belief, founded on *experience*, that God is indeed a God of Love and hence that there must be justice in the universe.

In his book, *An Interpretation of Religion: Human Responses to the Transcendent*, Hick defends his theodicy and the notion of an afterlife which is necessary to it, with his usual vigour. First, he accuses the non-realist philosophers of religion (singling out D.Z. Phillips and Don Cupitt) of "an unintended élitism" in relying on political change alone to bring about the conditions in which all can lead happy and fulfilled lives, for "even if the human situation should presently change markedly for the better, so that a much greater proportion of people are able to find inner peace and fulfilment, it would still be true that thousands of millions have already lived and died, their highest potentialities unfulfilled — and if the non-realists are right, permanently and irrevocably unfulfilled. This would negate any notion of the ultimate goodness of the universe". He then draws a comparison between this 'élitism' and "the strand of Augustinian and Calvinist theology which consigned the large majority of human beings to a predestined eternal damnation whilst a minority were recipients of an arbitrary and unmerited divine grace". He adds, "whereas the Augustinian-Calvinist doctrine "was developed explicitly, and its horrifying implications frankly accepted, the advocates of non-realist spirituality seem not yet to have noticed the harsh implication of their own teaching."[302] Finally, he points out that this represents a radically different vision to that of the great spiritual traditions of the world, "a reversal of their faith, from a cosmic optimism to a cosmic pessimism". For Quakers his words would mean that Fox's 'infinite ocean of light and love' had been overcome after all by his 'ocean of darkness and death'.

Although not affecting the logic behind Hick's theodicy, it might be thought there is still something distasteful about a readiness to see evil as ultimately productive of good when we consider the intensity and sheer scale of suffering in the world. Here we are reminded of the famous exchange between the worldly Ivan and the saintly Alyosha in Dostoyevsky's *The Brothers Karamazov*. In the course of this conversation, Ivan puts the following question to Alyosha:

> Imagine that you yourself are erecting the edifice of human fortune with the goal of, at the finale, making people happy, of at last giving them peace and quiet, but that in order to do it it would be necessary and unavoidable to torture to death only one tiny little creature, that same little child that beat its breast with its little fist, and on its unavenged tears to found that edifice, would you agree to be the architect on those conditions, tell me and tell me truly?"[303]

If Ivan can be thrown into such agony of mind over the fate of one hypothetical child, what would he think today, faced with the countless thousands dying of malnutrition in parts of Africa? What of the children thrown *alive* into the furnaces at Auschwitz, or those torn to shreds in the Israeli bombing of Gaza? What of the thousands of children made to endure months, years of sexual abuse at the hands of the priests they were taught to trust, the boy soldiers forced to murder

---

[302] Hick, *An Interpretation of Religion: Humanist Responses to the Transcendent* (London: Macmillan, 1989), pp. 207-8. It is ironic that Boulton, having been brought up by the Plymouth Brethren, who preached the one kind of élitism, should later in his life become a champion of the other kind.

[303] Fyodor Dostoyevsky, *The Brothers Karamazov*, trans. David McDuff (London: Penguin Books, 2003), p.321.

their parents — what chance of moral development had any of these? Is it surprising that some anti-theodicists have asked if any kind of happiness or 'development' for the individual, or even the whole of humanity, could be worth having at such a cost?

It may be that there is no theodical answer, only the answer that Alyosha finally gives, the kiss which replicates the kiss that Christ, in another of Ivan's parables, leaves on the mouth of the Grand Inquisitor. The message is clear: it is not human intellect, nor human imagination, but the love learnt from Christ that finally brings good out of evil and guarantees in the words of Julian of Norwich that "all shall be well and all manner of thing shall be well". Indeed one could speculate that if European Christianity, whose very representative the Grand Inquisitor is, had not rejected that kiss there might have been no arms trade, no First World War, no Hitler, no Second World War, no Holocaust, certainly no Grand Inquisitor, and perhaps no need of theodicy. It is our unfaithfulness, not God's generous gift, which must bear the responsibility for much of the evil in the world. Perhaps God *has* intervened between the intention and the act by providing us with the example of Jesus, but from Nicea onward we have been brushing Jesus to one side.

The problem with theodicies is that they seem to be trying to read the mind of God as if it were a mind similar to our own — they are overly anthropomorphic. Nevertheless they are useful in that they show that the problem of evil as presented by the opponents of religion is not as intractable and as self-evidently contradictory as it may seem. In fact, it could be argued that the shoe is now on the other foot, for how does the atheist account for moral evil other than as actions that one person abhors and another approves and enjoys? This is what Chad Meister calls the 'grounding problem': "If rape, torture, murder, government-sanctioned genocide, and so forth are objectively evil — evil for all persons in all times and places whether they recognise them as such or not — then what makes them so on the naturalist's account? . . . If there are no objective moral values, then there must be some basis — some metaphysical foundation or grounding — for their being so. It seems to me that naturalism lacks such a foundation or grounding or explanation, for on naturalism the cosmos is not morally good per se, nor is there a morally good being sufficient to ground evil or to bring real objective goodness out of evil".[304] The atheist is then left with a burden greater than any the theist has to bear — how to accommodate to and find meaning in "a world that, to quote Richard Dawkins, 'has precisely the properties we should expect if there is, at bottom, no design, no purpose, no evil, no good, nothing but pitiless indifference'".

While theodicy has been around for centuries, the newer arguments presented above (and these are not the only ones) do show that theology can make progress. Ultimately it is not a question that can be resolved by theological speculation, but is more about faith. For those who have been touched by the sense of God's loving presence, the logical contradictions inherent in the problem of evil like many other problems posed by religious faith are of little account and, as William James recognised, simply vanish away. Formidable as they are, they do not require us to replace our experience of the Real Presence in prayer and worship with the only God affirmed by Quaker non-theism, the God whose reality is restricted to what Robert Barclay described as "the natural mind and will of man."

Conclusion

There is not sufficient space here to discuss all the possible objections to theism and I am not suggesting that I have dealt fully or adequately with those I have covered. I have said nothing, for example, about religion as a force for evil in the world or about the claim that it conflicts with the methods and findings of science. Boulton tells us that "what links Bush and bin Laden, church, synagogue and mosque, Bible and Koran, is the conviction that there is an Ultimate Authority in human affairs; [and] that this Ultimate

[304] Meister, "God and Evil" in Moreland *et al* (eds.), *Debating Christian Theism* (Oxford: OUP, 2013), p. 217.

Authority is transcendent, super-human and absolute". [305] I will not attempt to analyse that statement here; but it highlights a pressing danger — the danger that we may be buying into a western and far-right narrative that sees Islam as the problem. To say 'Je suis Charlie' could be to align oneself with those who place freedom of speech and freedom of expression — important as these most certainly are — above the social courtesy and love of their neighbour that a postmodernist and post-Christian society seemingly finds so difficult. To make it the theme of a vast demonstration in Paris attended by the world's leading politicians is to exclude virtually the entire Muslim population of Europe who could not possibly identify with the obscenities depicted in the Charlie Hebdo cartoons, however sadly they may deplore the actions of their violent co-religionists.[306] And how can we say that theism is the problem when it is honouring the image of God in all others that is the real solution to so many of our problems?

Here I want to ask, is it reasonable to condemn religion *as a whole* on the basis of its more distorted expressions? Boulton says nothing about the enormous contribution of religion to the care and support of the most vulnerable in society, the many faith-based organisations dedicated to promoting community cohesion, the part played by bodies like the World Council of Churches and the Catholic Commission for Justice and Peace in bringing healing and reconciliation where it is most needed. Today social historians treat mono-causal explanations with caution but Boulton's rhetoric fails to identify any factor other than religion or to evaluate the importance of religion alongside, for example, ethnicity, racism, social marginalisation, poverty, unemployment, poor quality education and the ruthless political and economic interests that so often are the real drivers behind religious conflict.

---

305 *Godless*, p. 10.

306 I am referring here to the Islamist attack on the Paris offices of the satirical magazine *Charlie Hebdo* (7th January, 2015) during which 11 staff members and one police officer were killed.

An example of how easily these other factors can be overlooked is provided (unwittingly) by Christopher Hitchens in his book, *God is Not Great*. Hitchens tells "an old Belfast joke" intended to illustrate the depths of the Irish obsession with religious identity. A man is stopped at a roadblock and asked his religion. When he replies that he is an atheist he is asked, "Protestant or Catholic atheist?" Hitchens says "this shows how the obsession has rotted even the legendary local sense of humour", but what I think it really shows is that it is not religious belief but ethnic and tribal identity that is the major factor underlying the words of the questioner; and underlying ethnic and tribal identity are political and economic rivalries.

The humanist or 'new atheist' strategy of associating theism and religion with images of fundamentalist violence has been criticized by popular theologians such as Alister McGrath and Keith Ward.[307] Both agree that organised religion has been the cause of much evil and conflict in the world, but also of much that is good, and they point out that in countries where it had been replaced by atheism, such as revolutionary France and Soviet Russia, what we have seen follow is inhumanity on an unprecedented scale. The root of the problem they argue lies in human nature and the way in which human institutions can go terribly wrong, whether those of a liberal democracy, a government founded on great revolutionary ideals, or the church itself. Here is Keith Ward:

> A general religious explanation is that humans are enslaved to hatred and passion. They will pervert even the highest principles to their selfish ends. So when they get hold of a religion, they will pervert that too. But it is not the religion that is causing the hatred. It is the hatred that is causing the religion to become perverse. That is what is happening in the modern world with Islamic jihadists. They hate the West because of the chaos and destruction that Western forces have, the jihadists believe, caused in the Middle East. Given such burning

[307] See McGrath, *The Dawkins Delusion: Atheist Fundamentalism and the Denial of the Divine* (London: SPCK, 2007); and Ward, *Is Religion Dangerous?* (Oxford: Lion Hudson, 2006).

> hatred, religious texts, taken out of context and without reference to centuries of careful scholarly interpretation, can be used to give a 'moral' justification for terrorism. Most Muslims recognise this as a perversion of Islam, even though some might sympathise with the desire for revenge that jihadists have. Jews and Christians have also had their terrorists. Yet with all of them, but especially strongly with Christianity, terrorism is clearly incompatible with the teaching of mercy and loving-kindness that is professed most explicitly in the Christian Sermon on the Mount, which seems to call for total non-violence.[308]

Ward also expresses the view that if religion "is dangerous at times, that is far outweighed by the fact that it is one of the last great hopes the world has for peace and a positive future", and he backs this up with a comment that should have some appeal for Friends with their belief in "that of God in every one" and their concern for the environment:

> For those who believe in the incarnation of God in human life [in whatever way 'incarnation' is conceived], all human life is made holy by the divine presence. This is the foundation for belief in the sanctity of the human person, and in the sacredness of the material world with which God united the divine being in the deepest possible way.[309]

I hope that the examples I have given of theistic religious experience demonstrate that theism, within the Christian *mystical* tradition, is essentially benign and incapable of leading to evil when accompanied by the spirit of Love. If religion is to be our salvation, rather than our problem, Being itself needs to be apprehended in depth; that is to say, we need to know one another in the Eternal Thou which is at the heart of everything, not only of ourselves but of the precious and fragile environment in which we live.

---

308 Ward, *Religion and Human Fulfilment* (London: SCM Press, 2008), pp. xiv-xv.
309 Keith Ward, *Is Religion Dangerous?*, pp. 188, 183.

Friends have never displayed that fear of the scientific that has troubled other more scripturally based denominations. On the contrary, many have been at the forefront of developments in science and some have even made original contributions to theology of science. Despite this we see today a growing and uncritical acceptance in the Society of the crude 'scientism' of Richard Dawkins and Christopher Hitchens, a duo whose depiction of religion as "a botched attempt to explain the world" was described by Terry Eagleton as "like seeing ballet as a botched attempt to run for a bus." [310] It is disappointing, therefore, to read in an Area Meeting journal (the words are taken from the write-up on his book, *God is not Great*) — "Hitchens makes the ultimate case against religion. He frames the argument for a more secular life based on science and reason, in which hell is replaced by the Hubble telescope's awesome view of the universe and Moses and the burning bush give way to the beauty and symmetry of the double helix". As a regular reader of *New Scientist* and a non-believer in the traditional 'hell', this 'either-or' type of argument, which sets science and religion in opposition, strikes me as not only unnecessary but curiously dated. What appears to underlie it is the Faustian dream that science will eventually yield answers to all the major questions of life in every area of human knowledge and experience — a dream which Wittgenstein dismissed with his customary candour: "We feel that even when all *possible* scientific questions have been answered, the problems of life remain completely untouched."[311]

The Society of Friends is nothing if not a coming together of people who choose to interpret their experience in religious or spiritual terms. We could do otherwise and choose a materialist framework for our experience, which is what humanism offers. Today, our meetings are full of cross-currents. Many Friends who now opt for non-theism, indeed the non-mystical, have given up on their own seeking, and in

---

[310] Eagleton, *Reason, Faith, and Revolution: Reflections on the God Debate* (New Haven, CT.: Yale University Press, 2009), p. 50.

[311] Wittgenstein, *Tractatus Logico-Philosophicus* (London: Routledge Classics, 2001), §6.52, p.88.

our present muddle of theological and a-theological viewpoints have lost any faith they might have had in the spiritual discoveries and revelations of others. Fox's saying, "This I have known experimentally", has been translated into "if I haven't experienced it for myself it's of no help". Yet someone like William James, who spent a considerable portion of his life studying the religious experiences of others, without ever having had one himself, was perfectly able to accept the majority of such accounts as authentic; and if James and others like him can trust the testimony of strangers, why cannot we show more trust in the testimony of our fellow Quakers? Here is James writing to his old friend, Edwin Starbuck:

> I think that the fixed point with me is the conviction that our 'rational' consciousness touches but a portion of the real universe and that our life is fed by the 'mystical' region as well. I have no mystical experience of my own, but just enough of the germ of mysticism in me to recognise the region from which their voice comes when I hear it.[312]

And asked in a questionnaire on religious belief whether, never having had an experience of God, he accepted the testimony of others who claim to have felt God's presence directly? he answered, "Yes! The whole line of testimony on this point is so strong that I am unable to pooh-pooh it away".[313]

When James refers to 'mystical experience', in all likelihood he is thinking of that discrete phenomenon with its four distinctive characteristics which he describes in his celebrated *Varieties*, a type of experience that dispels all doubt about the nature of the "region from which it comes" and similar to those quoted earlier in this chapter. Yet innumerable as they appear when gathered together in a single volume such experiences are comparatively rare. For most of us the experience is cumulative, deepening with practice over a long period of time, even a whole lifetime, but nonetheless real and personally and *corporately*

---

[312] H. James (ed.), *The Letters of William James* (London: Longmans, Green and Co., 1926), p. 210. Vol. 2.
[313] *ibid*, p. 213.

transformative. James remained a seeker all his life, never finding what he longed for, "a living sense of commerce with a God", but not content to give up the search or take a fixed position along the way. Instead, he treasured his 'mystical germ', acknowledging that it "creates the rank and file of believers", and stoutly maintaining that "it withstands . . . all purely atheistic criticism."[314]

James saw that mysticism must have a goal. And until recently, this was also the position of Friends. Truth is a path not a possession, but a path that leads somewhere. There is no final destination, not because the path is endless, or peters out or goes round in circles, but because God is infinite and God's demands on us unceasing. Finders are still seekers and we are on a journey where there are no permanent stopping places. Without hampering ourselves with abstractions and definitions, we need our journey to have a direction. The words of Evelyn Underhill still speak to us today: "There are diversities of gifts, but the same Spirit" and "we shall not be able to make order, in any hopeful sense, of the tangle of material before us, until we have subdued it to this ruling thought". We need, she wrote, to conceive of one immanent and transcendent Mystery "towards which all our twisting pathways run, and one impulsion pressing us towards it".[315] None of this is possible without an initial openness to the experience of the Divine Presence, an attitude of the spirit which is essentially theist in orientation.

We are not speaking here of a GCHQ in the sky, noting down our every thought, nor an 'external' intelligence supervising the machinery of the universe in accordance with cold mathematical laws, but the Presence of Love sustaining all that is. If there is an intelligence at work — and it would follow from our understanding of God as in some way including the quality of personhood that there is — it is the intelligence of Love. It is this overflowing Presence which "pours into our fainting wills the elixir of new life and strength, and

[314] *ibid.*, p. 211.

[315] Underhill, *The Life of the Spirit and the Life of Today* (London: Methuen 1936 [1922]), p. 2.

into our wounded hearts the balm of a quite infinite sympathy" that we think of as God,[316] and if the word 'personal' sounds too provincial for such a Presence it is only because we have forgotten that our personhood participates in the personhood of God rather than the other way round.

The Thomist attributes of omnipotence, omniscience, omnipresence etc. may or may not be deducible from the encounter with such a creative and sustaining Power; one can be a theist and yet disagree over these kind of ascriptions. But an openness to the possibility of actual relationship with the immanent-transcendent God would seem to be fundamental. Without that central and leading core of Friends who are essentially theist in orientation there can be no true discernment, no recognisable divine guidance, no Quaker method and the Testimonies can have no other sanction than our collective approval. What we believe does matter if our faith is to have any content that is recognisably Christian-Quaker or Quaker-theist and if we are once again to have something in particular to say to a world which is sorely in need of the values embedded in our tradition. The alternative is to continue our secular drift in a spirit of nebulous amiability towards every conceivable point of view regardless of whether it leads us away from or nearer to God.

---

316 *ibid.*, p. 8.

Endpiece

SINCE THE INCEPTION of the Quaker movement in the 17th century, meeting for worship has been predicated on the reality of the immanent and transcendent God.[317] A God that is immanent only, however appealing the idea may be to non-theist and humanist Friends, is not one whose Presence can be shared. Without the transcendent element, there can be no rational ground for saying that what *I* experience in meeting for worship bears any relation to what *you* experience. Indeed, as the immanent-only God takes hold in our Society, it will become increasingly difficult for Friends and enquirers to see any lasting significance in the Quaker form of worship at all. As it is gradually emptied of the traditional contents, we will be left with only a faint echo of that noble and purposive life-giving endeavour, witnessed down the years, to be one with each other in the Spirit — in the things that are *Eternal*.

Representatives of non-theism declare, as did David Boulton, "I am not myself much at home with current Quaker-speak, with its 'gathered meetings' and 'centring down'". That is not surprising. Both these well-loved Quaker sayings presuppose some sense of transcendent being, and for humanists and many non-theists that is emphatically a red line. Together with such terms as the 'Real Presence', the 'Inner Light', 'waiting on God', they form a cluster of meanings which suggest that in worship we can rise above 'our individual centres of consciousness' to an encounter with that which is beyond anything we could hope to generate from within ourselves, even from within our own *collective* consciousness or subconscious. Of course, in the last resort, none of these phrases really matters.

---

[317] For an extended discussion of the meaning of the terms 'immanent' and 'transcendent' see below, pp. 208-9.

Words are the shadow, not the substance.[318] As we surrender to the silence of worship, we provisionally set aside all such formulations , striving to become, in Paul's words, "a letter written not with ink but with the Spirit of the living God, written not on stone tablets but on the pages of the human heart" (2 Cor. 3:3).

The kind of diversity energetically pursued by the Friends of the Nontheist Network, many of whom believe the world would be a better place *without* God, leaves us with 'nothing in particular' to say to a global community whose fundamental problems are spiritual rather than political and social — serious as these are. We can unite around a framework for action, but this in itself will not stop the drift towards secularism. We will still have our testimonies, but we will have them as "thieves", no longer knowing them, and no longer being able to proclaim them, "in the Spirit that gave them forth".[319]

Further, a diversity that elevates the immanent at the expense of the transcendent threatens the very existence of Quakerism in Britain, not only because it undermines the basis of our worship, but because it is the more easily manipulated. It provides the ideal conditions for the growth and spread of an alien set of beliefs and values which are clearly antithetical to the theism, mysticism and 'theological modernism' of many who currently hold membership of the Society.[320]

---

[318] See Isaac Penington: "Truth is a shadow except the last — except the utmost, yet every Truth is true in its kind. It is substance in its own place, though it be but a shadow in another place (for it is but a shadow from an intenser substance); and the shadow is a true shadow, as the substance is a true substance". Quoted in *CFT,* p. 10. A similar thought may be found in Philo, the contemporary of Jesus, who "compares the literal sense of Scripture to the shadow which the body casts, finding its authentic, profounder truth in the spiritual meaning which it symbolises"; see J. Kelly, *Early Christian Doctrines* (London: Adam & Charles Black 1977 [1958]), pp. 8-9.

[319] Margaret Fell and George Fox, *QFP*, §19.07.

[320] 'Theological modernism', the last in the long list of beliefs and perspectives to be 'swept away' by the 'avowed humanist', presumably refers to contemporary theologies that are not *postmodern* in outlook. The term is also used by scholars to describe the liberal theology of the late nineteenth and early twentieth centuries which was an early influence on the organisers of the Manchester Conference.

A large part of what I have been arguing in this book is that the immanence-transcendence debate needs re-balancing. In pursuit of this goal, it will not be enough to appeal only to the emotions, the heart. We must engage in reasoned discussion with those who place reason above all other forms of knowing. We will be in a much stronger position to defend our tradition when we have appreciated the weaknesses in the non-realist philosophy which has given humanism a wholly undeserved status in Britain Yearly Meeting; and when we have also grasped the materialist implications of the pantheism which identifies a finite and eventually lifeless universe with the impersonal attributes of a wholly immanent 'Divinity'.

As soon as there is talk of 're-balancing', we may expect the cry, "there can be no going back". However, it is not a question of 'going back', or for that matter of 'moving forward', but of 'going deeper', and this has always been the case when Quakerism has undergone conscious reform rather than mere drift. In the years following the Manchester Conference, a renewed attention to the Inner Light was felt to be a necessary corrective to the over-determined stress on the transcendent that held sway during the evangelical period of Quakerism. So we had a re-balancing in favour of immanence, and this set the tone for decades to come. However, we are told that Rufus Jones, the Quaker historian of mystical religion, and one of the most influential figures behind this movement, "in his later years, began to realise that his views had become too immanentist, to the devaluing of the transcendence of God".[321]

Has the time now come for a change of emphasis? If so, we could make a start by replacing the term *Inner Light* with what the early Quakers more appropriately called the *Inward Light*. By 'Inward Light' they meant the revelation that comes *to* us rather than that produced *by* us. For his part, Rufus Jones was clearly concerned that the pendulum had swung too far the other way. He would have been horrified to think that his life's work was but a first step towards the

---

[321] See W. Cooper in *Friends Journal* (26th Oct., 1957) and quoted in A. Roberts, *Through Flaming Sword* (Portland, OR.: Barclay Press, 1959), p. 111 (at note 60).

pantheism and non-realism we see in so much Quaker writing at the present day.

It is the immanence-transcendence distinction that now marks a major faultline in our Religious Society, zigzagging through all the diverse theological viewpoints, including the various forms of non-theism. However, it would be an over-simplification to associate immanence solely with humanism. A more subtle distinction is that offered by the noted philosopher and historian of secularism, Charles Taylor. While emphasising the importance of the immanence-transcendence divide, he finds the real faultline between what he calls the open and closed reading of immanence. 'Open' here means immanentist but open to the *possibility* of transcendence — an attitude rather than a credal statement or belief , and an attitude which I have suggested might be a minimal criterion for membership.

For Taylor, the really important gaps in our contemporary culture are those which appear in our moral and aesthetic vision as we opt for 'the *closed* reading of immanence', the humanistic stance that rules out the tiniest 'sliver' of transcendence and, as we saw in Chapter 9, leaves us with very shaky moral foundations on which to build our lives. He says: "A major question for all positions which take their stand in immanence, whether materialistic or not, is: how can one account for the specific force of creative energy, or ethical demands, or for the power of artistic experience, without speaking in terms of some transcendent being or force which interpellates us?"[322]

Humanism has a proud history, but what we usually think of as humanism, the humanism of the Renaissance, of Erasmus and Dean Colet, is about as far removed from Boulton's 'radical religious humanism' as, for instance, Thomas More's *Utopia* from the annual general meeting of the Blackburn Rationalist Society. Humanism as theology has been condemned by writers as various as Alexander Solzhenitsyn and Henri de Lubac who have argued that without God the sense of the sacredness of human life is vulnerable to "new and

[322] *A Secular Age*, p. 597. I take 'interpellate' in this context to mean interact with, inspire, transform, the equivalent of the poet's 'Muse'.

unimaginable inhuman ideologies and technologies". It is our recognition of 'that of God', the sacred, in every one and in the environment that saves us from ourselves.[323]

The sub-title I chose for this book is 'Standing up for God'. Drawing on the knowledge and thinking of some of the most prominent theologians writing today, I have tried to show that trust in the God of experience (including the experience enshrined in scripture) is not unreasonable and certainly not prevented by what is still a wide-open debate in philosophical theology. Theism — belief or trust in a God on whose love and guidance we depend, the God "whose Light shows us our darkness and brings us to new life" — is not the lie or threat that humanism claims, but the very foundation and cornerstone of our religious faith and the justification for our existence as a Religious Society.

In my last chapter I barely scratch the surface of what I describe as 'mystical theism' — a belief, a practice, and an attitude of mind which is open to the transcendent, but which looks for it within: 'the transcendent in experience', as the French existentialist philosopher, Gabriel Marcel, described it. Or as William Blake proclaimed in his poem, *Jerusalem*:

> I am not a God afar off, I am a brother and a friend:
> Within your bosoms I reside, and you reside in me.[324]

There is nothing narrow or confining in such a conception of God, nor in the expansive idea of personhood which it embraces, for the encounter with that which the early Quaker, Isaac Penington, called 'incomprehensible mystery' lets in the light and space, the joy, the loss, the penitential sorrow and, most poignant of all, the Love that

---

[323] See A. Riches, "Christology and Anti-Humanism", *Modern Theology* (July 2013), p. 312.

[324] G. Keynes (ed.), *Poetry and Prose of William Blake* (Oxford: The Nonesuch Library, 1961), p. 435. Blake probably had in mind Jn. 17:23 — "I in them, and thou in me, that they may be made perfect in one; and that the world may know that thou hast sent me, and hast loved them, as thou hast loved me".

bears with us and gives us strength to overcome our inadequacies in the face of worldwide suffering and injustice. How often have we heard of people weeping during their first experience of the 'gathered' meeting? What is it that touches them in their depths and opens them to all the joy and sorrow of the world? An impersonal force? The company of like-minded people? For some, perhaps, but almost certainly for others an experience so profound that the word 'God' may be the most suitable and awe-inspiring term we have for it.

Appendix A: Knowing, thinking and perceiving without language

From Bryan Magee, *Confessions of a Philosopher* (London: Phoenix, 1998 [1997]), pp. 96-9.

IF I LOOK up from the writing of this sentence, my view immediately takes in half a room containing scores if not hundreds of multicoloured items and shapes in higgledy-piggledy relationships with one another. I see it all clearly and distinctly, instantly and effortlessly. There is no conceivable form of words into which this simple, unitary act of vision can be put. For most of my waking days my conscious awareness is a predominantly visual experience — as Fichte puts it, 'I am a living seeing' — but there are no words to describe the irregular shapes of most of the objects I see, nor are there any words to describe the multiple, co-existing three-dimensional spatial relationships in which I directly see them as standing to one another. There are no words for the infinitely different shadings and differentials of colour that I see, not for the multifarious densities of light and shadow. Whenever I see, all that language can do is indicate with the utmost generality and in the broadest and crudest of terms what it is that I see. Even something as simple and everyday as the sight of a towel dropped on to the bathroom floor is inaccessible to language — and inaccessible to it from many points of view at the same time: no words to describe the shape it has fallen into, no words to describe the degrees of shading in its colours, no words to describe the differentials of shadow in its folds, no words to describe its spatial relationships to all the other objects in the bathroom. I see all these things at once with great precision and definiteness, with clarity and certainty, and in all their complexity. I possess them all wholly and securely in direct experience, and yet I would be totally unable, as would anyone else, to put that experience into words. It is emphatically not the case, then, that 'the world is the world as we describe it', or that I experience it through linguistic categories that help to shape the experiences themselves' or that my 'main way of dividing things up is in language' or that my 'concept of reality is a matter of linguistic categories'.

Corresponding things are true of our direct experience through all five of our senses. Imagine applying the phrases just quoted to the experiences I have when eating my dinner! Eating, like seeing, is part of our most elemental, everyday contact with the world of matter, even more necessary to our survival than seeing. I distinguish instantly, effortlessly and pleasurably between the taste of meat, the taste of potatoes, the taste of each vegetable, the taste of ice cream, the taste of wine . . . Can there be anyone who seriously maintains that the categories in which these experiences come to me are linguistic, or that my main way of distinguishing between them is linguistic? Is there even anyone who can put these experiences into words after he has had them — who can describe the taste of boiled potato, of lamb, of parsnip, in such a way that anyone who had not tasted those things would know from the descriptions what each of them tasted like? . . . How does one say the *Mona Lisa*, or Leonardo's *Last Supp*er? The assumption that everything of significance that can be experienced, or known, or communicated, is capable of being uttered in words would be too preposterous to merit a moment's entertainment were it not for the fact that it has underlain so much philosophy in the twentieth century, and so much literary theory too.

What I am saying has radical implications for any philosophy that holds that empirical knowledge must derive from experience. For it means that this direct experience which is never adequately communicable in words is the only knowledge we ever fully have. *That* is our one and only true, unadulterated, direct and immediate form of knowledge of the world, wholly possessed, uniquely ours. People who are rich in that are rich in lived life. But the very putting of it into words translates it into something of the second order, something derived, watered down, abstracted, generalised, publicly sharable. People who live most of their outer or inner lives in terms that are expressible in language — for example, people who live at the level of concepts, or in the world of ideas — are living a life in which everything is simplified and reduced, emptied of what makes it *lived*, purged of what makes it unique and *their*s. But although the unique character of lived experience cannot be communicated by concepts it can be communicated: by works of art. This explains why it is impossible to say what it is that a work of art 'means' or 'expresses' or 'conveys', even when that work is itself made up of words.

Appendix B: God as Energy and God as Person'

From Rachel Britton : text of a talk to Colchester Friends

GOD IS INFINITELY greater than all we can know or imagine. All we say about God can only be in the form of metaphors from our so-limited human experience. Given these axioms as starting points, it is not surprising that different people choose different sorts of metaphor, or that religious traditions offer such a wide range. For the purposes of this article, let us divide the commonly used language about God into two groups, that based on natural forces and energies, and that based on human life, and consider the uses and limits of each.

People talking of God often use words like Light, Fire, Power, Force, Energy and so on. If this language is taken literally, "God" becomes another natural force like gravity or radioactivity, and loses all spiritual reference. But as metaphors for God, as ways of pointing towards, and relating ourselves to, the ultimate mystery, they have great value. On the one hand, they suggest vastness and universality as opposed to calling up an image of something as small and bounded as ourselves. They give the soul room to breathe. Those who feel the action of God on themselves as being like expanding into a huge space, who sit in Meeting for Worship in an all-encompassing and boundless silence which itself is filled with God, need such language.

On the other, they suggest very well the enlightening, burning, energising, powerful action of God in us. People who prefer this sort of metaphor tend to say that they don't believe in a "personal" God, because it seems far too limited and parochial. It makes them feel claustrophobic.

Some may also say that we as human individuals are of much too little consequence to merit any attention from God. They may, for the same reason, reject Jesus as having anything at all adequate to say about God. This strikes me as rather like the Jewish and Moslem concerns about the traditional Christian view of Jesus. How can a single human on a tiny planet at one short moment of time possibly be held to express the nature of God? "Allahu Akhbar!", "God is Greater!"

The trouble with this approach comes when we want to speak of God's encounter with us. Wind and fire can be awesome, but unless we anthropomorphise them, they cannot represent purpose or love. If the God we point towards by such metaphors were impersonal in the way that natural forces are impersonal, God could not reach out to us. It is no good saying vaguely that the God-force "is positive". In relation to impersonal energies, that has no meaning except in the sense that one end of a battery "is positive". No force is in all circumstances good for us. All can be destructive as well as beneficial. Where they are of benefit, there is no intention in it. We may have a relationship, a response to, such forces, but they have no relationship or response to us. If these were the only valid metaphors for God, we would be in precisely the same state of desolation in the universe as if there were no God at all. We would be random happenings swept by powerful forces which neither know nor care about us.

So we need personal language too. If personal language about God is taken too literally, the anti-personal criticisms are entirely valid. God becomes an old man in the sky, or at least something very like us who we can be chummy with and almost keep in our pockets. The image called up is far too small. But our experience of God is not all about awe and worship of the immensely Other. It is also an experience of being summoned and led, being welcomed and fulfilled, of meeting and merging with the divine in our own depths which we must in some way have a likeness to. All this aspect of experience can only be represented in personal terms.

The person is the richest metaphor we have for God, because only the person is conscious, is self-aware, only the person can know and love persons, can discern the truth or have purposes. S. L. Frank, a Russian philosopher of the early 20th century, compares our awareness of God as relating to us, to that of our knowledge of other people as persons. This, he says, comes from the very first meeting of glances, which conveys to us irrefutable knowledge that we are in touch with another person, a knowledge which cannot be scientifically verified, but of which we are quite sure: "the confession of faith in a personal God is not a thought about the existence of a certain transcendental object, . . . it is the confession of our actual encounter and living bond with Him".

If ever we feel, in Meeting for Worship or in our own private experience, that our deepest longings are in some way met and answered, are even something given us to draw us in a certain direction, then the metaphor of the personal acquires value. If there were no sense of direction, if we could not feel that Ultimate Reality was the source of our desire to love, to be just, to heal rather than afflict, then we could trust no testimonies, we could only look at the world and despair.

This is very far from saying, of course, that God feels what we call "love". It is saying that although the nature of God is unimaginably beyond us, yet it is such that the faint reflection of it in the tiny mirror of human consciousness draws us to love, not to hate, to seek the truth rather than invent what suits us. Because this Reality, which we can only point towards, not fully name, is, though infinitely beyond us, beyond in the direction of what we call love and truth, we in our little way can love and know.

A person is outwardly a small and insignificant thing, so that it seems truly amazing that such things should find contact with God.

But inwardly, the human spirit is bounded neither by space nor time. The glance lights on us because and insofar as we are in fact capable of receiving it. Personal language leads us further into the nature of God than any other, because it expresses the most crucial aspects of what we experience of God.

Nevertheless we need both types of language, and both have always been used. Impersonal language is only lacking if that is all we have. Personal language without the corrective of the impersonal, too easily slides into the limited and sentimental. May we keep the balance, so that fusing the great with the personal "we may be enabled to measure in all its breadth and length and height and depth, the love of Christ, to know what passes knowledge".

Lightning Source UK Ltd.
Milton Keynes UK
UKOW04f1009170216

268540UK00001B/272/P